Easy English
STEP-BY-STEP

for ESL Learners

Premium Second Edition

Danielle Pelletier

D0731542

Mc
Graw
Hill

New York   Chicago   San Francisco   Athens   London   Madrid
Mexico City   Milan   New Delhi   Singapore   Sydney   Toronto

1 2 3 4 5 6 7 8 9   LHS   24 23 22 21 20 19

ISBN   978-1-260-45518-2
MHID   1-260-45518-1

e-ISBN   978-1-260-45519-9
e-MHID   1-260-45519-X

Interior artwork by Progressive Publishing Alternatives

McGraw-Hill products are available at special quantity discounts to use as premiums and sales promotions or for use in corporate training programs. To contact a representative, please visit the Contact Us pages at www.mhprofessional.com.

McGraw-Hill Language Lab App

Extensive audio recordings and review quizzes are available to support your study of this book. Go to mhlanguagelab.com to access the online version of this application. A free mobile version of the app can be found in the Apple app store and Google Play store (for Android devices).

Note: Internet access required for streaming audio.

To every teacher I've ever had, thank you!
To all of my students past and present, you've taught me well.
I am forever grateful.
To all who use this book, happy learning!

Contents

5 Recreation and Hobbies   165

Introduction

Welcome to *Easy English Step-by-Step for ESL Learners*! This book is for high-beginner-level, nonnative English speakers who want to improve their English communication skills.

- **English learners:** Are you living and working in an English-speaking country? Do you want to live in an English-speaking country? This book will help you build confidence as you speak English for everyday activities such as greeting and meeting people and asking for directions. You will also learn reading, writing, and grammar skills.

- **Teachers:** This book uses a pragmatic approach to teaching English to nonnative speakers. Easy-to-understand grammar explanations are illustrated in tables and reinforced with multiple examples and a variety of exercises to give the learner maximum practice. Common everyday expressions are put into context in realistic conversation for learners to become familiar with and practice using in the classroom as well as out there in the world. Use this book to teach speaking, pronunciation, grammar, reading, and writing skills to your beginner to high-beginner ESL students in an unintimidating way. *Easy English Step-by-Step for ESL Learners* provides the communication skills instruction, practice, and homework activities necessary for your students to speak English confidently and competently in daily activities.

 ## About This Book

The best way to use this book is to progress through the chapters sequentially. The content and skills in each chapter build on those of the previous chapters. So start with Chapter 1 and end with Chapter 8. The book is organized by theme, with each focusing on an area of life.

- **Chapter themes:** Each chapter focuses on a theme, such as daily activities, food shopping, transportation, recreation, health, and clothes shopping. In every one of these areas of life, helpful, authentic language that you can use immediately is introduced and practiced.

- **Functions:** You will learn real language that native speakers of English use in each of these areas of life. In this book, you will study ways to ask for and give information and express thoughts and emotions. For example, find out how to start a conversation, ask how to do things, order a meal in a restaurant, request directions, express your likes and dislikes, accept and decline invitations, talk to a doctor, and agree or disagree politely.

- **Conversation:** Each chapter includes a conversation between two people. Each conversation provides a variety of expressions, vocabulary, definitions, and idioms you need to communicate successfully in different situations. As a bonus, streaming audio recordings of these conversations are available to you. Practice listening, speaking, and your pronunciation skills with these recordings. See the copyright page for information on how to access the recordings online and via mobile app.

- **Pronunciation Tips:** Helpful pronunciation tips are given in every chapter. Audio recordings of many of the tips in the book are available for you to use while practicing your pronunciation of English. See the copyright page for information on how to access the recordings online and via mobile app.

- **Grammar:** Each chapter teaches one or more verb tenses and other grammatical structures such as pronouns, contractions, and articles. Grammar is the foundation upon which language is used and understood. When you understand the grammar, you can make better choices when speaking and writing.

- **Reading:** Reading skills are essential to living and working in an English-speaking country, so every chapter has a reading passage. You will learn skills to help you read effectively and comprehend the paragraph, while also discovering new vocabulary. Practicing reading will strengthen your writing skills.

- **Phrasal verbs:** Phrasal verbs are informal expressions native English speakers use in conversation. Understanding and using phrasal verbs will help you participate in conversations more naturally.

- **Writing:** You will learn how to write sentences and paragraphs, as well as how to use punctuation. Practicing writing also strengthens your reading skills.

- **Exercises:** The many exercises throughout this book allow you to practice every skill you learn and help you learn English more quickly. Do each exercise and then check the answers in the Answer Key at the back of the book. When you discover incorrect answers, revisit the lesson and try to figure out how to correct the incorrect answers. This strategy will strengthen your ability to correct yourself, which is a vital skill in language learning.

- **Body language:** Many chapters show appropriate body language and gestures to use when speaking in different situations. Using appropriate body language will help you communicate naturally and effectively in English-speaking countries.

- **Chapter quizzes:** There is a quiz at the end of every chapter, so test yourself! These tests help you review and remember the skills you have learned. Answer the ten questions and then check the answers in the Answer Key. When you discover incorrect answers, revisit the lesson and try to figure out how to correct the incorrect answers.

- **Do It Out There:** After each chapter quiz, there is a homework section. Find activities to do out in the world—outside of the classroom and away from your desk. These sections give you the opportunity to *use* the language you learn. These activities are a great way for you to build your confidence. Confidence comes from *doing*. So, get out there and use English!

- **A word about confidence-building:** This book provides the skills you need to use English to communicate successfully in life and at work. To build these skills, you must use the English you are learning *out there in the world*. The book cannot do that for you. You must do this. To build your confidence, you must use English. You may make mistakes and that is okay! Expect that you will make some mistakes. This is a normal part of learning and practicing. Practice, make mistakes, and practice some more. Then practice again. Practice will build your confidence. And practice makes perfect.

- **Answer Key:** The Answer Key at the end of the book provides answers for most exercises in the book. Do each exercise *first*, then look at the answers in the Answer Key. If you get something wrong, review the corresponding chapter section so you understand the correct answer. This is a practical learning strategy.

- **Appendix:** The Appendix at the back of the book gives you more helpful information. It shows how to write capital and lowercase letters; provides a list of vowels and consonants, phonetic symbols, and pitch patterns for conversation; describes the different parts of speech, stative verbs, irregular verbs, and WH question words; and provides lists of spelling rules, prepositions, and punctuation marks. Review the Appendix often.

Tips to Help You Learn English Quickly

To improve your English skills, practice *every day*. Here are some suggestions for practicing in your daily life. Increase your practice time as the skills become easier.

Listening

- Watch TV shows or movies in English with English subtitles (also known as closed captions) for 15 to 45 minutes every day—on TV, the Internet, or a smartphone.

- Listen to talk shows and news on the radio or Internet for 15 to 30 minutes every day in your car, at home, or on a smartphone.

- Listen to audio books and read the books at the same time.

- Listen to people speaking English at cafés, at work, at the bus stop—everywhere. It's OK if you do not understand much at the beginning. The more you listen, the more you will learn and the faster your English will improve.

Speaking and Pronunciation

- Create reasons to speak English: ask questions at the market, a restaurant, and work. Ask two questions every day. As you build your confidence, ask more questions.

- Call a store on the phone and ask for the price of a product. This is a good way to measure your listening and speaking skills. As you increase your fluency, this task will become easier.

- Practice pronunciation tips aloud in the shower, while driving, and when you are alone at home or work. Sing the English language! You can begin practicing by singing your phone number. See Chapter 6 for more information on how to sing your phone number.

- Practice pronunciation tips silently anytime in public—walking down the street, on the bus or train, or while waiting in line. Even singing in your mind is an effective strategy for practicing pronunciation.

Reading and Vocabulary

- Read part of the newspaper every day. Choose a section you enjoy, such as sports, business, or fashion, and read for 10 to 20 minutes at a time.

- Read and say aloud every street sign you see.

- Read menus at restaurants to learn food vocabulary.

- Read one children's book every day. If you have children, read with them!

- Keep a notebook or make flash cards of new vocabulary. Review these words and expressions every day.

- Use each new vocabulary term five times to learn it well.

Writing and Grammar

- Practice writing the alphabet (both capital and lowercase letters) in your notebook.

- Write five sentences in your notebook every day. Use a period at the end of each sentence.

- Write five questions in your notebook every day. Use a question mark at the end of every question.

- In these sentences, use the grammar and verb tenses you learned in each chapter.

- Check the subject-verb agreement in every sentence.

Companion Audio Recordings

Easy English Step-by-Step for ESL Learners features companion audio recordings that include conversations, pronunciation tips, and many example sentences for each chapter. See the copyright page for information on how to access the McGraw Hill Language Lab app.

How to Use These Recordings

Practice listening and speaking with these recordings as you work through the book:

- Locate the list of audio recordings within the Language Lab app. These are grouped by chapter and include reference to the corresponding page number in the book.

- Go through the book and mark each exercise/section in the book that has an accompanying audio recording.

- When you come to that section in the book, listen to the audio as you do the work.

How to Listen Effectively and Build Your Listening Skills

1. Listen and read along in the book 2–3 times.

2. Close the book and close your eyes and listen (do not read) as many times as you like (1–5 times).

3. Open the book and listen as you read along one time. Try to figure out what you can and cannot hear when you were listening with your eyes closed.

4. Repeat step #2 and try to hear what you could not hear before.

5. Repeat steps #1–4 often.

Advanced Listening Strategies

1. **Shadowing:** As you use the book, read and listen to the accompanying audio files at the same time. You want to "shadow," or follow the reading and mimic the sounds you hear. Pretend you are a movie actor and you need to sound like the person on the audio recording. Keep practicing until you can imitate the recorded voice well. To shadow, follow these steps:

   a. Read and listen to the recording simultaneously.

   b. Pause the recording (for longer recordings).

   c. Repeat exactly what you hear with your voice.

   d. Repeat steps a–c many times until you are satisfied that you sound like the recorded voice.

2. **Tracking:** Tracking is similar to singing along with your favorite song when you know the words. The singer is singing the song, and you are listening and singing the same words at the same time in the same way. Do this with the sentences, conversations, and readings in the book. Practice tracking each audio section many times to begin to know the "song" of the voice in the recording. Then, sing along with the voice! To learn how to track, follow these steps:

   a. Listen and speak along with the voice you hear (at the same time.)

   b. Try to speak at the same pace and rhythm as the speaker.

   c. If the speaker's voice is too fast or slow, pause and begin speaking again when you can.

   d. Repeat this many times until you know the "song" of the voice on the audio recording and you can imitate it almost perfectly in pace, rhythm, and sound.

1

Meeting People

In this chapter you will learn about:

Speaking
✓ How to greet people
✓ How to start a conversation
✓ How to use small talk
✓ How to talk about the weather
✓ How to introduce yourself

Vocabulary, Reading, and Writing
✓ Adjectives about your state and the weather
✓ Adverbs used with adjectives
✓ Phrasal verbs
✓ How to read effectively
✓ How to begin and end a sentence

Grammar
✓ How to use subject pronouns
✓ How to use the BE verb (affirmative and negative forms with contractions)

Body Language
✓ How to shake hands
✓ Nodding
✓ How to wave to say hello and good-bye
✓ How to point politely
✓ How to make eye contact when meeting someone

We will begin with greeting and meeting people. In this chapter, you will practice expressions, vocabulary, and body language for greetings, introductions, and small talk. To improve your reading skills, you will study three steps to effective reading. To practice writing, you will learn how to begin and end a sentence properly.

Greeting People

We greet people when we see them. We always greet people we know. We sometimes greet people we don't know. To **greet** someone is to say hello in a friendly way. There are many ways to greet someone. What expressions do you use? Make a list of them.

_____   _____   _____

_____   _____   _____

_____   _____   _____

Here are some common greetings. Read them aloud.

> To read **aloud** means to speak what you read with your full voice.

Hello.	Hi there.	How are you doing?	Long time no see!
Hello there.	Hey.	How are you?	Good morning.
Howdy.	Hey there.	What's up?	Good afternoon.
Hi.	Hey, how are you doing?	What's happening?	Good evening.

Tip

For greetings at different times of day, use these time tips:

Good morning: use before noon (12:00 P.M.)
Good afternoon: use from 12:01 P.M. until approximately 5:00 P.M.
Good evening: use from approximately 5:00 P.M. until midnight (12:00 A.M.)

> **Culture Note:** *Howdy* is used only in North America.
> **Pronunciation Tip:** Most speakers link words together. A phrase of three words can sound like one long word. For example, "How are you?" may sound like "Howaya?" and "What's up?" may sound like "Wassup?"
> **Tip:** "Good night" is *not* used to greet someone. It does *not* mean "hello." It means "Good-bye" or "Have a good sleep" / "I am going to bed."

Formal and Informal Greetings

Some greetings are formal, and some are informal. **Formal greetings** are more polite and used with people to whom we want to show respect, such as a boss or a teacher. **Informal greetings** are casual and used with friends and other people with whom we feel comfortable.

Culture Note

In the United States, men and women generally greet each other similarly: They use the same greetings and they shake hands the first time they meet. See Meeting People, Step 3.

Exercise 1.1

*Which of the greetings previously listed are formal and which are informal? A couple of greetings are **neutral**, meaning they can be used in most situations. Note each greeting in the appropriate column.*

Formal	Informal	Neutral
_____	_____	_____
_____	_____	_____
_____	_____	_____
_____	_____	_____
_____	_____	_____
_____	_____	_____

Exercise 1.2

Look at the following situations and decide if the greeting is appropriate or inappropriate for the situation. Follow the example. When the greeting is inappropriate, think of a better one.

An **appropriate** greeting is proper and suitable for the situation. An **inappropriate** greeting is improper and unsuitable for the situation.

EXAMPLE   It's 5:00 P.M. Gabrielle is at school and greets her friend. She says, "Good morning!"

"Good morning" is inappropriate because 5:00 P.M. is in the evening, not in the morning.

Appropriate   Inappropriate   *Inappropriate.*
Better greetings: Hey! How are you? How's it going? What's up?

1. It's 10:00 A.M. Brenda is at work and greets her supervisor. She says, "Hey, what's up?"

   Appropriate   Inappropriate   _____

2. It's 1:45 P.M. Jason is a student in the school cafeteria. He sees his good friend José and greets him by saying, "What's happening?"

   Appropriate   Inappropriate   _____

3. It's 9:00 P.M. Harry has just arrived at his night job and sees his supervisor. He greets him by saying, "Good night."

   Appropriate   Inappropriate   _____

Culture Note
Use formal language with a superior, such as a boss or a teacher. Use neutral and informal language with coworkers. Use informal language with friends.

Exercise 1.3

Read the following situations and create appropriate greetings. Follow the example, using the rules in the preceding note.

EXAMPLE   It's 10:00 A.M. Mohammed is at work and sees his coworker. How does he say hello?

Good morning. / Hello there! / How are you? / How are you doing?

1. It's 4:00 P.M. Brenda is at work and greets her supervisor. What expressions can she use to say hello?

   _____

2. It's 12:30 P.M. Dan sees his friend Sunil. How does he say hello?

   _____

3. It's 7 P.M. Klara greets her teacher in night class. How does she say hello?

   _____

4. It's 8 A.M. Maura sees her friend Isaac. How does she greet him?

   _____

5. It's 9 A.M. Belinda sees her boss at work. How does she greet her?

   _____

Conversation: Greeting People

Read the following conversations aloud.

DAN: Hey, Sunil. What's up?

SUNIL (friend): Nothing. What's happening with you?

DAN: Oh, not much. Just having some lunch.

MARGARET (teacher): Good evening, Klara.

KLARA (student): Hello!

MARGARET: How is everything?

KLARA: Good, thank you. Uh, I have a question about the homework.

MARGARET: Yes?

BELINDA: Good morning, Laura.

LAURA (boss): Good morning, Belinda. And how are you today?

BELINDA: Fine, thank you.

MAURA: Isaac! How's it going?

ISAAC (friend): Hey, Maura. Not bad. What about you?

MAURA: All right. Where are you going?

ISAAC: To class.

MAURA: Me too.

Here are some responses to common questions in greetings. See Grammar: Adjectives for information on adjectives for states of health.

QUESTIONS	OPTIONAL BEGINNING	RESPONSES (USE ADJECTIVES FOR STATE OF HEALTH)	EXAMPLES
How are you?	I'm . . .	great / excellent / very	I'm great!
How are you doing?	I'm doing . . .	good / good / fine /	I'm doing okay.
How are things?	Things are . . .	pretty good* / okay / all right / not bad* well** / very well**	Things are pretty good.
How's it going?	It's going . . .	And you? / What about you?	It's going well.
What's happening?*		Not much* / Nothing* /	Nothing much.
What's been happening?*		Nothing much*	
What's new?*		And you? / What about you?	
What's going on?*			
What's been going on?*			

*Informal.

**Only used with *How's it going?* and *How are you doing?*

Tip
To greet someone, we often ask questions. However, we usually do *not* engage in long conversations during a greeting. Give brief responses and keep them positive.

Exercise 1.4

Complete the following conversations with appropriate greetings and conversation. Use a variety of expressions.

1. It's 7 A.M. Brenda arrives at work and sees her supervisor, Donald.

   Brenda greets him: _____

   Donald greets Brenda with a question: _____

   Brenda replies: _____

2. It's 1:45 P.M. Jason is a student in the school cafeteria. He sees his friend José.

   Jason greets José: _____

   José replies with a greeting and a question: _____

   Jason replies: _____

3. It's 9 P.M. Harry has just arrived at his night job and sees his supervisor, Miguel.

   Miguel greets Harry with a question: _____

   Harry replies and asks a question: _____

   Miguel replies: _____

4. It's 10 A.M. Mohammed is at work and sees his coworker, Shannon, in the hallway.

   Mohammed greets her: _____

   Shannon replies and asks a question: _____

   Mohammed responds: _____

Saying Good-Bye

When we leave or when others leave, we say good-bye. There are many ways to do this. What expressions do you use to say good-bye? Make a list of them.

_____   _____   _____

_____   _____   _____

_____   _____   _____

Here are some common ways to say good-bye. Read them aloud.

Good-bye.	See you later/soon.	Later. (*informal*)
Bye.	See you (day/time) Monday/next week.	Talk to you later.
Bye-bye. (*informal*)	See you. (*informal*)	Take care.

If you meet someone new, you can use these phrases to say good-bye. Read them aloud.

It was nice meeting you.	Nice meeting you.
Great meeting you.	Good meeting you.
It was a pleasure meeting you.	A pleasure meeting you.

 Wave Hello and Good-Bye
When we see someone we know and they are too far away to talk to, we often wave. To **wave** is to swing a hand or an arm from left to right with the palm facing the person. There are different ways to wave. You can wave with just your hand near your body.

Or you can wave with your whole arm extended high above your head. The farther away a person is, the bigger the wave is.

Meeting People

Sometimes you will be around people you have never met. For example, you may be near a person you don't know at school, at work, or at a party. How do you meet this new person? How do you introduce yourself? What do you say when you meet someone new? Think of some examples.

_____

_____

The Six Steps to Meeting Someone

When we meet someone new, we usually follow these six steps:

1. Make eye contact.
2. Make small talk.
3. Introduce yourself.

4. Look for a connection.
5. Learn about each other.
6. End the conversation.

We usually follow these steps at school and when socializing. At work, we sometimes do not follow all six steps. We sometimes know the connection, so we skip Step 4. Let's learn more about these steps.

Step 1: Make Eye Contact

It is common to make eye contact with someone you are meeting for the first time. To **make eye contact** means that two people look directly into each other's eyes. Usually, we make eye contact and then begin speaking. We often smile. Sometimes, we speak and make eye contact at the same time. Steps 1 and 2 are often done at the same time.

Culture Note

In North America, eye contact is expected and acceptable during a conversation. When listening, we often watch someone's mouth, and when speaking, we look directly in the person's eyes.

Step 2: Begin the Conversation with Small Talk and Be Positive

You can begin a conversation with someone by using small talk. **Small talk** is informal discussion about topics that are simple, nonpersonal, and noncontroversial. When you use small talk, speak about things in a positive way. Do *not* say negative things.

> Topics are **nonpersonal** when they are about general ideas and things; they are *not* about specific people. Topics are **controversial** when they are taboo or when people often disagree about them. Examples of controversial topics include money, politics, and religion. **Noncontroversial** topics are topics that many people can easily discuss without arguing.

Culture Note: Making Small Talk

Common small talk topics in North America include:

- The weather—*Nice weather we're having. Beautiful day, isn't it?*
- Your surroundings, such as the venue, drinks, food, and music—*Great music!*
- The latest technology—*Is that the newest smartphone?*
- Current movies or TV programs—*Have you seen (name of the movie or TV show)?*
- Any topic relevant to the situation, such as homework if you are in a classroom—*Did you do the homework?*—or the music and food at a party—*The food is really good.*

Common small talk topics in the United Kingdom include:

- The weather—*Nice weather we're having. Beautiful day, isn't it?*
- Something you have in common—*Have you been standing here long?*—if you are standing behind someone in a queue.

Step 3: Introduce Yourself—Smile and Shake Hands

To introduce yourself, say your name. Use the following expressions:

I'm (*say name*).

(*Say name.*)

Less common: My name is (*say name*).

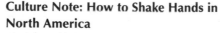

Culture Note: Giving Your Name
In North America, we say just our first names in informal situations. In business or formal situations, we give our first and last names.

When you introduce yourself, shake hands. Follow the rules in the following chart.

Culture Note: How to Shake Hands in North America
Shake with your right hand. Stand one arm's length away from the other person, and extend your arm. Your elbow should be close to your body. Put the palm of your hand firmly in the other person's hand and shake up and down once or twice. Do not shake too quickly. Hold the person's hand firmly, but not too tightly or too lightly. Then let go. Look the person in the eye and smile when shaking hands.

In general, it is impolite to *not* shake if another person extends a hand. However, if you do not want to shake hands because of your religious beliefs, you may smile and nod with your hands behind your back while you introduce yourself. If you have a cold, you can smile and say, "I'm sorry. I have a cold."

> To **initiate** something is to begin something.

Handshake Rules in North America	Handshake Rules in the United Kingdom
Women and men both initiate handshakes.	Women should initiate a handshake with men.
Handshakes should be firm, not light.	Handshakes should be light, not firm.
Shake hands when meeting someone and *usually* when leaving someone you have just met.	Shake hands when meeting someone and *always* when leaving someone.

Step 4: Look for a Connection or Common Interest—Ask Information Questions

After you meet someone, continue the conversation by asking questions. (Learn more about asking questions to keep a conversation going in Chapter 6. In addition to the "BE: Forming WH Questions" section later in this chapter, you can find more about information questions in Chapters 2, 3, 5, and 7.) A **connection** refers to how people know each other through places or other people like friends, coworkers, family members, and neighbors. For example, Maribel works with Lee. They are connected through work. Having a **common interest** means that two or more people like the same thing. For example, Carlos and Jane both enjoy science fiction movies. So their common interest is science fiction movies.

Two Types of Questions

Information questions are questions that begin with WH—words and phrases such as *who, what, when, where, why, how, what kind, which one, how many,* and *how much.* These questions ask for more information about a topic. Here are some examples of information questions: *How do you know Susan? / Who do you know here? / Where are you from?*

Yes/no questions require either a yes or a no answer. They begin with words such as the BE verb and auxiliary verbs such as *do, did, have, has, had, should, can, could, will,* and *would.* Here are some examples of yes/no questions: *Do you know Susan? / Have you been here long? / Is the food good?*

Step 5: Learn About Each Other—Ask Information and Yes/No Questions

After you find a connection, learn more about the person. However, do not ask for or give too many details. This deeper level of conversation may happen later but usually not the first time you meet. For example, it's okay to say in what neighborhood you live but do not give your street address.

Example Questions to Ask
Here are some common topics and information questions for getting to know someone in the United States. Read each question aloud. Speak clearly and slowly.

> To **get to know someone** is to learn about that person by communicating with him or her.

- **Country of origin:** *Where are you from?*
- **Residential area or neighborhood:** *Where do you live? / Do you live around here?*
- **Your job:** *What do you do? / Where do you work?*
- **Areas of interest such as sightseeing, restaurants, or recreational activities:** *What do you do for fun? / What's your favorite restaurant?*

In the United States, we often discuss jobs when getting to know someone. It is considered a neutral topic. It's okay to ask about someone's job, but do not ask about his or her position or title. In the United Kingdom, do *not* discuss jobs; this is considered a private topic, and people value their privacy highly. It is impolite to ask someone personal questions. A **personal question** is a question about someone's private or home life. Do *not* ask someone where he or she lives or what he or she does for work.

Step 6: End the Conversation Politely and with a Smile

Ending a conversation can be awkward, so it is helpful to know how to do it politely. Say that you have enjoyed meeting the person. Then give a brief reason why you are ending the conversation. Here are some common and acceptable reasons for ending a conversation: to find someone, to use the restroom, to get some food or drink, or to leave the event. In North America, shaking hands is optional in social situations and expected in professional situations. In the United Kingdom, always shake hands when ending a conversation and leaving.

> If something is **awkward**, it is difficult and sometimes uncomfortable.

Exercise 1.5

What are the six steps to meeting someone new?

1. _____   4. _____

2. _____   5. _____

3. _____   6. _____

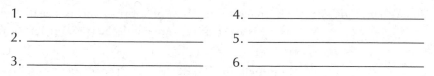

Conversation: Meeting People

Let's look at a sample conversation between two people at a party. They don't know each other and are meeting for the first time. The conversation includes all six steps. Read the conversation aloud.

CONVERSATION	CONVERSATION GUIDE
DONNA (making eye contact with Brad[1]): The food is good.[2]	1. **Step 1: Make eye contact.** Smile and look at the other person.
	2. **Step 2. Begin the conversation with small talk and be positive.** Other opening expressions include *Great party/food, isn't it? / What a nice party. / Enjoying the party?* Or you can talk about the weather.
BRAD: Yeah, it is.[3]	3. *Yeah* is an informal expression that means "yes." To agree with someone is polite. You may also use expressions such as *It is! / Isn't it? / You're right. / Yum!*
	Yum and **yummy** are informal expressions meaning that something tastes good.
	Tip: If someone is uninterested in speaking, he or she may ignore you or smile briefly but say nothing. When this happens, you can decide whether to continue speaking or stop.
	To **ignore** someone is to not look at nor talk to that person.
DONNA: Have you tried the cake?[4] It's delicious.[5]	4. To continue the conversation about food, you can ask a question using the expression *Have you tried the [food/drink name]?* with rising pitch. **Pitch** measures how high or low a sound is. The sound of a person's voice gets higher with rising pitch and lower with falling pitch. See the pitch chart in the Appendix for more information. See the following pronunciation tips to learn how to use pitch appropriately.
	Pronunciation Tip: Rising pitch shows that you are waiting for a response.
	5. Next, comment on the taste. Talk about what tastes good.
	Tip: Do not talk about things that taste bad.
BRAD: No.[6] What kind is it?[7]	6. Respond to the question affirmatively or negatively. If the answer is affirmative, agree with the speaker: *Yes, I have. It **is** delicious.*
	Pronunciation Tip: Stress *is* to show agreement. To **stress** a word means you say the word more loudly.

CONVERSATION | **CONVERSATION GUIDE**

7. If the answer is negative, ask more questions about the food: *Is it homemade? / Is it vegetarian/vegan? / Have you tried the apple pie?*

DONNA: Chocolate.[8]

8. Answer in a friendly way. If you don't know the answer, you can use the following: *I'm not really sure. / I don't know what it's called. / I don't know. I've never had it before.*

BRAD: It looks delicious.[9]

9. Respond to continue the conversation: *Maybe I'll try it. / I should try it. / I love cake. / Cake is my favorite! / I'm allergic to chocolate, so maybe I'll pass on the cake.*

To **pass on** something is to decline it.

DONNA (smiling): I'm Donna.[10] (Extends hand to shake[11])

10. **Step 3: Introduce yourself—smile and shake hands.**

Introduce yourself by saying your first name and putting your hand out to shake.

Tip: It is less common to say, "My name is . . ."

11. See the earlier Culture Note on shaking hands.

BRAD (smiling): Brad.[10] Nice to meet you, Donna. (Shakes Donna's hand[11])

If you have a long name or a name that is uncommon in this country, say it slowly. You may need to repeat it or even spell it—for example, "I'm Rasheed. R-a-s-h-e-e-d."

DONNA: Very nice to meet you,[12] Brad.[13]

12. Other expressions you can use when meeting someone for the first time include *It's very nice to meet you, (name). / Nice to meet you, (name). / So nice to meet you, (name). / It's good to meet you. / Good to meet you. / It's a pleasure to meet you, (name). / It's a pleasure meeting you, (name).*

13. **Tip:** Repeat a person's name during the introduction to be polite and to help you remember the name.

BRAD: Who do you know here?[14]

14. **Step 4: Look for a connection or common interest—ask information questions.** Brad is looking for a connection with Donna. Other expressions he might use include: *So, what's your connection to this event? / Do you know (person's/host's name)?*

DONNA: Oh, I know Susan.[15] She's sitting over there (points at Susan[16]). We're neighbors.[15] How about you?[17]

15. Explain your connection briefly. Be friendly. In North America, use first names only. In the United Kingdom, use first and last names.

16. Point politely. (See the illustrations in Chapter 6 for pointing.)

17. Continue the conversation with a question, such as *What about you? / And you? / And what's your connection to this party?*

(continued)

CONVERSATION	CONVERSATION GUIDE
BRAD: I came with Juan. He's the host of this party.[15]	
DONNA: How do you know Juan?[18]	18. Ask about the connection. A common expression for this question is *How do you know (name)?*
BRAD: We work together.[15]	
DONNA: Oh.[19] So, what do you do?[20]	19. To show that you are listening, say, "Oh," "Ah," "Mm," or "Hm," or nod your head occasionally. To **nod** is to move your head up and down. Nodding shows agreement and understanding.
	20. **Step 5: Learn about each other—ask information and yes/no questions.** Continue the conversation by asking other information questions. *What do you do?* is a question about someone's job.
	Culture Note: In the United Kingdom, do not ask about people's jobs.
BRAD: I work in health care. I work with nurses.[21]	21. Answer the question generally and briefly. Do not discuss details.
DONNA: That sounds interesting.[22] Do you like it?[23]	22. Comment to show that you are interested. Another expression to show interest is *Oh, really?*
	23. Ask another question to continue the conversation, such as *How do you like it? / Have you been doing this long?*
BRAD: It's okay.[24] What about you? What do *you* do?[25]	24. Answer the question. If your answer is negative, speak neutrally about it. **Important:** Do not speak about negative things when meeting someone for the first time in a social situation.
	25. Ask a similar question to continue the conversation. Stress *you.*
DONNA: I just moved here.[24]	
BRAD: Oh, where did you move from?[26]	26. Moving from a different country usually generates questions: *Where did you move from? / How long have you been here? / How do you like it? / Did you come with family?*
	To **generate** something is to create it.
DONNA: Shanghai.	
BRAD: How do you like it here?[26]	
DONNA: I like it. But sometimes I miss my friends.[27]	27. Answer honestly but not negatively. Continue being positive.

CONVERSATION	CONVERSATION GUIDE
BRAD: I bet.[28]	28. Show empathy or understanding. To have **empathy** is to have the ability to share the feelings of another. You might nod or use other expressions, including: *I would too. / That's understandable. / I'm sure you do. / Sure.*
DONNA: Well, it's been very nice talking with you, Brad.[29] I'm going to go find Susan.[30] (Extends hand to shake and smiles)	29. **Step 6: End the conversation with a smile**. To end a conversation, say that you have enjoyed meeting the other person. 30. Give a brief reason why you are ending the conversation, such as *Excuse me, I must find the restroom. / Pardon me, but I need to get something to drink.*
BRAD (nodding and smiling[31]): Nice meeting you too, Donna.[32] (Shakes her hand[33])	31. Nodding is a common way to show agreement or understanding. 32. Respond politely by saying that meeting the other person has been a pleasure. 33. When someone extends his or her hand, it's impolite not to shake hands. See the earlier Culture Note about shaking hands.

Culture Note: Introducing Yourself

In North America and the United Kingdom, it is customary to introduce yourself to people you do not know when you are in a shared situation. It is not common to introduce yourself to strangers in public.

General Rules in North America	General Rules in the United Kingdom
We usually say just our first name at social gatherings. For example, *I'm Donna*. At professional gatherings, we often say both our first and last names. Titles are not usually used in professional situations. For example, if someone has a PhD, she will not use *Dr. McRobie*. Instead, she will give her first and last name: *Katherine McRobie*.	In the United Kingdom, you should say both your first and last name when introducing yourself. For example, *I'm Donna Greene*. Use titles and last names when meeting someone until he or she invites you to use his or her first name only. For example, Donna might say, "It's nice to meet you, Mr. Smith."

Culture Note: Pointing
It is impolite to point at people. It is especially impolite to point at someone using your **index finger**, the first finger closest to your thumb. To point politely, use an open hand with the palm turned slightly upward.

Now that you have read a conversation between two people meeting at a party, let's review.

Exercise 1.6

Read the conversation between Donna and Brad again aloud. Then answer the following questions. Use the Conversation Guide to help you.

1. What is the first step in meeting someone new?

   _____

2. What is the second step in meeting someone new?

   _____

3. Donna started a conversation with Brad. What small talk topic did she use?

   _____

4. Donna asked a common question about food. How does that question begin?

   _____

5. What is the most common way to introduce yourself? Choose the correct answer:

   My name is . . . / I'm . . .

6. Should you shake someone's hand when you first meet him or her? Choose the correct answer:

   Yes   No

7. Where do you look when you shake someone's hand?

   _____

8. What is a connection?

   _____

9. What types of questions can you ask to learn more about the other person?

_____

10. What are some common and acceptable reasons for ending a conversation?

_____

Now that you understand how to meet someone, let's review appropriate topics for small talk.

Exercise 1.7

Read the following situations. Choose the best small talk topics for each situation. Review appropriate topics in the "Communication Strategy: Small Talk" section of Chapter 6. Follow the example.

EXAMPLE   You are at a bus stop.

  a. The weather

  b. Politics

  c. The bad bus driver

The best answer is the weather because politics is controversial (taboo) and the bad bus driver is negative.

1. You are in the cafeteria at work.
   a. Your terrible boss
   b. Your family
   c. The food in the cafeteria

2. You are in the registration line at school.
   a. The weather
   b. The registration process
   c. The long line

3. You are at your community center.
   a. Misbehaving children
   b. The weather
   c. Lack of money

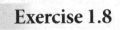

Exercise 1.8

Complete the conversations with appropriate expressions for meeting someone new.

1. In the cafeteria at work, Alex is sitting at a table with someone she doesn't know.

   ALEX (makes eye contact): The pizza is really good here.

   MARION: Is it? I haven't had it. The salad is pretty good.

   ALEX (extends her hand): _____

   MARION (shakes hands): _____

2. You are at the park near your community center. There is a new person sitting on the bench.

   YOU (make eye contact): It's a beautiful day, isn't it?

   SHARON: Yes, it really is.

   YOU (extend your hand): _____

   SHARON (shakes your hand): _____

3. You are in the registration line at school.

   LARRY (makes eye contact): _____

   YOU: _____

   LARRY (extends his hand): _____

   YOU (shake his hand): _____

Grammar: Subject Pronouns

We sometimes use a pronoun in place of a noun. A **noun** is a person, place, or thing. A **pronoun** replaces a noun. A **subject pronoun** replaces a noun in the subject position of the sentence. The **subject** is usually at the beginning of a sentence; it is usually before the verb. Do you know any subject pronouns? Note the ones you know.

> A **noun** is a person, place, or thing.

_____   _____   _____

_____   _____   _____

_____   _____   _____

Study the following chart of subject pronouns. Read them aloud.

Subject Pronouns

	SINGULAR	PLURAL
First person	I	We
Second person	You	You
Third person	He (male)	They
	She (female)	They
	It	They

Tip: *He* refers to a male subject; *she* refers to a female subject. These are the only gender-specific pronouns. All other subject pronouns can be used for either gender. *It* refers to things and animals. *They* can refer to things and people. When *they* refers to people, it can refer to men, women, or a combination of both. *They* can also refer to things, which are not gender-specific.

Culture Note: In the United States, *he*, *she*, and *they* also refer to pets.

Here are some example sentences:

I like English. / *You* are my friend. / *He* is strong. / *She* is funny.

It is sunny. / *We* are family. / *You* make delicious cake. / *They* work together.

NOTE: In English, use only a noun *or* a pronoun as the subject. Do *not* use both.

INCORRECT: **Mr. Jones ~~he~~** lives here. / **He ~~Mr. Jones~~** lives here.
CORRECT: *Mr. Jones lives here. / He lives here.*

Exercise 1.9

Choose the correct subject pronoun for each sentence. Refer to the preceding pronoun chart for help, and follow the example. Practice speaking: read the correct sentences aloud twice.

Twice means two times.

EXAMPLE   Taylor (female):   She   He   It   *She* works at the library.

1. Jack and Jill (male + female):   We   They   You   _____ attend college.

2. Fred and I (male + male):   We   They   You   _____ go to the movies on Fridays.

3. Solomon (male):   She   He   It   _____ has two children.

4. Sienna (female):   She   He   It   _____ goes to school on Tuesday nights.

5. My car (gender neutral):   She   He   It   _____ drives well.

6. Beau and Nancy (male + female):   We   They   You   _____ exercise every morning.

Exercise 1.10

Complete the following sentences with the correct subject pronoun. Study the people in the conversation, and follow the example.

Professor Williams (male)   Mr. Somers (male)   Dr. Velling (female)

Aidan (male)   Ms. Brown (female)   Noda (female)

Sasha (male)   Emma (female)

EXAMPLES   Professor Williams → Sasha: *You* are in my class.

Sasha → Mr. Somers (about Noda): *She* is my wife.

1. Aidan → Ms. White (about Emma and Noda): _____ are my coworkers.

2. Emma → Noda (about Professor Williams): _____ is my professor.

3. Dr. Velling → Ms. Brown (about Mr. Somers): _____ is my patient.

4. Dr. Velling → Mr. Somers (about Mr. Somers): _____ need to exercise more.

5. Professor Williams → Sasha (about Sasha): _____ passed the class!

6. Noda → Emma (about Noda and Emma): _____ should go shopping.

7. Noda → Mr. Somers (about Sasha): _____ is my husband.

8. Ms. Brown → Mr. Somers (about Ms. Brown): _____ work at the bakery.

Practice speaking: read the correct sentences aloud twice.

> **Tip:** *Mr.* is male: it is used for both unmarried and married men. *Miss, Mrs.,* and *Ms.* are used for females: *Miss* = unmarried; *Mrs.* = married; and *Ms.* = unknown marital status. Other titles such as *Dr.* and *Professor* are used for both men and women.
>
> **Pronunciation Tip:** *Mr.* is pronounced "mister," *Mrs.* is pronounced "missiz," and *Ms.* is pronounced "mizz."
>
> **Culture Tip:** In North America, *Mr., Miss, Mrs.,* and *Ms.* are rarely used in social situations. These titles are used mostly by children when addressing their teachers at school or elders in their community. Titles are rarely used in business or among adults.
>
> In some parts of North America, it is considered impolite to make assumptions about whether someone is married or single by using *Mrs.* or *Ms.* If you are meeting someone for the first time, they will tell you what name to call them. If you don't know their name, don't use one and don't use a title.

Exercise 1.11

Study the following people, and create sentences using subject pronouns. Follow the examples.

Roberto (male student)   Muhab (male engineer)   Roger (male mechanic)

Jessica (female student)   Maya (female chef)   Rani (female dog walker)

Yin (female author)   Somsak (male police officer)

NOTE: Maya and Roger are married.

EXAMPLES   Jessica → Rani (about Muhab)   *He is an engineer.*

              Roger → Muhab (about Yin)   *She is an author.*

1. Yin → Maya (about Roger) _____

2. Roberto → Roger (about Roberto and Jessica) _____

3. Roger → Yin (about Roger and Maya) _____

4. Muhab → Maya and Yin (about Rani) _____

5. Rani → Jessica (about Rani) _____

6. Somsak → Muhab (about Somsak) _____

7. Roberto → Yin (about Yin) _____

8. Jessica → Roberto (about Muhab) _____

9. Maya → Somsak (about Roger) _____

10. Yin → Maya and Roger (about Maya and Roger) _____

Now that you have learned subject pronouns, let's study the BE verb.

Grammar: BE Verb

In English, we often use the **BE verb** to describe people, places, and things. In this section, we will practice using the BE verb. Read the following sentences aloud.

> I *am* a student. / His hair *is* brown. / Sue and Bob *are* at work. / It *is* broken.
> I *am* fine. / Sue *is* excited. / We *are* great! / They *are* tall. / Abe *is* a doctor.

BE: The Affirmative Form

To write the BE verb in the affirmative form, use the following chart. Read the example sentences aloud.

SUBJECT PRONOUN	BE VERB FORM	EXAMPLE SENTENCES
I	am	I am fine.
You/We/They	are	You are fine. / We are fine. / They are fine.
He/She/It	is	He is fine. / She is fine. / It is fine.

Exercise 1.12

Choose the correct form of the BE verb in the following sentences. Use the preceding chart for guidance, and follow the example.

EXAMPLE   The hospital am/are/is big. *is*

1. The cafeteria (am/are/is) noisy. _____

2. Ronnie (am/are/is) a nurse. _____

3. I (am/are/is) hungry. _____

4. Jimmy and Young (am/are/is) students. _____

5. Mrs. White (am/are/is) a teacher. _____

6. We (am/are/is) cousins. _____

7. She (am/are/is) at work. _____

8. It (am/are/is) red and blue. _____

9. The books (am/are/is) heavy. _____

10. English (am/are/is) useful. _____

Practice speaking: read the correct sentences aloud.

Exercise 1.13

Complete the following sentences with the correct affirmative BE verb form. Follow the example, and review the BE verb chart.

EXAMPLE   Sandra *is* my neighbor.

1. I _____ okay.

2. Salvatore _____ my coworker.

3. We _____ friends.

4. Alvin and Sam _____ brothers.

5. Sarah _____ an employee there.

6. Dierk and I _____ neighbors.

7. He _____ fine.

8. It _____ rainy today.

9. Joan and Mei _____ at school now.

10. I _____ busy this week.

Practice speaking: read the correct sentences aloud.

Affirmative: BE Contraction

In English, we often use contractions by combining two or more words. When words are combined, they are shortened with an **apostrophe** ('). Look at the following chart to see how to form a contraction with an apostrophe and the BE verb. Read the example sentences aloud.

BE: Affirmative Contraction (Subject Pronoun + BE Verb)

SUBJECT PRONOUN	BE VERB FORM	CONTRACTION = SUBJECT PRONOUN + BE	EXAMPLE SENTENCES
I	am	I'm	I'm fine.
You/We/They	are	You're / We're / They're	You're fine. / We're fine. / They're fine.
He/She/It	is	He's / She's / It's	He's fine. / She's fine. / It's fine.

 # Exercise 1.14

Create sentences using the following words. Use the correct form of the BE verb. Then form the sentence again using a subject pronoun and a contraction. Follow the example, and use the preceding chart for help. Read the correct sentences aloud.

EXAMPLE   Jenny / BE / my coworker. *Jenny is my coworker. She's my coworker.*

1. Tomas / BE / my supervisor.

   _____

2. Gerald and I / BE / great today.

   _____

3. My sisters / BE / here.

   _____

4. Mary and Will / BE / my friends.

   _____

5. Today / BE / a great day!

   _____

BE: The Negative Form

To form the BE verb in the negative, use the following two charts. Read the example sentences aloud.

BE: Negative Contractions (BE + Negative)

SUBJECT PRONOUN	BE VERB FORM	NEGATIVE	CONTRACTION = BE VERB + NEGATIVE	EXAMPLE SENTENCES
I	am	not		No contraction
You/We/They	are	not	aren't	You aren't sad. / We aren't sad. / They aren't sad.
He/She/It	is	not	isn't	He isn't sad. / She isn't sad. / It isn't sad.

BE: Negative Contractions (Subject Pronoun + BE)

SUBJECT PRONOUN	BE VERB FORM	CONTRACTION = SUBJECT + BE VERB	NEGATIVE	EXAMPLE SENTENCES
I	am	I'm	not	I'm not tall.
You	are	You're	not	You're not tall.
We	are	We're	not	We're not tall.
They	are	They're	not	They're not tall.
He	is	He's	not	He's not tall.
She	is	She's	not	She's not tall.
It	is	It's	not	It's not tall.

Exercise 1.15

Read the following sentences. Choose the correct negative BE verb contraction. Follow the example.

EXAMPLES   Joseph (am not/isn't/aren't) an engineer. _isn't_

They ('m not/'s not/'re not) coworkers. _'re not_

1. Audrey (am not/isn't/aren't) a ballerina. _____

2. We (am not/isn't/aren't) in that class. _____

3. Josephine (am not/isn't/aren't) blonde. _____

4. My parents (am not/isn't/aren't) here. _____

5. Sandra and Ella (am not/isn't/aren't) cousins. _____

6. You ('m not/'s not/'re not) brunette. _____

7. I ('m not/'s not/'re not) a baker. _____

8. She ('m not/'s not/'re not) short. _____

9. We ('m not/'s not/'re not) siblings. _____

10. He ('m not/'s not/'re not) serious. _____

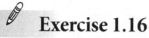

Exercise 1.16

Form sentences using both types of contractions shown in the preceding charts. Use a subject pronoun in the second sentence. Follow the example.

EXAMPLE   Joan and Deb / BE / not / sisters. *Joan and Deb aren't sisters.* / *They're not sisters.*

1. Marty and Joe / BE / not / cousins.

   _____

   _____

2. You / BE / not / a mechanic.

   _____

   _____

3. Cheryl and I / BE / not / siblings.

   _____

   _____

4. Mr. Jones / BE / not / happy.

   _____

   _____

5. My computer / BE / not / old.

   _____

   _____

6. Mrs. Weatherby / BE / not / strict.

   _____

   _____

7. The road / BE / not / straight.

   _____

   _____

8. I / BE / not / a teacher.

_____

_____

9. Francisco / BE / not / a student.

_____

_____

10. Rose / BE / not / sleepy.

_____

_____

Practice speaking: read the correct sentences aloud.

Exercise 1.17

Create two sentences about yourself using the affirmative BE verb. Then create two sentences about yourself using the negative BE verb.

Affirmative BE verb

1. _____

2. _____

Negative BE verb

3. _____

4. _____

Exercise 1.18

Create affirmative sentences using subject pronouns. Follow the example.

Affirmative BE Verb (No Contraction)

EXAMPLE: They: _They are students._

1. She: _____

2. He: _____

3. It: _____

4. You: _____

5. We: _____

6. They: _____

Affirmative BE Verb (with Contraction)

They: _They're students._

7. She: _____

8. He: _____

9. It: _____

10. You: _____

11. We: _____

12. They: _____

Exercise 1.19

Now create negative sentences using subject pronouns. Follow the example.

Negative BE Verb (No Contraction)

Negative BE Verb (with Two Types of Contractions)

EXAMPLE   They: *They are not students.*

They: *They're not students.* /
They aren't students.

1. She: _____

7. She: _____   _____

2. He: _____

8. He: _____   _____

3. It: _____

9. It: _____   _____

4. You: _____

10. You: _____   _____

5. We: _____

11. We: _____   _____

6. They: _____

12. They: _____   _____

BE: Forming Yes/No Questions

When we meet people, we ask questions. We use yes/no questions to get information. **Yes/no questions** can be answered with either *yes* or *no*. See how to form these questions in the following chart. Read the example sentences aloud.

BE VERB	SUBJECT OR SUBJECT PRONOUN	REST OF THE SENTENCE	EXAMPLE SENTENCES
Am	I	a student?	Am I a student?
Are	you/we/they	happy?	Are they happy?
Is	he/she/it	okay?	Is it okay?

Pronunciation Tip

Use rising pitch at the end of yes/no questions. Yes/no questions indicate uncertainty. Therefore, we use rising pitch to show that we would like an answer. (See the pitch chart in the Appendix for more information.)

You can answer a yes/no question with a long answer, using the complete verb tense and all parts of the sentence; you can give a short answer that includes only part of the verb tense; or you can give a quick answer using only *yes* or *no*. All of these answers are acceptable. The most common type of answer is a short answer. See the following examples.

YES/NO QUESTION: Is she happy today?

Affirmative Answers

LONG ANSWER: *Yes, she **is** happy today. / Yes, she**'s** happy today.*

SHORT ANSWER: *Yes, she **is**.*

QUICK ANSWER: *Yes.*

Negative Answers

LONG ANSWER: *No, she **is not** happy today. / No, she **isn't** happy today. / No, she**'s not** happy today.*

SHORT ANSWER: *No, she **is not**. / No, she **isn't**. / No, she**'s not**.*

QUICK ANSWER: *No.*

BE: Short Answers to Yes/No Questions

Here are some rules we use in short answers with yes/no questions.

> **Pronunciation Tip**: For long affirmative answers, stress the BE verb when not contracted: *Yes, she **is** happy today*. Also stress the BE verb for short affirmative answers: *Yes, she **is**.* For long and short negative answers, stress the negative contraction or *not*: *No, she is **not** happy today. / No, she **isn't**.* **Note**: Do not stress the quick answers.

Rules

- Omit the main verb in short answers.

- Do not contract *am* and *not*.

- Do not contract the affirmative short answer.

YES OR NO + COMMA	SUBJECT OR SUBJECT PRONOUN	BE VERB FORM	NEGATIVE	NEGATIVE CONTRACTION*
Yes,	I	am.		~~Yes, I'm.~~
No,	I	am	not.	No, I'm not.
Yes,	you/we/they	are.		~~Yes, they're.~~
No,	you/we/they	are	not.	No, they aren't.
				No, they're not.
Yes,	he/she/it	is.		~~Yes, he's.~~
No,	he/she/it	is	not.	No, he isn't.
				No, he's not.

*No contraction for affirmative answers.

Caution

A quick answer can sometimes be perceived as abrupt or rude. Always give quick answers in a polite tone. When giving a negative answer, you may often offer more information as an explanation. For example, you might say, "No, I'm not happy today. I'm sick."

When the answer is negative, you can sometimes omit the negative answer and use the word *actually* instead. For example, you might say, "Actually, I'm sick today."

✎ Exercise 1.20

Form yes/no questions with the BE verb using the words given. Then create long, short, and quick answers to each question. Answer the questions affirmatively (yes) or negatively (no) as indicated. Use a subject pronoun and contractions for the short answers. Follow the examples shown.

EXAMPLE 1   BE verb / Barbara / a teacher? (yes)

QUESTION: *Is Barbara a teacher?*

LONG ANSWER: *Yes, she is a teacher.*

SHORT ANSWER: *Yes, she is.*

QUICK ANSWER: *Yes.*

EXAMPLE 2   BE verb / Ted and Sally / married? (no)

QUESTION: *Are Ted and Sally married?*

LONG ANSWER: *No, they aren't married. / No, they're not married.*

SHORT ANSWER: *No, they aren't. / No, they're not.*

QUICK ANSWER: *No.*

1. BE verb / Alejandrina / an employee? (yes)

   QUESTION: _____

   LONG ANSWER: _____

   SHORT ANSWER: _____

   QUICK ANSWER: _____

2. BE verb / Dean / late? (no)

   QUESTION: _____

   LONG ANSWER: _____

   SHORT ANSWER: _____

   QUICK ANSWER: _____

3. BE verb / Jenna / your sister? (yes)

   QUESTION: _____

   LONG ANSWER: _____

   SHORT ANSWER: _____

   QUICK ANSWER: _____

4. BE verb / you / a student / at the community college? (no)

QUESTION: _____

LONG ANSWER: _____

SHORT ANSWER: _____

QUICK ANSWER: _____

5. BE verb / you / a student / at the nursing school? (yes)

QUESTION: _____

LONG ANSWER: _____

SHORT ANSWER: _____

QUICK ANSWER: _____

BE: Forming WH Questions

When we meet people, we ask questions. We use **WH questions**, or **information questions**, to ask about time, location, and the manner of and reason for an action. WH questions begin with WH question words or phrases such as *who, what, when, where, why, how, what kind, which one, how long, how many*, and *how much*. (For a list of WH question words, refer to the Appendix.) The following chart shows how to form these information questions. Read the example sentences aloud.

WH QUESTION WORD/PHRASE	BE VERB	SUBJECT OR SUBJECT PRONOUN	REST OF SENTENCE	EXAMPLE SENTENCES
When	am	I	at school?	When am I at school?
Where	are	you/we/they	right now?	Where are they right now?
Why	is	he/she/it	sad?	Why is she sad?

Pronunciation Tip

We usually use falling pitch at the end of WH questions. However, if you didn't hear or understand some information and you need repetition, use rising pitch. See the pitch chart in the Appendix for more information.

You can answer WH questions using the BE verb in different ways. You can give a long answer, which is a complete sentence and usually uses subject pronouns and contractions with the BE verb. You can also give a short answer with only the essential information that answers the question.

Exercise 1.21

Form WH questions with the BE verb using the words given. Form long and short answers. Follow the examples.

EXAMPLE 1   Where / BE verb / Felipa / today? (at school)

QUESTION: *Where is Felipa today?*

LONG ANSWER (COMPLETE SENTENCE): *She is at school. / She's at school.*

SHORT ANSWER (NOT A COMPLETE SENTENCE): *At school.*

EXAMPLE 2   Why / BE verb / Marciano / late? (because there is a lot of traffic)

> When we use the WH question word *why*, we usually use *because* in the answer.

QUESTION: *Why is Marciano late?*

LONG ANSWER (COMPLETE SENTENCE): *He is late because there is a lot of traffic. / He's late because there's a lot of traffic.*

SHORT ANSWER (NOT A COMPLETE SENTENCE): *Because there is a lot of traffic.*

1. When / BE verb / Xin / home? (at 3:00 P.M.)

   QUESTION: _____

   LONG ANSWER: _____

   SHORT ANSWER: _____

2. Why / BE verb / Michael / unhappy? (because he failed the test)

   QUESTION: _____

   LONG ANSWER: _____

   SHORT ANSWER: _____

3. How often / BE verb / Harry and William / at baseball practice? (every day after school)

   QUESTION: _____

   LONG ANSWER: _____

   SHORT ANSWER: _____

4. Where / BE verb / he / now? (at home)

   QUESTION: _____

   LONG ANSWER: _____

   SHORT ANSWER: _____

5. How / BE verb / she? (fine)

QUESTION: _____

LONG ANSWER: _____

SHORT ANSWER: _____

6. Who / BE verb / he? (the boss)

QUESTION: _____

LONG ANSWER: _____

SHORT ANSWER: _____

Grammar: Adjectives

Adjectives describe nouns. **Nouns** are people, places, and things.

PUT THE ADJECTIVE *BEFORE THE NOUN:* ADJECTIVE + NOUN		USE ADJECTIVES TO DESCRIBE HOW YOU FEEL: SUBJECT + STATIVE VERB* + ADJECTIVE	
*It's a **sunny day**.*	*He has a **red** car.*	*I **feel fine**.*	*She **is happy**.*
sunny = adjective	red = adjective	feel = stative verb	is = stative verb
day = noun	car = noun	fine = adjective	happy = adjective

*A **stative verb** is used to describe a state or condition. See the Appendix for a list of common stative verbs.

We usually use adjectives like the following ones, along with the BE verb, to describe how we feel. Read these words aloud. The adjectives are in order from best to worst. Informal expressions have an asterisk (*) next to them.

Best ————————————————————————————————→

Excellent / Great / Very good / Good / Fine / Pretty good* / Okay / All right / Not bad* / So-so*

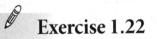 ## Exercise 1.22

Create sentences describing how people feel. Use the correct form of the BE verb.

EXAMPLE   Katie / BE / pretty good.   *Katie is pretty good.*

1. Benjamin / BE / great. _____

2. Evelyn and Rocco / BE / okay. _____

3. Diana / BE / all right. _____

4. Sonja and I / BE / excellent. _____

5. They / BE / good. _____

6. I / BE / very good. _____

Talking About the Weather

Weather is a common topic for small talk. It is a neutral topic and is easy to discuss. When we talk about the weather, we usually say, "It's + (adjective)." For example, we might say, "It's sunny." Here are some common adjectives to describe the weather. Read them aloud.

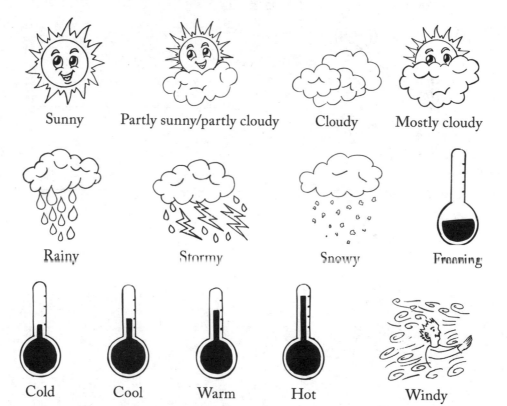

When we talk about the weather, this is the form we use:

It + is + adjective. / It's + adjective.

EXAMPLE SENTENCES: *It is cloudy. / It is windy. / It's chilly. / It's sunny.*

We may add a word or phrase to the sentence to give more information.

It's hot *out there*! / It's rainy *today*. / It's snowy *outside*.

We may also add an adverb to emphasize the adjective:

It's *so* hot out there! / It's *too* cold today. / It's *very* windy!

Exercise 1.23

Create a sentence describing the weather. Use the illustrations to help you, and follow the example.

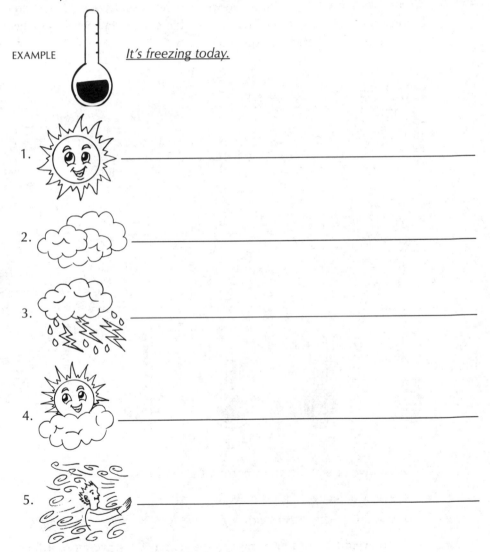

EXAMPLE   *It's freezing today.*

1. _____

2. _____

3. _____

4. _____

5. _____

Read the correct sentences aloud twice.

Using the Negative

Another way to talk about the weather is to use the negative form:

It is not + adjective. / Contraction: It's not + adjective. / It isn't + adjective.

EXAMPLE SENTENCES: *It is not cloudy. / It's not freezing today. / It isn't sunny now.*

Exercise 1.24

Create negative sentences describing the weather. Form two sentences for each answer: Create the full sentence and then the sentence using a contraction. Following the example, use the illustrations and clue words to help you.

EXAMPLE  (cold) *It is not cold today.*
Contraction: *It's not cold today. It isn't cold today.*

1.  (rainy)

_____

_____

2. (sunny)

_____

_____

3.  (hot)

_____

_____

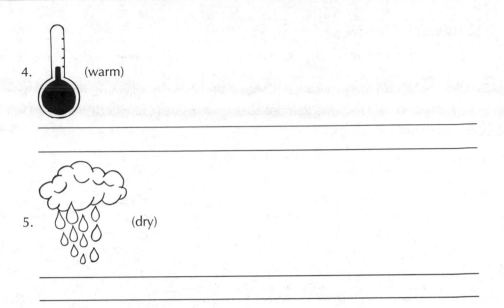

4. _____ (warm)

_____

_____

5. _____ (dry)

_____

_____

Practice speaking: read the correct sentences aloud twice.

Using Intensifier Adverbs

In English, we use adverbs to intensify an adjective. To **intensify** something is to make it stronger. To use an adverb with an adjective, put the adverb first:

Adverb + adjective

EXAMPLE SENTENCES: Read the sentences aloud.

The soup is **very hot**.   _The pasta is **so delicious**._   _The bread is **really soft**._

very = adverb   so = adverb   really = adverb

hot = adjective   delicious = adjective   soft = adjective

Here are some adverbs we use with adjectives. They decrease in intensity from left to right.

Intense ──→

Very / Quite / Really / So / Pretty* / A bit / A little / A little bit / A tad

*"Pretty" is an informal expression used in North America.

Tip

The adverb _too_ gives any adjective a negative meaning.

This bread is too hard. _(It's harder than you like, and you want it softer.)_

This soup is too hot. _(It's hotter than you want, and you want it cooler.)_

This coffee is too bitter. _(It's more bitter than you like, and you want it sweeter.)_

Culture Note: In North American English, _quite_ means "very." In British English, _quite_ means "a little."

Exercise 1.25

Choose the adverb that best completes the sentence. Use the illustrations to help you.

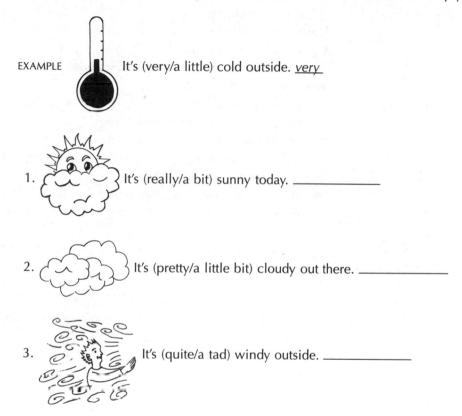

EXAMPLE   It's (very/a little) cold outside. *very*

1.   It's (really/a bit) sunny today. _____

2.   It's (pretty/a little bit) cloudy out there. _____

3.   It's (quite/a tad) windy outside. _____

Vocabulary: Phrasal Verbs

Phrasal verbs are usually composed of two words: a verb and a preposition. An example of a two-word phrasal verb is *run into*, which means to unintentionally meet someone you know. A phrasal verb sometimes has three words: a verb, a preposition, and another preposition. An example of a three-word phrasal verb is *run out of*, which means to deplete the supply of something. Phrasal verbs are informal and used often in English. Let's examine the phrasal verbs in the following chart.

PHRASAL VERBS	
Common form	Verb + preposition (+ preposition)
Pronunciation	Stress on preposition: turn *off* / break *down*
Grammar	May require an object:
	Turn off *the radio*. (object) / The car broke down. (no object)
Pronoun	Replace object with pronoun:
	Correct: Turn *it* off. (Pronoun separates phrasal verb.)
	Incorrect: ~~Turn off it.~~
Meaning 1	The verb and preposition may create a new meaning that is different from the verb's original meaning.
	Example: He came across an old photograph.
	To **come across something** means to find something unintentionally.
Meaning 2	The preposition may intensify the verb.
	Example: He *spread* the research papers *out* on the desk.
	To **spread out** means to distribute something widely over an area.

Some phrasal verbs have multiple meanings. Let's look at examples of phrasal verbs:

To check out—to look at	To drop in on—to visit
To look up to—to admire	To find out—to discover
To look down on—to regard with contempt	To look up—to look in a dictionary for
To be fed up with—to be intolerant of	To cut off—to interrupt
To cut down on—to reduce consumption of	To break into—to enter forcibly

Now, let's practice using phrasal verbs.

Exercise 1.26

Complete the following sentences with the correct phrasal verb from the preceding list.

EXAMPLE   Joanna *looks up to* her supervisor because he is honest.

1. My mother is _____ my sister's bad behavior.

2. Shirley must _____ fatty foods. She's trying to lose weight.

3. Ned and Owen should _____ new vocabulary.

4. The robber will _____ the car and steal the stereo.

5. _____ the new car. It's beautiful!

6. We have to _____ Grandma and bring her lunch.

Reading About It

This section introduces the steps for reading effectively. In later chapters of the book, you will practice these steps. For now, let's learn what the three steps are.

Step 1: Pre-Read

Pre-reading quickly helps you understand the topic and main idea of the passage. When you pre-read, you quickly scan the text *before* you read the passage. Spend only a few minutes pre-reading. Do not read everything!

> A **passage** is a segment of writing. It can be short or long.

To Pre-Read

- Read the title.

- Look at the pictures or charts.

- Look for key words.

- Read the first and last sentences of every paragraph.

- Read the first and last paragraphs of long passages.

> **Key words** are important words that are usually repeated.

Step 2: Read Actively

Active reading helps you remember the information you read. While you read, use a pencil, pen, or highlighter to label important information, such as the topic and the main idea. You should also identify key words, new vocabulary, and parts you find unclear.

To Read Actively

- Underline the topic.
- Circle new vocabulary.
- Put a question mark (?) next to unclear parts.
- Take notes.
- Highlight the main idea and key words.
- Mark examples with "Ex."

- Number main points, lists, or ideas.
- Write comments or questions.

Step 3: Understand What You Read

After you have actively read the passage, check your understanding. Be sure you understand what you read. There are many ways to check your understanding.

To Check Your Understanding

- Answer questions and score your answers.
- Summarize the passage.
- Respond to what you read by giving your opinion on the topic.
- Discuss the passage with a partner.
- Outline the passage.

Let's Read Together

Let's practice the three steps for reading effectively. First, pre-read the following passage. As you do, identify the topic and main idea of the passage. Spend one to two minutes pre-reading.

> The **topic** is the subject of the passage. It is usually in the title and in the first sentence. The **main idea** is the primary point about the topic.

 Rita Learns English

Rita is learning English. She is from Italy. She moved to an English-speaking country. She goes to school at night. Rita practices English every day. She studies at home. Her English is improving.

Now answer the following two questions. Remember: the topic and the main idea are usually in the title and the first sentence.

What is the topic? _____

What is the main idea? _____

To find the topic of a reading, ask this question: *Who or what is the passage about?* The subject of the passage is Rita. You can see *Rita* in the title and also in the first sentence. So Rita is the topic.

To find the main idea of a reading, ask these questions: *What about Rita? What important information do we learn about her?* We find out that she is learning English. The main idea is she is learning English.

The answers to the two questions are:

What is the topic? *Rita*

What is the main idea? *She is learning English.*

Next, **actively read** the passage. Read it carefully. Use your pencil, pen, and highlighter to label examples, key words, new vocabulary, and confusing parts. (If you are reading this as an e-book, copy the passage onto your own paper first.) When you are finished, your passage might look like the example shown.

Rita is learning English. She is from Italy. She moved to an English-speaking country. She goes to school at night. Rita practices English every day. She studies at home. Her English is improving.

Finally, **check that you understand what you read**. Answer the following questions to check your comprehension. In later chapters, you will learn other ways to check your understanding.

 ## Exercise 1.27

Answer the questions.

1. What is the title of this passage? _____

2. Who moved to a new country? _____

3. When does Rita go to school? _____

4. Note all that are true about Rita.

   a. She is learning English.   c. She studies at home.

   b. She is from Spain.   d. She practices English every day.

5. What is the main idea of this passage? _____

Writing About It

In this section, you will learn how to begin and end a sentence.

How to Begin a Sentence

Every sentence must begin with a capital letter. A **capital letter**, also called an **uppercase letter**, is the large version of a letter. A capital letter is the opposite of a **small letter**,

Tip: All capital letters are larger than small letters. Make all capital letters bigger than small letters when you write.

which is also called a **lowercase letter**. Study the complete uppercase and lowercase alphabets in the Appendix.

Exercise 1.28

Now that you have studied the section on capital letters and lowercase letters, see what you remember. Use the Appendix to help you.

1. What is the capital for *n*? _____

2. What is the lowercase letter for *H*? _____

3. What is the lowercase letter for *P*? _____

4. What is the capital for *b*? _____

5. What is the capital for *q*? _____

6. What is the lowercase letter for *E*? _____

7. What is the capital for *k*? _____

8. What is the capital for *w*? _____

9. What is the lowercase letter for *Y*? _____

10. What is the capital for *d*? _____

Look at the following example sentences. The correct sentences begin with a capital letter. The incorrect sentences begin with a small letter.

CORRECT: *L*earning a new language takes time.

INCORRECT: *l*earning a new language takes time.

CORRECT: *I*t is exciting to live in a new country.

INCORRECT: *i*t is exciting to live in a new country.

Exercise 1.29

Complete the following sentences with a capital letter. Refer to the uppercase alphabet in the Appendix for examples, and see the reading passage about Rita for clues.

1. _____ita is learning English.

2. _____taly is her home country.

3. _____he studies every day.

4. _____er English will be better soon.

5. _____hen do you practice English?

6. _____ou should practice English every day.

Practice speaking: read the correct sentences aloud twice.

Exercise 1.30

Create three sentences about yourself. Begin each sentence with a capital letter.

1. _____

2. _____

3. _____

How to End a Sentence

Every sentence in the English language must end with punctuation. **Punctuation marks** are the marks used in writing. There are three ways to end a sentence: with a period (.), with a question mark (?), or with an exclamation point (!).

1. A **period** (.) ends every statement. It is also called a **full stop**.

2. A **question mark** (?) ends every question.

3. An **exclamation point** (!) shows emphasis with interjections, demands, or declarations.

The most commonly used end-of-sentence punctuation marks are the period and the question mark. In this chapter, we will focus on those marks.

The Period

A period ends every statement. A **statement** is a declarative sentence, or a telling sentence. A statement does *not* ask a question. Let's look at some example statements. Read them aloud.

Learning English is fun.   She is a student.

It is raining.   James works at the hospital.

The Question Mark

A question mark ends every **direct question**, including information questions, yes/no questions, and tag questions. We will study questions in Chapters 2, 3, and 5. Let's look at some examples here. Read them aloud.

Where are you going?   Is he a student?

Mary's a doctor, isn't she?   What time is it?

Exercise 1.31

Look at the following sentences and decide if the end-of-sentence punctuation is correct. If it is incorrect, write the sentence correctly. See the example sentences.

Correct: *It is sunny today.*

Incorrect: ~~What do you do.~~ *What do you do?*

1. _____ Is it rainy out there? _____

2. _____ My friend is from Morocco? _____

3. _____ What time does the restaurant open. _____

4. _____ It is freezing outside. _____

5. _____ Are you happy today. _____

6. _____ Stanley is a student. _____

7. _____ Nodira is from Russia. _____

8. _____ This is my brother? _____

9. _____ Maura is a student, isn't she. _____

10. _____ Where is Vivek. _____

Practice speaking: read the sentences aloud twice.

Exercise 1.32

Indicate the correct punctuation at the end of every sentence.

1. She is a teacher_____

2. Where does Joe live_____

3. Isabella lives in the city_____

4. Matt and Carla are students, aren't they_____

5. Is that your dog_____

6. Is Omar your friend_____

7. What time does work begin_____

8. We are at the store_____

9. My car is red_____

10. Who is she_____

Practice speaking: read the correct sentences aloud twice.

Exercise 1.33

Unscramble the words to make a statement or a question. Be sure every sentence begins with a capital letter and ends with a period or a question mark. Follow the examples.

EXAMPLES   does / How often / study / she   *How often does she study?*

studies / She / day / every   *She studies every day.*

1. you / live / Where / do _____

2. I / in / Lakeview / live _____

3. that / dog / your / Is _____

4. it / Yes, / is _____

5. do / study / you / When _____

6. study / I / night / every _____

7. does / cost / How much / it _____

8. a lot / It / costs _____

9. he / a / student / Is /good _____

10. Ali / good / a / is / student _____

Practice speaking: read the correct sentences aloud twice.

Exercise 1.34

Create two questions and two statements. Use correct end-of-sentence punctuation.

Statements	Questions
1. _____	1. _____
2. _____	2. _____

Quiz

Check your understanding of Chapter 1.

1. Which of these is *not* an informal greeting?

   Hi.   What's up?

   Good morning.   Howdy.

2. What's the best way to say good-bye to someone you have just met?

   Later.   A pleasure meeting you.

   Take care.   Bye.

3. What's the first step in meeting someone?

   Make small talk.   Introduce yourself.

   Say hello.   Make eye contact.

4. How do people shake hands in North America?

   Firmly   Firmly, with five shakes up and down

   Quickly   Lightly

5. What is the correct subject pronoun for *Denny and Suzuki*?

   She   He

   It   They

6. What's the correct form of the BE verb in this sentence? She _____ happy.

   is   be

   am   are

7. What is the correct negative contraction of BE in this sentence? The books
   _____ heavy.

   isn't   aren't

   's not   're not

8. Which is *not* an example of pre-reading?

   Reading the title   Circling new vocabulary

   Looking at the pictures and charts   Reading the first and last sentences of
                                                   every paragraph

9. Which is *not* an example of reading actively?

   Underlining the topic   Highlighting the main idea and key
                                                   words

   Taking notes   Reading the first and last paragraphs
                                                   of long passages

10. Which punctuation mark is *not* used at the end of a sentence?

    ?   ,

    !   .

Do It Out There!

Now that you have learned how to greet and meet people, try it out in the
world. Review this chapter, and go out and use English! Put a check mark
next to each activity as you complete it.

To Do This Week

❑ Greet five people using appropriate phrases. ("Formal and Informal
  Greetings" section)
❑ Wave hello and good-bye to three people you know. ("Wave Hello and
  Good-bye" sidebar)
❑ Meet two people. Use two different types of small talk. ("Culture Note:
  Making Small Talk" sidebar)
❑ Shake hands with two people. ("Culture Note: How to Shake Hands"
  sidebar)
❑ Speak using subject pronouns and the correct form of the BE verb.
  (Grammar sections on subject pronouns and BE verb)

Weekly Log

Keep a weekly log of your progress. Make notes on how your practice went. What happened? Was it successful? How do you know it was successful? Was it unsuccessful? How do you know? Review all the instructions, tips, and culture notes in Chapter 1.

_____

_____

_____

_____

_____

_____

_____

2

Habits, Customs, and Routines

In this chapter you will learn about:

Speaking
✓ How to talk about habits, customs, and routines
✓ How to introduce two people to each other

Vocabulary, Reading, and Writing
✓ Adverbs of frequency
✓ Vocabulary for family members
✓ Vocabulary related to daily activities
✓ How to read actively
✓ The difference between a passage's topic and main idea
✓ Subject-verb agreement
✓ Proper nouns
✓ Phrasal verbs related to routines

Grammar
✓ The simple present verb tense
✓ How to ask questions about frequency with non-BE verbs using *do*
✓ Third person singular with the simple present
✓ *Who* questions with the simple present verb tense
✓ Yes/no questions with answers for the simple present

Body Language
✓ To wave someone over (to you)

In this chapter, you will practice the grammar, spelling rules, and vocabulary to describe your habits, customs, and routines. To improve your reading skills, you will practice reading actively and discover the difference between a topic and a main idea. To practice writing, you will learn subject-verb agreement and how to capitalize proper nouns.

Talking About Habits, Customs, and Routines

We often talk about habits and activities. We do some activities every day. We do some activities every week, every month, or every year. What activities do you do regularly? Identify your habits, customs, and routines and how often you engage in them. Create a list of them. See the examples.

Activities I Do Every Day	Activities I Do Every Week	Activities I Do Every Year
Brush my teeth	*Go to the park*	*Visit my family in Mexico*
_____	_____	_____
_____	_____	_____
_____	_____	_____
_____	_____	_____
_____	_____	_____
_____	_____	_____

Now, look at the following list of habits, customs, and routines. How often do you perform them?

Exercise 2.1

Match the activities and customs on the right with the frequency on the left.

Every day   Take a shower
Every week   Go to work/school
Every six months   Go to the dentist
Every year   Celebrate your birthday
                     Eat lunch
                     Take a vacation
                     Play in the park
                     Exercise

Now that you have been introduced to habits, customs, and routines, let's learn some vocabulary about family.

Talking About Family

Meet the Anderson family.

Let's practice vocabulary for family members.

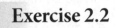

Exercise 2.2

Look at the Anderson's family tree. Complete the sentences about their relationships using the vocabulary given.

grandfather	grandmother	grandparents	mother	father
wife	husband	parents	sister	brother
child	children	aunt	uncle	niece
nephew	granddaughter	grandson	grandchild	grandchildren
cousins	sister-in-law	brother-in-law	siblings	relatives

Remember

To show possession in English, we use an apostrophe and the letter *s*. For example, to show that Martha is the mother of Mary, we write *Martha is Mary's mother.*

1. Howard and Martha are Mary's _____.

2. Mary and Jim are _____.

3. Cindy is Jim's _____.

4. Madeleine and Mason are Jim and Cindy's _____.

5. Jack is Aidan's _____.

6. Madeleine is Mason's _____.

7. Howard and Martha's grandchildren are _____, _____, _____, and _____.

8. Madeleine is Mary and Carl's _____.

9. Aidan is Jim and Cindy's _____.

10. Carl is Jim's _____.

11. Cindy is Carl's _____.

12. Jack and Mason are _____.

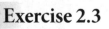

Culture Note

In North America, the word *kid* is often used instead of *child*, and *kids* is often used instead of *children*.

Exercise 2.3

Create a family tree for your family. Place each person's name under his or her picture.

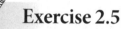 ## Exercise 2.4

Create sentences showing the relationships of your family members. Use the vocabulary for family members listed in Exercise 2.2. Remember to use an apostrophe + s to show relationships.

1. _____

2. _____

3. _____

4. _____

5. _____

Exercise 2.5

Let's look at the daily activities that Cindy and Jim Anderson do. Some of the verbs describing their activities are missing. Complete the sentences with the verbs given.

| gets up | finishes | walk | arrives | makes | picks up |
| eats | goes | puts | relax | watches | |

Cindy   Jim

Morning

Jim (1) _____ at 5:00 A.M. He goes to the gym and exercises for an hour. At 6:30 A.M., he showers at the gym. Cindy wakes up at 6:00 A.M. She (2) _____ breakfast for the family. At 7:30 A.M., Cindy, Madeleine, and Mason (3) _____ to the bus stop. Cindy goes home and takes a shower at 7:45 A.M. For breakfast, Jim always drinks a protein shake. He drives to work, where he (4) _____ at 7:00 A.M. At 8:30 A.M., Cindy catches the bus to work.

Noon

Cindy usually has lunch with coworkers. Jim often goes to a restaurant for lunch.

> **Culture Note**: In English, people *have* and *eat* lunch. They do not *take* lunch.

Afternoon

Cindy (5) _____ work at 5:00 P.M. and goes home. Sometimes, she takes a walk in the park after work. Jim leaves work at 3:30 P.M. and (6) _____ his kids at school. He takes Mason to baseball practice and Madeleine to soccer practice.

Evening

Jim and the kids go home for dinner. At 6:30 P.M., Cindy (7) _____ dinner with her family. After dinner, she helps her children with their homework, while Jim (8) _____ TV.

Nighttime

At 8:30 P.M., Cindy (9) _____ her kids to bed. After Madeleine and Mason go to bed, Jim and Cindy (10) _____. Jim (11) _____ to bed around 10:30 P.M., and Cindy follows around 11:00 P.M.

> **Around** and **about** mean "approximately."

Culture Note

In North America, the suffix **-ish** may be used for estimating times; for example, *Jim goes to bed at 10:30**ish***.

Grammar: Using the Simple Present Verb Tense

In English, we use the simple present verb tense to talk about habits, customs, and routines. Let's look at some example sentences.

EXAMPLE 1: *Cindy wakes up at 6:00 A.M.*

	X	X	X		X		X	
Sunday	Monday	Tuesday	Wednesday	Thursday	Friday	Saturday

Cindy doesn't wake up early on weekends, but she wakes up at 6:00 A.M. every weekday. It's a habit.

EXAMPLE 2: *Jim visits his parents in Florida every winter.*

X		X		Illness		X		X
2012	2013	2014	2015	2016

Jim usually visits his parents in Florida every year, although one year, he is sick and doesn't go. His visit is an activity he plans every year.

EXAMPLE 3: *They barbecue every weekend in the summer.*

X X X X X X X X X X

← —————————————————————————————————— →

Winter   Spring   Summer   Fall

The Anderson family makes dinner on the barbecue every Saturday and Sunday during the summer. They don't barbecue in the winter, and they sometimes barbecue in the fall and spring, but they always barbecue in the summer. It's a custom.

> To **barbecue** means to cook food outside on a grill. A **barbecue** is an outdoor grill. **Culture Note:** In Australia, the slang expression for a *barbecue* is a *barbie*.

Simple Present: Forming the Affirmative
Read the example sentences in the following table aloud.

SUBJECT OR SUBJECT PRONOUN	VERB IN SIMPLE PRESENT FORM	EXAMPLE SENTENCES
I/You/We/ They	take	They *take* the bus to work. / Jim and Cindy *take* the bus to work.
He/She/It	take**s**	She *takes* the bus to work. / Cindy *takes* the bus to work.

Important: With *he, she,* and *it,* you must use the third person singular verb tense. To form the third person singular with most verbs, you add **-s** at the end of the verb. See more spelling rules in the Appendix.

Simple Present: Irregular Verb Forms
Some verbs are irregular, meaning they do not follow the normal rules. See the following list of common irregular verbs. See a list of irregular verbs in the Appendix.

I/YOU/WE/ THEY	HE/SHE/IT
have	has
do	does
go	goes

> **Pronunciation Tip:** *Do* and *does* are pronounced with different vowel sounds: *do* is pronounced /du/, and *does* is pronounced /dəz/. However, the vowel sounds in *go* and *goes* are the same: /goʊ/ and /goʊz/. See the Appendix for a complete list of International Phonetic Alphabet symbols.

Exercise 2.6

Complete the sentences with the correct simple present verb form.

EXAMPLE   She _relaxes_ after she puts the children to bed.   relax   relaxes

1. Mason _____ baseball after school.   play   plays

2. Madeleine _____ soccer after school.   play   plays

3. They all _____ dinner at around 6:30 P.M.   eat   eats

4. Mason and Madeleine _____ their homework every night.   do   does

5. Every year, they _____ Cindy's birthday in the park.   celebrate   celebrates

6. The kids _____ to the dentist every six months.   go   goes

7. Jim _____ five days a week.   work   works

8. Cindy and her children _____ to the bus stop on school days.   walk   walks

9. Madeleine _____ more homework than Mason.   have   has

10. Mason _____ younger than Madeleine.   are   is

Pronunciation Tip: Three Different -s Ending Sounds

In English, we make three different sounds for the final -s in plural count nouns, such as toys and pets. It is also found in possessive nouns and pronouns, such as its and Jane's, and in third person singular simple present verbs, such as takes and gives.

The sound of the -s ending is determined by the last consonant sound in the word. For example, let's look at the word *take*. The last consonant sound in *take* is /k/. The /k/ sound is voiceless, so the sound of the -s ending will be /s/. Another example is the word *give*. The last consonant sound in *give* is /v/. The /v/ sound is voiced, so the sound of the -s ending will be /z/.

The following table provides a list of the sounds and rules.

SOUND	/s/	/z/	/ɪz/
Examples	takes, stops, puts, makes, starts, its, Pat's, Jeff's, tips, socks	drives, gives, does, says, shows, loves, homes, schools, rings, Rob's	wishes, misses, watches, chooses, judges, Mitch's, Jones's, houses
Final consonant sounds	/t/; /f/; /p/; /k/; /θ/	/m/; /n/; /d/; /v/; /b/; /g/; /l/; /w/; /y/; /ŋ/; /ð/; all vowel sounds	/s/; /z/; /tʃ/; /dʒ/; /ʃ/; /ʒ/
Rules and notes	This final -s sounds like a snake: *sss*. It is a **voiceless sound** because it does not engage the vocal cords; only air is used to make the sound. Put your hand on your throat as you make this sound; there is no vibration.	This final -s sounds like a /z/. It is a **voiced sound** because it engages the vocal cords, meaning the vocal cords vibrate. Put your hand on your throat and feel the vibration as you make the sound *zzz*.	This ending adds a syllable to the word. It is a voiced sound and pronounced like the BE verb *is*.

Exercise 2.7

Look at the third person singular verbs, plural count nouns, and possessives that follow. Identify the last consonant sound each has before the -s ending. Then check the preceding table. Does the -s ending sound like /s/, /z/ or /ɪz/? Choose the correct sound. The first one has been done for you.

1. decides /s/ /z/ /ɪz/ _/z/_
2. starts /s/ /z/ /ɪz/ _____
3. dances /s/ /z/ /ɪz/ _____
4. cars /s/ /z/ /ɪz/ _____

5. problems /s/ /z/ /ɪz/ _____
6. Mary's /s/ /z/ /ɪz/ _____
7. Peng's /s/ /z/ /ɪz/ _____
8. Jack's /s/ /z/ /ɪz/ _____

Exercise 2.8

Think of two plural count nouns, two possessives, and two third person singular simple present verbs. Then choose the correct -s ending sound for each.

PLURAL COUNT NOUN			POSSESSIVE			THIRD PERSON SINGULAR VERB		
_____ /s/ /z/ /ɪz/			_____ /s/ /z/ /ɪz/			_____ /s/ /z/ /ɪz/		
_____ /s/ /z/ /ɪz/			_____ /s/ /z/ /ɪz/			_____ /s/ /z/ /ɪz/		

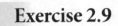

Exercise 2.9

Create sentences about your habits, customs, and routines. Think about your family's habits too. You may use the following verbs or other verbs. Use the third person singular in two of the sentences.

go   do   walk work play exercise   eat sleep wake up make
arrive leave relax cook visit celebrate get drive get up   take catch

1. _____
2. _____
3. _____
4. _____
5. _____
6. _____

Simple Present: Forming the Negative

To form the negative simple present verb tense, you must use the verb helper *do* plus *not*. The main verb must take the base form. The following table shows how to form the negative simple present tense. Read the example sentences aloud.

SUBJECT OR SUBJECT PRONOUN	DO OR DOES	NEGATIVE	BASE FORM OF VERB	EXAMPLE SENTENCES
I/You/We/ They	do	not	take	I do not take the bus to work.
He/She/It	does	not	take	He does not take the bus to work.

Important: Do not add **-s** to the main verb if it's negative. See the example sentences.

INCORRECT: *He does not ~~takes~~ the train to work.*

CORRECT: *He does not take the train to work.*

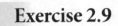

Exercise 2.10

Complete the sentences with the correct negative form of the simple present verb.

EXAMPLE   Joseph <u>*does not*</u> play basketball after school.   do not   does not

1. Miriam _____ work on weekends.   do not   does not

2. Abdul and Moe _____ study every night.   do not   does not

3. Mr. Shane _____ work on Mondays.   do not   does not

4. Ms. Schuler _____ teach in the summer.   do not   does not

5. They _____ go to the movies every weekend.   do not   does not

6. Pamela and Jasper _____ play soccer.   do not   does not

Simple Present: Forming Negative Contractions

In English, we often speak using contractions. It's less formal. We also use contractions when writing informally. Read the example sentences aloud.

SUBJECT OR SUBJECT PRONOUN	DO OR DOES	NEGATIVE	CONTRACTION OF DO AND NEGATIVE	BASE FORM OF VERB	EXAMPLE SENTENCES
I/You/We/They	do	not	don't	take	I don't take the bus to work.
He/She/It	does	not	doesn't	take	He doesn't take the bus to work.

Now that you know how to form negative contractions in the simple present verb tense, let's practice.

Exercise 2.11

Form sentences using the words given. First, create the negative form of the simple present verb, and then create the negative contraction.

EXAMPLE   Griffin / NEGATIVE / go / to school on weekends.

Griffin **does not go** to school on weekends.

Griffin **doesn't go** to school on weekends.

1. Charlie / NEGATIVE / play / hockey.

_____

_____

2. Cindy / NEGATIVE / drive / to work.

_____

_____

3. Jack / NEGATIVE / play / a musical instrument.

_____

_____

4. Joshua and Sybil / NEGATIVE / go / to college.

_____

_____

5. Sharon and her sister / NEGATIVE / work / at night.

_____

_____

6. I / NEGATIVE / exercise / in the morning.

_____

_____

7. We / NEGATIVE / finish / work at the same time every day.

_____

_____

Grammar: Using Adverbs of Frequency

When we talk about habits, customs, and routines, we use adverbs of frequency. In most cases, the adverb of frequency is placed *before the verb*. However, if the BE verb is the main verb, then the adverb of frequency is placed *after the BE verb*. The following chart shows common adverbs of frequency organized by meaning. Read the example sentences aloud.

100%

  ↑ Always
     Almost always
     Often
     Usually
     Frequently
     Sometimes
     Occasionally
     Seldom
     Not often
     Hardly ever
     Rarely
  ↓ Never

0%

EXAMPLE 1:   Jim *never* **takes** the bus to work.

EXAMPLE 2:   Mason *always* **does** his homework after dinner.

EXAMPLE 3:   Madeleine **is** *usually* finished with her homework before Mason.

Culture Note: In the United States, we can use the adverbs of frequency *always* and *never* to complain. **Pronunciation Note:** We stress *always* and *never* whenever we use them to make a complaint. See the examples of complaints using these two adverbs of frequency:

- Complaint: He ***always*** loses his keys!
- Complaint: She is ***never*** on time to meetings.

Now, let's practice using adverbs of frequency in sentences. Be sure to put the adverb in the correct place. Use the example sentences to guide you.

Exercise 2.12

Create sentences using the words given. Be sure to use the correct form of the simple present verb tense. He, she, *and* it *require the third person singular form.*

EXAMPLE   Shelby / ADVERB OF FREQUENCY / go / to school on weekends. (never)
Shelby never goes to school on weekends.

1. Takako and Jun / ADVERB OF FREQUENCY / eat / breakfast. (always)

   _____

2. Solomon / ADVERB OF FREQUENCY / take / a shower / in the morning. (often)

   _____

3. They / ADVERB OF FREQUENCY / drive / to work / Monday through Friday. (usually)

   _____

4. I / BE / ADVERB OF FREQUENCY / late / for work. (hardly ever)

   _____

5. She / ADVERB OF FREQUENCY / walk / to work. (seldom)

   _____

6. Hildegard / ADVERB OF FREQUENCY / exercise / before work. (sometimes)

   _____

7. Julius and his brother / ADVERB OF FREQUENCY / take / the bus to school. (frequently)

   _____

8. You / BE / ADVERB OF FREQUENCY / late for school. (occasionally)

   _____

9. We / ADVERB OF FREQUENCY / miss / class. (hardly ever)

_____

10. Oscar / BE / ADVERB OF FREQUENCY / tired / by 9:00 P.M. (always)

_____

Exercise 2.13

Create sentences about your habits, customs, and routines using the adverbs of frequency given. Remember that the adverb of frequency usually goes before the verb. However, if you are using the BE verb, the adverb of frequency follows it.

1. often _____

2. sometimes _____

3. seldom _____

4. never _____

Asking About the Frequency of Activities with the WH Question *How Often*

In conversation, we ask questions about the frequency at which someone does an activity. We use *how often* to start these questions. As you review the following table, read the example sentences aloud.

WH QUESTION PHRASE—HOW OFTEN	DO OR DOES	SUBJECT OR SUBJECT PRONOUN	BASE FORM OF VERB	REST OF SENTENCE + QUESTION MARK	EXAMPLE SENTENCES
How often	do	I/you/we/they	take	the bus to work?	How often do you take the bus to work?
How often	does	he/she/it	take	the bus to work?	How often does she take the bus to work?

Pronunciation Tip

Use falling pitch with information questions, which begin with a WH question word such as *who, what, when, where, why, how, which one, how many, how much, what kind*, and *how often*. See the pitch chart in the Appendix for more information.

Let's look at some examples of questions about frequency:

How often does she play basketball after school?

How often does he finish his homework before dinner?

How often do they play volleyball in the park?

How often do you take singing lessons?

How often does Nate help you clean?

How often do the kids watch movies?

How often does Li vacuum the house?

How often does she play with her friends?

Now, let's practice writing questions of frequency using the simple present verb tense.

Exercise 2.14

Create sentences using the words given. Be sure to use the correct form of do. *Review the table on how to form questions of frequency, and use the example sentences to guide you.*

EXAMPLE   How often / DO / John / play / baseball?

How often does John play baseball?

1. How often / DO / Etta / watch / TV?

   _____

2. How often / DO / Jay and Marcy / go / to the mall?

   _____

3. How often / DO / Mom / shop / for groceries?

   _____

4. How often / DO / you / do / your homework?

   _____

5. How often / DO / they / eat / dinner at restaurants?

   _____

6. How often / DO / your sister / make / your breakfast?

   _____

7. How often / DO / we / miss / the bus?

   _____

8. How often / DO / Adele / visit / her grandparents?

   _____

Now let's learn how to answer questions of frequency. You can use a complete sentence; this is called a long answer. You can also give a short answer, which uses only the adverb of frequency. Examples are shown here.

QUESTION OF FREQUENCY: How often does she take the bus to work?

LONG ANSWER: She always takes the bus to work.

SHORT ANSWER: Always.

Exercise 2.15

Form questions of frequency about the Anderson family's activities. The long answers are done. Use these long answers to help you form the questions. Then create short answers.

Madeleine   Mason   Cindy   Jim

EXAMPLE   QUESTION: *How often does Mason play baseball after school?*

LONG ANSWER: Mason often plays baseball after school.

SHORT ANSWER: *Often.*

1. QUESTION: _____

   LONG ANSWER: Cindy never drives to work.

   SHORT ANSWER: _____

2. QUESTION: _____

   LONG ANSWER: Jim often has lunch at a restaurant.

   SHORT ANSWER: _____

3. QUESTION: _____

   LONG ANSWER: Madeleine always does her homework after dinner.

   SHORT ANSWER: _____

4. QUESTION: _____

    LONG ANSWER: Cindy and Jim always relax before going to bed.

    SHORT ANSWER: _____

5. QUESTION: _____

    LONG ANSWER: Cindy sometimes takes a walk in the park.

    SHORT ANSWER: _____

Now that you have practiced asking questions of frequency, let's practice asking other WH questions.

Grammar: Asking WH Questions in the Simple Present Tense

In conversation, we ask many kinds of questions. We can ask about the location of, reason for, or manner of an occurrence. Let's look at some different WH question words we use.

WH QUESTION WORD	WHAT IT ASKS ABOUT	WH QUESTION WORD	WHAT IT ASKS ABOUT
Where	Location, place	Who*	People
When	Time, day, date	What time	Time
What	Something	Why/What for (informal)	Reason
How many	Quantity (countable)	How much	Amount (uncountable)
How old	Age	How long	Duration
Which/Which one	Choice	How	Manner, condition, quality

*See the "*Who* Questions: The Simple Present" section later in this chapter for an explanation of how to form questions with *who*.

WH Questions: The Simple Present

Now, let's learn how to form questions with these WH words. Read the example sentences aloud.

WH QUESTION WORD	DO OR DOES	SUBJECT OR SUBJECT PRONOUN	BASE FORM OF VERB	REST OF SENTENCE + QUESTION MARK	EXAMPLE SENTENCES
Where	do	I/you/we/they	catch	the bus to work?	Where do they catch the bus to work?
How many siblings	does	he/she	have	?	How many siblings does she have?
Which dog food	does	Rex	like	?	Which dog food does Rex like?
Who/whom (object of verb)	does	Grandma Jo	pick up	at school?	Who/whom does Grandma Jo pick up at school?

Here are some examples of these different WH questions:

Where does he go every day after school?

Which bus does he catch to work?

Which one does she want?

Why does Mike walk to work? / *What* does Mike walk to work *for*?

When does Sally ride her bike to work?

How many children do they have?

How much time does Monica need to get to work?

How old is Xavier?

How does she get to school?

How long does the train ride take?

What time does he leave work?

> *Who* refers to the subject of a sentence, while *whom* refers to an object of a sentence. In North America, these two words are often used interchangeably when referring to an object. See the Appendix for more information.

Now let's practice forming different WH questions using the simple present verb tense.

Exercise 2.16

Create sentences using the words given. Be sure to use the correct form of do. *Review the table on how to form WH questions with the simple present verb tense, and use the preceding example sentences to guide you.*

EXAMPLE   Why / DO / Mack / work / on Saturdays?

Why does Mack work on Saturdays?

1. When / DO / your mother-in-law / arrive?

   _____

2. What time / DO / your children / get / home from school?

   _____

3. What / DO / Peter, Paul, and Mary / do / on the weekends?

   _____

4. Where / DO / Donna / play / hockey?

   _____

5. Which day / DO / you / sleep / late?

_____

6. How many employees / DO / the company / have?

_____

7. How much time / DO / we / get / for each break?

_____

8. How long / DO / summer vacation / last?

_____

 ## Exercise 2.17

Form five questions using different WH question words. Be sure to follow the correct sentence structure and word order. Review the table, and use the example sentences to guide you.

1. _____
2. _____
3. _____
4. _____
5. _____

Who Questions: The Simple Present

When _who_ is the subject of the sentence, we do not add another subject, such as _I_, _you_, _we_, _they_, _he_, _she_, or _it_. In these questions, we do _not_ use _do_. As you look at the following examples, read the example sentences aloud.

WHO (SUBJECT OF SENTENCE)	MAIN VERB IN SIMPLE PRESENT THIRD PERSON SINGULAR FORM	REST OF SENTENCE + QUESTION MARK	EXAMPLE SENTENCES
Who	goes	to work on Sunday?	Who goes to work on Sunday?
Who	wants	to have pizza for lunch?	Who wants to have pizza for lunch?

Now let's read some example sentences:

Who bakes cookies every Saturday evening?

Who knows the bus schedule?

Who exercises every morning?

Who has the ball?

> **Note:** When _who_ is the subject of the sentence, we use the third person singular form with the simple present verb tense.

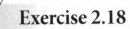

Exercise 2.18

Create sentences using the words given. Review the table on how to form Who *questions with the simple present verb tense, and use the preceding example sentences to guide you. Be sure to use the third person singular form of the verb.*

EXAMPLE   Who / give / Olaf / a ride to work every day?

Who gives Olaf a ride to work every day?

1. Who / want / vanilla ice cream for dessert?

   _____

2. Who / need / the car tomorrow?

   _____

3. Who / need / to sleep more than six hours a night?

   _____

4. Who / take / a vacation every year?

   _____

5. Who / get / paid on Fridays?

   _____

6. Who / visit / the zoo every year?

   _____

Exercise 2.19

Form three questions using who. *Be sure to follow the correct sentence structure and word order. Review the table, and use the example sentences to guide you.*

1. _____
2. _____
3. _____

Now that you know how to form WH questions, let's see how to form yes/no questions.

Grammar: Yes/No Questions with Non-BE Verbs in the Simple Present Tense

In conversation, we ask questions about what people do. We frequently talk about our habits, customs, and routines. We use yes/no questions to start or maintain a conversation and answer these questions with either *yes* or *no*. Use *do* for yes/no questions in the simple present.

DO OR DOES	SUBJECT OR SUBJECT PRONOUN	BASE FORM OF MAIN VERB	REST OF SENTENCE	EXAMPLE SENTENCES
Do	I/you/we/they	study	every day after school?	Do you study every day after school?
Does	he/she/it	go	on vacation every year?	Does she go on vacation every year?

Pronunciation Tip
Use rising pitch at the end of yes/no questions, which usually indicate uncertainty. See the pitch chart in the Appendix for more information.

Let's look at some example sentences:

Does she play the tuba in the school band?

Do they attend religious classes every week?

Does she understand the homework assignment?

Do you know math really well?

Does it require technical assistance?

Do Mary and Jill have bicycles?

Exercise 2.20

Create sentences using the words given. Review the preceding table on yes/no questions with the simple present verb tense, and be sure to use the correct form of do. *Use the example sentences to guide you.*

EXAMPLE   DO / Ellen / go / to the movies every Friday?

Does Ellen go to the movies every Friday?

1. DO / Marjorie and Tomas / sing / in the choir?

2. DO / your parents / go / on vacation to Europe every year?

_____

3. DO / Davida / have / the same work schedule?

_____

4. DO / Michel / play / football?

_____

You can answer yes/no questions with long answers that use the complete verb tense and the rest of the sentence. Or you can give a short answer that includes only part of the verb tense. You can also give a quick answer of *yes* or *no*. All of these types of answers are acceptable. Note that long answers use the simple present tense form of the verb. Also note that the short answer uses only *do* or *does*.

YES/NO QUESTION: Does she like parties?

Affirmative Answers

LONG ANSWER: Yes, she *does like* parties.

SHORT ANSWER: Yes, she *does*.

QUICK ANSWER: Yes. (See Chapter 1 for alternatives for *yes*.)

Negative Answers

LONG ANSWER: No, she *doesn't like* parties.

SHORT ANSWER: No, she *doesn't*.

QUICK ANSWER: No. (See Chapter 1 for alternatives for *no*.)

> When the answer is negative, we often provide a reason or cause for the negative answer. For example, we might say, "No, she doesn't. *She prefers to be alone.*"

Short Answers to Yes/No Questions: The Simple Present

We usually omit the main verb in short answers, as shown in this table.

YES OR NO + COMMA	SUBJECT OR SUBJECT PRONOUN	DO OR DOES	NEGATIVE	NEGATIVE CONTRACTION*
Yes,	I/you/we/they	do.		Yes, they do.
No,		do	n't.	No, they don't.
Yes,	he/she/it	does.		Yes, he does.
No,		does	n't.	No, he doesn't.

*There are no contractions for affirmative answers.

Exercise 2.21

Form yes/no questions with the simple present verb tense using the words given. Then create long, short, and quick answers to each question. Answer the questions affirmatively (yes) or negatively (no) as indicated.

EXAMPLE 1   DO / Karen / attend / the meetings / every week? (Yes)

QUESTION: *Does Karen attend the meetings every week?*

LONG ANSWER: *Yes, she does attend the meetings every week.*

SHORT ANSWER: *Yes, she does.*

QUICK ANSWER: *Yes.*

EXAMPLE 2   DO / Tad and his cousin / work out / every evening? (No)

QUESTION: *Do Tad and his cousin work out every evening?*

LONG ANSWER: *No, they don't work out every evening.*

SHORT ANSWER: *No, they don't.*

QUICK ANSWER: *No.*

1. DO / Felicity and her boyfriend / go / to an art museum / every month? (Yes)

   QUESTION: _____

   LONG ANSWER: _____

   SHORT ANSWER: _____

   QUICK ANSWER. _____

2. DO / Alexandra and Petrov / vacation / in Thailand / every winter? (No)

   QUESTION: _____

   LONG ANSWER: _____

   SHORT ANSWER: _____

   QUICK ANSWER: _____

3. DO / Minzhi / play / on a tennis team? (Yes)

   QUESTION: _____

   LONG ANSWER: _____

   SHORT ANSWER: _____

   QUICK ANSWER: _____

4. DO / Chun-Chieh / attend / music school? (No)

QUESTION: _____

LONG ANSWER: _____

SHORT ANSWER: _____

QUICK ANSWER: _____

Vocabulary: Phrasal Verbs for Daily Activities

In this section, we will learn some more phrasal verbs. In Chapter 1, we discovered that phrasal verbs are verbs + prepositions and may have more than one definition. Let's look at some phrasal verbs related to daily activities and habits.

Exercise 2.22

*Read the phrasal verbs on the left, then read the definitions on the right. You may know some of these verbs. Match each phrasal verb with the appropriate definition. For the verbs you do not know, take a guess. Some phrasal verbs can be separated with both a noun or pronoun. These are shown in **bold**.*

1. _____ to take **someone** out

2. _____ to dress up / to dress **someone** up

3. _____ to work out

4. _____ to wake up / to wake **someone** up

5. _____ to get up

6. _____ to hang out

7. _____ to get away

a. to stop sleeping

b. to go on vacation

c. to relax and socialize

d. to go on a date and pay for someone

e. to dress formally

f. to exercise

g. to get out of bed

Exercise 2.23

Complete the sentences with the correct phrasal verb. Be sure to use the correct verb form, including the third person singular when necessary.

EXAMPLE   They want to *get away* for the weekend.

1. He usually _____ with the alarm every day at 6:00 A.M.

2. Cassandra _____ with her friends every Saturday night.

3. David frequently _____ Julia _____ for dinner and a movie.

4. Mrs. Wilson seldom _____ when her alarm sounds. She likes to stay in bed for a few extra minutes every morning.

5. Debra _____ for church every Sunday morning. She wants to look very nice.

6. Anna and her brother _____ at the gym four days a week.

Introducing Someone

In the first chapter, you learned how to introduce yourself to someone. Now let's discuss what to do when you are talking to someone and want to introduce him or her to a third person. For example, Cindy and Jim are at a party, and Cindy's friend Arielle arrives. Cindy waves Arielle over, because she wants to introduce Arielle to Jim. Cindy can use the expression *This is* or *I want you to meet*. See the example conversation that follows.

Wave Someone Over
To **wave someone over** is to use your body language to ask someone to join you. We use our hand and arm to wave someone over. The farther away someone is, the bigger the movement can be. We usually wave someone over with one hand—either the right or the left is acceptable. Start the wave with your hand extended at arm's length from your body. With your palm facing inward, bring your hand toward your chest by bending your elbow. Your hand should not touch your chest. You can repeat this gesture two times quickly.

Conversation: Introducing Someone to Someone Else

Jim   Cindy   Arielle

CONVERSATION

CINDY: Hello, Arielle! (Waves Arielle over. Arielle walks toward Cindy.)[1]

ARIELLE: Hi, Cindy. How's it going?[2]

CINDY: Great, thanks! Jim, I want you to meet my friend.[3] This is Arielle. Arielle, this is[4] my husband, Jim. Arielle is my coworker who I often have lunch with.[5]

JIM: Very nice to meet you, Arielle.[6] (Extends his hand.)

ARIELLE (shaking hands): Nice to meet you too, Jim. I've heard a lot about you.[7]

CONVERSATION GUIDE

1. Greet and wave your friend over.

2. Your friend greets you. (See Chapter 1 for more greetings and expressions.)

3. Use the expression *I want you to meet* _____ or *I'd like you to meet* _____ and explain your relationship with him/her (*my friend*).

4. Immediately follow with the expression *This is* _____, and use the person's name. Repeat the process to introduce the second person to the first.

5. You can further explain your relationship with the new person. **Note:** This can also happen after the two people shake hands.

6. See Chapter 1 for more expressions.

7. *I've heard a lot about you* is a common expression when the relationships are constant and ongoing such as those between coworkers, colleagues, and close friends. This expression usually means that one person has heard positive things about the other.

CONVERSATION	CONVERSATION GUIDE
JIM (smiling): Really? I hope it's all good.[8]	8. The expression *I've heard a lot about you* can also refer to negative things. Here, Jim is friendly and joking when he says, "I hope it's all good." He knows his wife would only say good things about him to a coworker.
ARIELLE (smiling): Oh, yes. Cindy speaks highly of you.[9]	9. To **speak highly of someone** is to say positive things about that person. Other, less formal expressions: *Only good things. / All good. / Of course!*

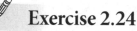

Exercise 2.24

Arielle and Cindy are eating lunch together in the cafeteria at work. Fatima enters the cafeteria and sees Arielle. Arielle waves Fatima over to the table, so she can introduce Fatima to Cindy. Create a conversation in which Arielle introduces Fatima to Cindy. Use the preceding steps as a guide. Include notes about shaking hands. The conversation has been started for you.

ARIELLE: Hi, Fatima! (Waves Fatima over)

FATIMA (arriving at the table where Arielle and Cindy are eating): _____

_____

ARIELLE (introducing Fatima and Cindy): _____

FATIMA: _____

ARIELLE: _____

CINDY: _____

FATIMA: _____

Reading About It

In this section, we'll practice identifying the topic and main idea of a passage while pre-reading. We will also practice reading actively. As you learned in Chapter 1, when you read actively, you remember what you read. Reading actively means that you interact with the passage by writing in the margins, highlighting important points, and marking up the text. To **mark up the text** means to write marks in the text. There are many ways to accomplish this. Marks may include circling a new word, underlining a phrase, or drawing a question mark in the margin.

Remember

The three steps to reading effectively are as follows:

1. Pre-read
2. Read actively
3. Check your understanding

(See Chapter 1 for more information on each step.) Before you read actively, you should pre-read the passage.

Let's Read Together

Pre-read the passage that follows. Remember: do not spend a lot of time pre-reading. We pre-read to find the topic and main idea of the passage quickly. Spend one to two minutes pre-reading. Follow these steps:

1. Read the title of the passage.
2. Read the first sentence of the paragraph.
3. Read the last sentence of the paragraph.

These sections are shaded for you.

> A **paragraph** is a section of writing that contains one main idea. It is usually 3 to 20 sentences long.

 José's New Job and New Life

José has a new job and a new life. Two weeks ago, he moved from Mexico to an English-speaking country. He moved because the job opportunities are better. He got a job with his brother's landscaping company, "Green Scapes." José and his brother, Carlos, make beautiful gardens for homes and businesses. They work very hard six days a week. José is also learning English so he can communicate with the customers. He goes to English class every Monday and Wednesday evenings. He studies his textbook and notes every day, and he practices speaking English every day at work. It is not easy, but he enjoys his new job and his new life.

Topics and Main Ideas

What is this story about? _____

You can see what the story is about by pre-reading the passage—reading the title, the first sentence, and the last sentence of the passage. The story is about José's new job and new life. Now, we must identify the topic and the main idea of the passage.

The **topic** is the subject of the reading. It is usually a broad category. The **main idea** is the primary point about the topic. It is a specific idea about the topic.

To find the topic of the passage, ask the question: *What is the subject of this passage?* The subject, or topic, in this passage is José.

To find the main idea of the passage, ask the question: *What about the topic,* or *What about José?* The main idea of the passage is José's new job and new life.

Now, what are the correct answers for these questions:

What is the topic? _____
What is the main idea? _____

 ## Exercise 2.25

Following are two passages. Spend one minute pre-reading each passage. Ask the appropriate questions to find the topic and the main idea of each. See the preceding example. Identify the topic and the main idea.

 Ravi and His Family

Ravi lives far away from his family in India. He misses his parents, siblings, and relatives. He moved to a new country for a job as a programmer at a computer company that makes software. Right now, the company is creating a new product. Ravi works on this product, so he is very busy. He works from 7:00 a.m. to 8:00 p.m. Monday through Friday. He usually works on Saturdays too. Sometimes he even goes to work on Sundays. Ravi wants to call his parents, but the time difference is big. They are usually sleeping when he calls. Ravi likes his new job, but he misses his family very much.

1. What is the topic? (What is the subject of this passage?)

_____

2. What is the main idea? (What about the topic?)

_____

_____

Peng Gets an Education

Peng is learning a new educational system. He moved to the United States six months ago and is studying business and finance at a university. In China, he didn't go to his undergraduate classes. Instead, he read and studied the textbook. Peng easily passed all of his exams. He has great memorization skills. In the United States, however, there is a different way of learning. At the university, he must attend classes. The professors talk about new ideas and discuss them with the students. They expect the students to have opinions about the topic. The exams are usually essay exams. Peng doesn't prepare for the exams by memorizing; he has a new way of studying. He reviews the annotations in his textbook and all of his class notes. He also discusses the topics with classmates. Peng practices writing for the essays too. He works hard to pass his exams. For Peng, this new way of learning is difficult but also fun.

3. What is the topic? (What is the subject of this passage?)

_____

4. What is the main idea? (What about the topic?)

_____

Let's look at some other examples of topics and main ideas. You will see two examples of a topic on the left and a few main ideas on the right. Notice that the topic is a large category, and the main ideas are specific ideas within that large category.

TOPICS (BROAD CATEGORIES)	MAIN IDEAS (SPECIFIC IDEAS ABOUT THE TOPIC)
Money	Investing money
	Saving money
	Getting a bank loan
	Making a profit in your business
	Getting out of debt
Exercise	How to exercise safely
	Types of exercises
	Exercising to gain strength
	Exercising in a gym versus outdoors
	Exercising to lose weight

Exercise 2.26

On the left are three topics. Create three main ideas for each topic.

TOPICS		MAIN IDEAS
School	1.	_____
	2.	_____
	3.	_____
Work	1.	_____
	2.	_____
	3.	_____
Hobbies	1.	_____
	2.	_____
	3.	_____

Reading Actively

After you pre-read and find the topic and main idea, read the passage actively by following these steps:

- Underline the topic.
- Circle new vocabulary.
- Put a question mark (?) next to unclear parts.
- Take notes.

- Highlight the main idea and key words.
- Mark examples with "Ex."
- Number main points, lists, or ideas.
- Write comments or questions.

Exercise 2.27

Go back to the passage titled "Peng Gets an Education" and actively read it. You already know the topic and the main idea. Now complete the tasks in the preceding list. (If you are reading this as an e-book, copy the passage onto your own paper first.) To guide you, answer the following questions.

1. What are the four different ways of learning in a U.S. university?

   a. _____

   b. _____

c. _____

d. _____

2. What are Peng's three new ways of studying?

    a. _____

    b. _____

    c. _____

Exercise 2.28

Now go back and review the passage and your notes and highlighting. Answer the following questions to check your understanding of the passage.

1. Where is Peng from? _____

2. Where does he live now? _____

3. What is he studying at the university? _____

4. In China, did he go to class? _____

5. How did Peng study for exams in China? _____

6. Does memorization help him in his U.S. classes? _____

7. Does he go to classes at the U.S. university? _____

8. What is Peng learning at the university? _____

9. Does he work hard to pass his exams at the university? _____

10. Does Peng like studying in the United States? _____

When you are done, look at the following passage. You can find the answers to the questions there. The answers are highlighted and marked with the numbers of the corresponding questions. Compare your answers to those shown. Then check the Answer Key.

 Peng Gets an Education

Peng is learning a new educational system.[8] He moved to the United States six months ago[2] and is studying business and finance[3] at a university. In China,[1] he didn't go to his undergraduate classes.[4] Instead, he read and studied the textbook. Peng easily passed all of his exams. He has great memorization skills.[5] In the United States, however, there is a different way of learning.[8] At the university, he must attend classes.[7] The professors talk about new ideas and discuss them with the students. They expect the students to have opinions about the topic. The exams are usually essay exams. Peng doesn't prepare for the exams by memorizing;[6] he has a new way of studying.[8] He reads the text-book and all of his class notes. He also discusses the topics with classmates. Peng practices writing for the essays too. He works hard to pass his exams.[9] For Peng, this new way of learning is difficult but also fun.[10]

Good work! We will continue to practice pre-reading and reading actively in later chapters because these are very important skills. Let's move on to writing skills.

Writing About It

In this section, you will learn about subject-verb agreement and proper nouns.

Subject-Verb Agreement with the Simple Present Verb Tense

In English, the subject and verb of every sentence must **agree**, meaning that **the verb must match the subject in number**. A singular subject takes a singular verb, and a plural subject takes a plural verb. See the chart for singular and plural subject pronouns.

	SINGULAR	PLURAL
First person	I go	We go
Second person	You go	You go
Third person	He goes	They go
	She goes	
	It goes	

For the simple present verb tense, it is especially important to check the third person singular subject-verb agreement. Be careful with any sentence that has the subject pronouns *he*, *she*, and *it*. See the following example sentences of subject-verb agreement with the simple present verb tense.

> A **verb** expresses the action taken by, condition of, or state of being of the subject in a sentence. A **subject** is a noun or pronoun that performs the verb in a sentence.

Subject-verb agreement: He goes to school.
(**He** = subject / **goes** = verb)

Does the verb *goes* match the subject *He*? Look at the preceding chart. From that chart, we see that the verb matches the subject. Therefore, there is subject-verb agreement. Let's look at another sentence:

They goes to work every day.

Does the verb *goes* agree with the subject *They*? Check the preceding chart. From that chart, we see that the subject and verb do *not* match. Therefore, there is *no* subject-verb agreement. The sentence is incorrect. How can we correct the sentence?

_____

The correct sentence is *They go to work every day.*

Exercise 2.29

Go back to the passage titled "Ravi and His Family." Find all the sentences containing the simple present verb tense. Then find the subject of each sentence. Notice that each verb agrees with the subject in that sentence. Review the chart to help you.

Exercise 2.30

Look at the following sentences. Identify the verb and subject of each sentence, and determine if there is subject-verb agreement. If there is not subject-verb agreement, correct the sentence. Follow the example.

EXAMPLES   I gives my homework to the teacher. <u>*Incorrect. / I give my homework to the teacher.*</u>

We go to computer class every Tuesday. <u>*Correct.*</u>

1. She want ice cream for dessert. _____

2. They meet every Friday to discuss the project. _____

3. The grocery store take cash only. _____

4. The professor lectures for 45 minutes every class. _____

5. The bus ride is 25 minutes long. _____

6. We drives 10 miles to work every day. _____

7. They celebrates every holiday with a big festival. _____

8. Renuka plays on the university soccer team. _____

Exercise 2.31

Create sentences using all forms: first person singular and plural, second person singular and plural, and third person singular and plural. Think about habits, customs, and routines such as school, work, and hobbies. Think about yourself, friends, family, and coworkers. The first one is done for you.

	SINGULAR	PLURAL
First person	1. I go	2. We go
Second person	3. You go	4. You go
Third person	5. He goes	8. They go
	6. She goes	
	7. It goes	

1. I *study English every day.*

2. We _____.

3. You _____.

4. You _____.

5. He _____.

6. She _____.

7. It _____.

8. They _____.

Proper Nouns

Proper nouns are nouns that name a person, place, or thing. These nouns are always capitalized. Each word in the proper noun begins with a capital letter except prepositions such as *of*. An example of a noun is *country*. An example of a proper noun is *Brazil*. The proper noun *Brazil* names a specific country, so it is capitalized. Look at the following list for more examples.

NOUN	PROPER NOUN
bridge	the Golden Gate Bridge
wall	the Great Wall of China
river	the Nile
ocean	the Atlantic Ocean
planet	Mars
road	Willow Road
family	the Andersons
man	Michael Jackson
city	Lisbon
state	Oaxaca
girl	Allison
building	the Empire State Building

In proper nouns, prepositions and the word *the* do not have to be capitalized. For example: **the** *United Arab Emirates* / **the** *Declaration* **of** *Independence*.

Practice 2.32

Look at the list and choose the items that are proper nouns.

Jennifer	Mr. Blumenthal	teacher	house	the White House
school	Whiting High School	bank	Flint Bank	Queen Elizabeth
queen	store	Nordstrom	city	Manhattan

Exercise 2.33

Think of proper nouns you know. Note the names of specific places, people, and things. Be sure to capitalize each word in the proper noun except for the *and the prepositions.*

People   **Places**   **Things**

_____   _____   _____

_____   _____   _____

_____   _____   _____

Exercise 2.34

Choose five of the proper nouns you just gave. Form a sentence using each of these nouns. Use the simple present verb tense form.

EXAMPLES   ***Boston*** *is a city in* ***Massachusetts***.

We go to the ***Museum of Modern Art*** *twice a year.*

The tower lights on the ***Empire State Building*** *change colors almost every night.*

1. _____

2. _____

3. _____

4. _____

5. _____

✎ Quiz

You have finished Chapter 2. Great work! Now take the quiz to see what you remember. Choose the correct answers for each question. There may be multiple correct answers.

1. For which activities do we use the simple present verb tense?

   Habits   Temporary situations

   Customs   Weekly activities

2. What word describes the relationship of your mother's sister to you?

   Uncle   Cousin

   Aunt   Niece

3. What are examples of third person singular pronouns?

   I   He

   She   It

4. Read this sentence: *We take classes on Tuesday nights.* What are the two correct negative forms of the verb in that sentence?

   do not take   don't take

   does not take   doesn't take

5. Jack goes to the movies about twice a year. What adverb of frequency describes this situation?

   Often   Occasionally

   Frequently   Hardly ever

6. What expressions do you use when you want to introduce someone to another person?

   That is   This is

   I want you to meet   I'd like you to meet

7. To wave someone over to you, you should use both arms. True or False?

8. To discover the frequency of someone's activities, which WH question word do you use?

   When   Which one

   How do   How often

9. The topic of a reading passage is the primary point of the topic. True or False?

10. *Subject-verb agreement* means that the subject and verb must agree in number. True or False?

Do It Out There!

Now that you have learned how to talk about the members of your family and your routines and how to introduce people, try it out in the world. Review this chapter again, and go out and use English! Put a checkmark next to each activity as you complete it.

To Do This Week

- ❏ Describe your family members to a friend, a coworker, or a colleague. ("Talking About Family" section)
- ❏ Talk about two things you do every day, every week, every month, and every year to two people you know. Be sure to pronounce the **-s** ending correctly. ("Grammar: Using the Simple Perfect Verb Tense" section and "Pronunciation Tip: Three Different **-s** Ending Sounds" section)
- ❏ Use three new phrasal verbs when talking about your routines. ("Vocabulary: Phrasal Verbs for Daily Activities" section)
- ❏ Talk about two things you do *not* do every day, every week, every month, and every year to two people you know. ("Simple Present: Forming the Negative" section)
- ❏ Ask a friend, coworker, or colleague how often he or she does activities such as going to the movies, playing in the park, going on vacation, and visiting family. ("Grammar: Using Adverbs of Frequency" section)
- ❏ Introduce someone to someone else at school, at work, or in your community. ("Conversation: Introducing Someone to Someone Else" section)

Weekly Log

Keep a weekly log of your progress. Make notes on how your practice went. What happened? Was it successful? How do you know it was successful? Was it unsuccessful? How do you know? Review all the instructions, tips, and culture notes in Chapter 2.

_____

_____

_____

_____

_____

_____

_____

3

Food: Shopping and Restaurants

In this chapter you will learn about:

Speaking
✓ How to make polite requests
✓ How to order food in a restaurant
✓ How to describe quantities
✓ How to ask about quantities

Vocabulary, Reading, and Writing
✓ Vocabulary related to cooking, food, eating, and restaurants
✓ How to discover vocabulary meaning from context
✓ How to practice finding the topic and main idea of a passage
✓ How to use commas in a list

Grammar
✓ The present progressive verb tense in affirmative and negative sentences
✓ Yes/no questions with the present progressive
✓ WH (information) questions with the present progressive
✓ *Who* questions with the present progressive
✓ Definite articles
✓ Indefinite articles
✓ Count and noncount nouns
✓ Questions using *how much* and *how many*

Body Language
✓ How to get a waitperson's attention and call him or her over

In this chapter, you will practice polite expressions and vocabulary for talking about food (shopping for it and preparing it) and eating in restaurants. To improve your grammar skills, you will learn the present progressive verb tense. To improve your reading skills and vocabulary, you will learn how to guess the meaning of new vocabulary from its context within a sentence. You will also review and practice identifying the topic and main idea of a passage. To practice writing, you will learn how to use commas in a list.

Talking About What People Are Doing Now

We often talk about activities that we are doing at the same time we are speaking. These are temporary actions in progress. They began before and continue, or progress, for some time. For example, at this moment, you are reading this sentence. You are also studying English. You are doing these activities right now. Let's look at examples of what other people are doing right now.

Sammy is cooking for the family.

Alice is chopping vegetables.

Joe is setting the table for dinner.

These actions began before now and will continue for some time. We use the present progressive verb tense to talk about these **activities in progress**. This verb tense is also called the present continuous tense.

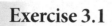

Exercise 3.1

Study the pictures on the left, then read the sentences on the right that describe what these people are doing. Match the picture with the correct sentence.

1.

a. Ari and Sue are reading the lunch menu.

2.

b. They are grocery shopping.

3.

c. Ralph is barbecuing/grilling steak.

4.

d. Jenny is ordering take-out food.*

Grammar: Using the Present Progressive Verb Tense

In English, we use the present progressive verb tense to talk about what we are doing now. Let's look at some example sentences.

---

*Called *takeaway* in the United Kingdom.

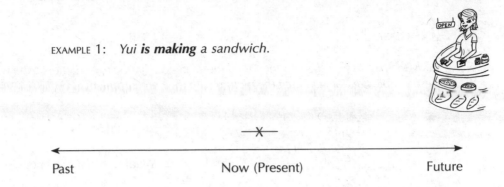

EXAMPLE 1:   *Yui **is making** a sandwich.*

←————————————⎯✗⎯————————————→

Past   Now (Present)   Future

At this moment, Yui is making a sandwich. The activity is not complete, and it is temporary. She started this activity five minutes ago. It may take her five more minutes. For these ten minutes, she is making a sandwich.

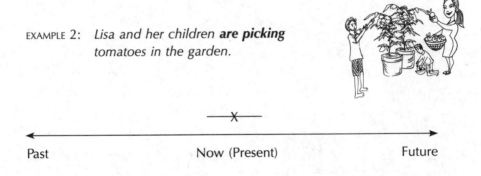

EXAMPLE 2:   *Lisa and her children **are picking** tomatoes in the garden.*

←————————————⎯✗⎯————————————→

Past   Now (Present)   Future

Right now, Lisa and her kids are picking tomatoes. The task is not complete, and it is temporary. They began this activity a few minutes ago. It may take a total of 20 minutes. So for 20 minutes, they are picking tomatoes in the garden.

EXAMPLE 3:   *Doug and Lisa **are growing** vegetables in their backyard.*

←————————————⎯✗⎯————————————→

Past   Now (Present)   Future

Doug and Lisa are growing vegetables in their backyard this summer. It is a temporary activity with a longer duration. It is a summertime activity. They began the garden in late spring. It is not complete yet, but it will be complete by autumn. This summer, they are growing vegetables in the garden.

EXAMPLE 4:   *These days, Nancy **is studying** at the community college.*

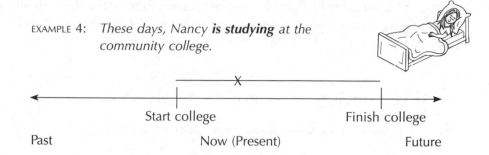

Start college   Finish college

Past   Now (Present)   Future

At this moment, Nancy is sleeping. *These days*, she is going to college. We use the present progressive to talk about temporary activities that have either a short or a long duration. Although Nancy is sleeping right now, nowadays she is attending a community college to receive a degree. It is a temporary but long activity—two to four years. She started her studies a few months ago, and they will not be complete for a few years. For a few years, Nancy is studying at the community college.

Temporary actions in progress are different from habitual actions, which we learned about in Chapter 2. We perform habitual actions regularly, such as every day, every week, every Sunday, every month, every winter, and every year. As you know from Chapter 2, we use the simple present tense for habitual actions. However, temporary actions in progress at the moment of speaking require the **present progressive verb tense**, which indicates that the action is current and will end at a future time. Let's look at how to form this verb tense.

Important
The present progressive verb tense is rarely used with stative, or nonaction, verbs. Common stative verbs include *be, seem, appear, understand, have, believe, like, dislike, love, hate, know, mean, remember,* and *want.* For a more comprehensive list of stative verbs, see the Appendix.

The Present Progressive: Forming Affirmative Statements
Now, let's see how to form the present progressive in affirmative statements. As you review the table, read the example sentences aloud.

SUBJECT OR SUBJECT PRONOUN	BE VERB	BASE FORM OF MAIN VERB + -ING	EXAMPLE SENTENCES
I	am	eating	I am eating a salad.
You/We/ They	are	eating	They are eating dinner right now.
He/She/It	is	eating	He is eating a pepperoni pizza.

Important: Be careful to use the correct form of the BE verb when forming the present progressive. With the pronoun *I*, use *am*. With *you*, *we*, and *they*, use *are*. With *he*, *she*, and *it*, you must use *is*.

Exercise 3.2

Complete the sentences with the correct form of the BE verb.

EXAMPLE   Audrey *is* making breakfast right now.   am   are   is

1. Marcia _____ planting herbs on her balcony.   am   are   is

2. Zoey and Bo _____ raising chickens.   am   are   is

3. Professor Gupta _____ reserving a table at the
   new restaurant.   am   are   is

4. Right now, we _____ getting lunch to go.   am   are   is

5. I _____ cooking pasta for dinner.   am   are   is

The Present Progressive: Spelling Rules
Here are common spelling rules for the progressive form of verbs:

1. Add **-ing** to the base form of the verb.
   Example: eat → eating

2. If the verb ends in a silent e, drop the e and add
   -ing. Example: mak<u>e</u> → making

3. In a one-syllable word, if the last three letters are a consonant-vowel-consonant (CVC), double the last consonant and add **-ing**.
   Example: <u>put</u> → pu<u>tt</u>ing

4. However, do *not* double the final consonant if it is a *w*, *x*, or *y*.
   Example: fix → fi<u>x</u>ing

> **Getting food to go** means that you do not eat at the restaurant. Rather, you go to the restaurant, buy food, and take it out to eat it somewhere else. **Dinner** is the evening meal and **lunch** is the midday meal.

Exercise 3.3

Spell the progressive form of the given verb correctly using these rules.

1. take → _____   4. drink → _____

2. buy → _____   5. stop → _____

3. choose → _____   6. show → _____

The Present Progressive: Expressions of Time

Here are some common time expressions we use with the present progressive:

> Now / right now
>
> At the moment / at this moment
>
> This week / this weekend / this month / this year / this semester / this season / this quarter
>
> These days / nowadays

Exercise 3.4

Complete the following sentences with the correct form of the BE verb and the present progressive form of the verb given.

> To **fix** a meal means to make it. We fix breakfast, lunch, and dinner.

EXAMPLE　Mr. Shumacher _is fixing_ lunch for his wife. (fix)

1. They _____ to a five-star restaurant right now. (drive)
2. At this moment, Dan _____ the restaurant to make reservations. (call)
3. Sal _____ culinary school nowadays. (attend)
4. Sofia _____ groceries for the family. (buy)
5. Right now, the chef _____ a special meal for this party. (cook)
6. We _____ the seeds for next year. (save)
7. The butcher _____ lamb this week. (sell)
8. I _____ dinner for everyone. (make)

Exercise 3.5

Create sentences about what you, your friends, and your family are doing right now or these days. Be sure to use the affirmative present progressive verb tense. Be sure to use the correct form of the BE verb.

_____

_____

_____

_____

The Present Progressive: Forming Negative Statements

To form the negative present progressive verb tense, you must use *not*, as shown in the table. As you review it, read the example sentences aloud.

SUBJECT OR SUBJECT PRONOUN	BE VERB	NEGATIVE	BASE FORM OF MAIN VERB + -ING	EXAMPLE SENTENCES
I	am	not	eating	I am not eating salad. I am eating a sandwich
You/We/They	are	not	eating	They are not eating dinner. They are making dinner right now.
He/She/It	is	not	eating	He is not eating a pepperoni pizza. He is eating a mushroom pizza.

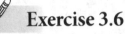

Exercise 3.6

Complete the sentences with the correct negative form of the present progressive verb.

EXAMPLE   Heidi *is not* driving to the restaurant.   am not   are not   is not
           She is walking.

1. Angela _____ working full time.   am not   are not   is not
   She is going to college.

2. Suri and Jaime _____ studying Italian.   am not   are not   is not
   They are studying English.

3. Dr. Palumbo _____ seeing patients today. am not   are not   is not
   It's Sunday.

4. I _____ working this summer.   am not   are not   is not
   I am vacationing in Spain.

5. Bob and Peter _____ eating out.   am not   are not   is not
   They are cooking at home.

6. Denise and I _____ enjoying the movie.   am not   are not   is not
   It's boring.

Exercise 3.7

> To **eat out** or **go out for dinner** means to eat at a restaurant.

Create sentences about what you, your friends, and your family are not *doing right now or these days. Be sure to use the negative present progressive verb tense. Use the preceding chart to help you. Use the correct form of the BE verb.*

_____

_____

_____

_____

Culture Note
In North America, we use the present progressive verb tense with the time words *always, constantly,* and *forever* to complain about someone or something. For example: *He is **always** leaving dirty dishes in the sink. / She is **constantly** playing her music too loudly at night.*

The Present Progressive: Forming Negative Contractions

In English, we often use contractions when we speak. For the present progressive verb tense, we can make a negative contraction two different ways: (1) combine the subject and the BE verb; or (2) combine the BE verb and the negative *not*. We also learned these contractions in Chapter 1.

The following charts show the two methods of forming negative contractions. As you review them, read the example sentences aloud.

Contraction: Subject Pronoun + BE Verb

SUBJECT PRONOUN + BE VERB	NEGATIVE	BASE FORM OF MAIN VERB + -ING	EXAMPLE SENTENCES
I'm	not	eating	I'm not eating a salad. I am eating a sandwich.
You're/We're/They're	not	eating	They're not eating dinner. They are making dinner right now.
He's/She's/It's/John's	not	eating	He's not eating a pepperoni pizza. He is eating a mushroom pizza.

Contraction: BE Verb + Negative

SUBJECT OR SUBJECT PRONOUN	BE VERB FORM + NEGATIVE	NEGATIVE	BASE FORM OF MAIN VERB + -ING	EXAMPLE SENTENCES
I*	am	not	eating	I am not eating a salad.* I am eating a sandwich.
You/We/They	aren't		eating	They aren't eating dinner. They are making dinner right now.
He/She/It	isn't		eating	He isn't eating a pepperoni pizza. He is eating a mushroom pizza.

*Note: There is no contraction with *am* and *not*.

Exercise 3.8

Create sentences describing what people are doing. Use the present progressive verb tense and the words given. Then create the negative form of the sentence using the two different ways to make contractions. Review the spelling rules if you need help.

EXAMPLE   Shauna / visit / her grandparents.

Shauna is visiting her grandparents.

Shauna isn't visiting her grandparents.

Shauna's not visiting her grandparents.

1. Hiro / play / soccer for the summer.

   _____

   _____

   _____

2. I / study / English these days.

   _____

   _____

   _____

3. Ian and Catherine / argue / at this moment.

   _____

   _____

   _____

4. My dog / chew / on a bone.

   _____

   _____

   _____

5. Sara and I / talk / on the phone.

   _____

   _____

   _____

Exercise 3.9

Use the negative contraction with the present progressive verb tense to create sentences about what you, your friends, and your family are not *doing right now or these days. Use the correct forms of the BE verb. Use both kinds of contractions.*

_____

_____

_____

_____

The Present Progressive: Forming Yes/No Questions

In conversation, we ask questions about what people are doing. We use yes/no questions to get this information. We answer these questions with either *yes* or *no*. For yes/no questions in the present progressive, we **invert** the subject and the BE verb, meaning we change the order of the subject and the BE verb. The BE verb begins the sentence and the subject comes after the BE verb. The following table shows how to form these questions. As you review it, read the example sentences aloud.

BE VERB	SUBJECT OR SUBJECT PRONOUN	BASE FORM OF MAIN VERB + -ING	REST OF SENTENCE	EXAMPLE SENTENCES
Am	I	eating	a salad?	Am I eating a salad?
Are	you/we/they	eating	dinner right now?	Are they eating dinner right now?
Is	he/she/it	eating	a pepperoni pizza?	Is he eating a pepperoni pizza?

Pronunciation Tip
Use rising pitch at the end of yes/no questions to indicate uncertainty. You use rising pitch to show that you would like an answer. See the pitch chart in the Appendix for more information.

You can answer a yes/no question with a long answer, using the complete verb tense and all parts of the sentence. You can also give a short answer, which includes only part of the verb tense. Or you can give a quick answer, saying only *yes* or *no*. All these types of answers are acceptable. Here are a couple of examples:

YES/NO QUESTION: Is she cleaning the house?

Affirmative Answers

LONG ANSWER: Yes, she is cleaning the house. / Yes, she's cleaning the house.

SHORT ANSWER: Yes, she is.   QUICK ANSWER: Yes.

Negative Answers

LONG ANSWER: No, she isn't cleaning the house. / No, she's not cleaning the house.

SHORT ANSWER: No, she isn't. / No, she's not.   QUICK ANSWER: No.

Pronunciation Tip

For long affirmative answers, stress the BE verb when it is not contracted: *Yes, she **is** cleaning the house.* For short affirmative answers, stress the BE verb: *Yes, she **is**.* For both long and short negative answers, stress the negative contraction or *not*: *No, she's **not** cleaning the house. / No, she **isn't**.* **Note:** Do not stress quick answers.

The Present Progressive: Short Answers to Yes/No Questions

There are a few rules when using the present progressive with short answers to yes/no questions:

- We usually omit the main verb in short answers.
- We never contract *am* and *not*.
- We do not contract the affirmative short answer.

The following chart shows how to form short answers.

YES OR NO + COMMA	SUBJECT OR SUBJECT PRONOUN	BE VERB FORM	NEGATIVE	NEGATIVE CONTRACTION*
Yes,	I	am.		
No,	I	am	not.	No, I'm not.
Yes,	you/we/they	are.		
No,	you/we/they	are	not.	No, they aren't. / No, they're not.
Yes,	he/she/it	is.		No, he isn't.
No,	he/she/it	is	not.	No, he's not.

*There are no contractions for affirmative answers.

Caution

A quick answer can sometimes be perceived as abrupt and rude, so give quick answers in a polite tone. When giving a negative answer, we often offer more information, or we can correct wrong information. For example, you might say, "No, I'm not cleaning the house. *I'm cooking dinner.*" Sometimes, we offer an explanation. For example, you might say, "No, I'm not cleaning the house *because I cleaned yesterday.*" When an answer is negative, we may omit the negative answer and instead correct with the word *actually*. For example, you might say, "Actually, I'm cooking dinner."

Exercise 3.10

Form yes/no questions with the present progressive verb tense using the words given. Then create long, short, and quick answers to the question. Answer the questions affirmatively (Yes) or negatively (No) as indicated.

EXAMPLE 1   BE verb / Naomi / teach / swim lessons this summer? (Yes)

QUESTION: *Is Naomi teaching swim lessons this summer?*

LONG ANSWER: *Yes, she is teaching swim lessons this summer.*

SHORT ANSWER: *Yes, she is.*   QUICK ANSWER: *Yes.*

EXAMPLE 2   BE verb / Lisa and Doug / grow / herbs in their front yard? (No)

QUESTION: *Are Lisa and Doug growing herbs in their front yard?*

LONG ANSWER: *No, they aren't growing herbs in their front yard. / No, they're not growing herbs in their front yard.*

SHORT ANSWER: *No, they aren't. / No, they're not.*   QUICK ANSWER: *No.*

1. BE verb / Miguel / go / to adult school for English? (Yes)

   QUESTION: _____

   LONG ANSWER: _____

   SHORT ANSWER: _____   QUICK ANSWER: _____

2. BE verb / Sheila / read / a book right now? (No)

   QUESTION: _____

   LONG ANSWER: _____

   SHORT ANSWER: _____   QUICK ANSWER: _____

3. BE verb / Jeff and Henry / work / at the ice cream shop? (No)

   QUESTION: _____

   LONG ANSWER: _____

   SHORT ANSWER: _____   QUICK ANSWER: _____

4. BE verb / you / study / at the community college? (Yes)

QUESTION: _____

LONG ANSWER: _____

SHORT ANSWER: _____ QUICK ANSWER: _____

5. BE verb / Bethany / learn / computer programming at school this year? (Yes)

QUESTION: _____

LONG ANSWER: _____

SHORT ANSWER: _____ QUICK ANSWER: _____

Grammar: Asking WH Questions in the Present Progressive Tense

In conversation, we ask questions about what people are doing. We use WH questions, or information questions, to ask about the time of, location of, manner of, and reason for an action. As mentioned in Chapter 2, WH questions begin with WH question words or phrases, such as *who, what, when, where, why, how, what kind, which one, how long, how many,* and *how much.* For a list of WH question words, refer to the Appendix. The following table shows how to form these questions. As you review it, read the example sentences aloud.

WH QUESTION WORD/PHRASE	BE VERB	SUBJECT OR SUBJECT PRONOUN	BASE FORM OF MAIN VERB + -ING	REST OF SENTENCE	EXAMPLE SENTENCES
When	am	I	eating	a salad?	When am I eating a salad?
Where	are	you/we/they	eating	dinner right now?	Where are they eating dinner right now?
Why	is	he/she/it	eating	a pepperoni pizza?	Why is he eating a pepperoni pizza?

Pronunciation Tip
We usually use falling pitch at the end of WH questions. However, if you didn't hear or understand some information and you need the speaker to repeat it, use rising pitch. See the pitch chart in the Appendix for more information.

We can answer WH questions in different ways using the present progressive verb tense. We can give a long answer, which is a complete sentence and usually uses subject pronouns and contractions with the BE verb. We can also give a short answer with only the essential information that answers the question.

Exercise 3.11

Form WH questions with the present progressive verb tense using the words given. Form both long and short answers.

EXAMPLE 1   Where / BE verb / Naomi / teach / swim lessons this summer? (at the Oakland Pool)

QUESTION: *Where is Naomi teaching swim lessons this summer?*

LONG ANSWER: *She's teaching swim lessons at the Oakland Pool.* (complete sentence)

SHORT ANSWER: *At the Oakland Pool.* (not a complete sentence)

EXAMPLE 2   Why / BE verb / Sammy / cook / dinner? (he enjoys cooking)

QUESTION: *Why is Sammy cooking dinner?*

LONG ANSWER: *He's cooking dinner because he enjoys cooking.*

SHORT ANSWER: *Because he enjoys cooking.*

> When we use the WH question word *why*, we usually use *because* in the answer.

1. When / BE verb / Miguel / go / to school? (at night)

   QUESTION: _____

   LONG ANSWER: _____

   SHORT ANSWER: _____

2. How many books / BE verb / Sheila / read / right now? (three)

   QUESTION: _____

   LONG ANSWER: _____

   SHORT ANSWER: _____

3. How often / BE verb / Jeff and Henry / work / at the ice cream shop? (every weekday)

   QUESTION: _____

   LONG ANSWER: _____

   SHORT ANSWER: _____

4. Why / BE verb / you / study / at the community college? (It's affordable.)

   QUESTION: _____

   LONG ANSWER: _____

   SHORT ANSWER: _____

5. How / BE verb / Bethany / do / in the computer programming class? (very well)

QUESTION: _____

LONG ANSWER: _____

SHORT ANSWER: _____

For the WH question *who*, there is a different structure. In questions that begin with *who* when *who* is the subject, we do *not* have another subject or subject pronoun. See the following chart for examples. As you review it, read the example sentences aloud.

WHO (SUBJECT OF SENTENCE)	BE VERB FORM (IS*)	BASE FORM OF MAIN VERB + -ING	REST OF SENTENCE	EXAMPLE SENTENCES
Who	is	slicing	the bread?	Who is slicing the bread?
Who	is	cutting	the cake?	Who is cutting the cake?

*__Note:__ Always use the BE form *is* with *who* and a main -ing verb.

When asking a *Who* question in response to something someone said, we can shorten the question. See the examples in Exercise 3.12. We can give long, short, or quick answers to *Who* questions. The long answer is a complete sentence. The short answer provides essential information + the BE verb. The quick answer gives only the essential information (who) that answers the question.

Exercise 3.12

Form Who *questions using the present progressive verb tense based on the statements given. Form long, short, and quick answers. Notice that the questions and long answers can often be shortened.*

EXAMPLE   Max and Mara are grilling salmon right now.

QUESTION: *Who is grilling salmon right now*? / *Who is grilling salmon?* / *Who is?*

LONG ANSWER: *Max and Mara are grilling salmon.* (complete sentence)

SHORT ANSWER: *Max and Mara are.* (essential information + BE verb)

QUICK ANSWER: *Max and Mara.* (essential information only)

1. Lara is going to dinner with Rex.

QUESTION: _____

LONG ANSWER: _____

SHORT ANSWER: _____

QUICK ANSWER: _____

2. Margarita and her son are eating dinner at her sister's house.

QUESTION: _____

LONG ANSWER: _____

SHORT ANSWER: _____

QUICK ANSWER: _____

3. Roshana's mother is cooking Sunday dinner.

QUESTION: _____

LONG ANSWER: _____

SHORT ANSWER: _____

QUICK ANSWER: _____

4. Lorraine and her friends are getting sandwiches at a deli.

QUESTION: _____

LONG ANSWER: _____

SHORT ANSWER: _____

QUICK ANSWER: _____

5. Ludwig and Cy are bringing food to the park.

QUESTION: _____

LONG ANSWER: _____

SHORT ANSWER: _____

QUICK ANSWER: _____

Grammar: Count and Noncount Nouns

In English, nouns are countable or uncountable. When we can count a noun (for example, one car, two apples, three drinks, 25 spoons), we call it a **count noun**. Count nouns can be singular (one car) or plural (two cars). When we can't count the noun because it's too difficult or impossible (rice, music, hair, milk, salt, rain, and so on), we call it a **noncount noun** or a **mass noun**. Noncount nouns name materials (plastic), liquids (water), abstract ideas (sadness), and other things we see as masses without clear divisions. They have only one form, not singular and plural forms. We can usually measure noncount nouns. For example, we might say, "two cups of rice," "three liters of milk," or "a pinch of salt." We don't say, "two rices," "three milks," or "three salts." Let's look at some examples of count and noncount nouns.

Reminder: Nouns are people, places, or things.

COUNT NOUNS	NONCOUNT NOUNS
Nouns that can be counted	Nouns that *cannot* be counted
Singular or plural forms	Only one form
Examples: person/people, car/cars, cookie/cookies, child/children, tooth/teeth, potato/potatoes, toy/toys, vegetable/vegetables, knife/knives	**Examples:** water, rain, air, rice, salt, oil, plastic, money, music, tennis, coffee, cheese, chocolate, sugar, cream, tea, hair, wood, sand, soap, happiness, peace, cheese, fish, furniture, luggage, equipment, information, weather, bread, news, fruit, meat, health

Example sentences:	
I have two dollars.	I have money.
	Not: ~~I have two moneys.~~
She owns a restaurant.	She wants some water.
Pamela eats an apple every day.	May I please have a piece of cake?
Joe has one car.	We breathe air.

Some words can be both count and noncount nouns. For example, the word *chicken* can be either count or noncount, depending on how it is used. If we are talking about a whole, complete chicken, it's countable. However, if it is divided into sections for cooking or eating, it is noncount, and you need to use a quantifier such as *a piece of*. The following chart illustrates different uses for the same word.

Count noun: a chicken
Celia raises hen-laying chickens in her backyard.
She has two chickens.

Noncount noun: chicken
Jasper is having chicken for dinner.
He is eating some chicken.
He is eating a piece of chicken.

Count noun: a pie
Julie made three pies for the party.

Noncount noun: pie
I would love a piece of blueberry pie.
I would love some blueberry pie.

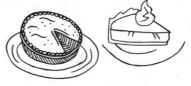

✎ Exercise 3.13

Read the following sentences, and identify the nouns as either count or noncount nouns.

EXAMPLE   I am shopping for coffee, apples, carrots, cheese, and bread.

Count nouns: apples, carrots / Noncount nouns: coffee, cheese, bread

1. I am ordering two pizzas, some soda, and a bag of potato chips for lunch.

   _____

2. Would you like coffee, tea, water, or juice?

   _____

3. I lost my luggage at the airport, so my friends are driving me to the store to get clothes.

   _____

4. Shana is reading about tennis in the news.

   _____

5. Tyler is eating chocolate, two apples, and a banana with some ice cream.

   _____

Spelling Rules for Plural Count Nouns

In English, we mark a plural count noun by spelling it differently. Regular count nouns are marked by adding -s or -es. Irregular count nouns have a variety of spellings, as shown in the following chart.

SPELLING RULES FOR REGULAR COUNT NOUNS	EXAMPLES
For most nouns, add -**s**.	house → house**s**; carrot → carrot**s**; meal → meal**s**
When the noun ends in a consonant + *y*, change the *y* to an *i* and add -**es**.	baby → bab**ies**; library → librar**ies**; berry → berr**ies**
For nouns ending in *sh*, *ch*, *tch*, *s*, *x*, or *z* add -**es**. (**Note:** For words ending in a single *z*, add -**zes**.)	watch → watch**es**; kiss → kiss**es**; box → box**es**; quiz → quiz**zes**
For some nouns ending in *o*, add -**es**.	potat**o** → potato**es**; tomat**o** → tomato**es**; her**o** → hero**es**; ech**o** → echo**es**

Some count nouns are marked by irregular plural forms, as you will see in the following chart.

SPELLING RULES FOR IRREGULAR COUNT NOUNS	EXAMPLES
Words ending in *f* or *fe* (change the *f* to a *v* and add **-es**)	calf → calves; knife → knives; half → halves; life → lives; loaf → loaves; shelf → shelves; elf → elves; self → selves; leaf → leaves; thief → thieves; wife → wives; wolf → wolves
Words derived from foreign languages such as Greek and Latin	analysis → analyses; bacterium → bacteria; datum → data; medium → media; fungus → fungi
Other irregular count nouns	child → children; foot → feet; man → men; woman → women; person → people; tooth → teeth; goose → geese; mouse → mice; ox → oxen

*Note: This is not a comprehensive list of the spelling rules.

Exercise 3.14

See Chapter 2 for Pronunciation Tips for words with **-s** endings.

Form the correct spelling of the plural for each count noun. Some of these nouns are regular and some are irregular. See the preceding charts for help.

EXAMPLE   orange → *oranges*

1. spoon → _____

2. fork → _____

3. knife → _____

4. egg → _____

5. child → _____

6. tooth → _____

7. batch → _____

8. recipe → _____

9. potato → _____

10. boysenberry → _____

11. hen → _____

12. loaf → _____

Quantifiers

When we talk about noncount nouns, we use quantifiers. For example, you can have *a glass of* milk, *a piece of* cake, or *a bowl of* ice cream. **Quantifiers** are countable. When you use them, you make the noncount noun countable, or measurable. If you have more than one, make sure to pluralize the quantifier. For example, you can eat *a piece of* pie or ***two** pieces of* pie.

Exercise 3.15

Look at the following list of quantifiers, and match the appropriate noncount noun to each. Some quantifiers have more than one correct answer.

Quantifiers	Noncount Noun
1. A slice of <u>bread</u>	a. milk
2. Two pieces of _____	b. soup
3. A bottle of _____	c. soda
4. Five cans of _____	d. water
5. A glass of _____	e. flour
6. A bag of _____	f. salt
7. Two pinches of _____	g. bread
8. A bowl of _____	h. cake

Determiners

Words such as *many*, *his*, *my*, *a lot of*, and *these* are **determiners**. They precede nouns and help us identify or quantify nouns. For example, in the sentence *My book is on the table*, **my** identifies which book. It's not *his book* or *a book*. It's *my book*. In the sentence *Many people are eating dinner now*, *many people* measures the number of diners. It's not *one person* or *two people* but *many people*. The following chart gives more examples of determiners.

DETERMINERS THAT IDENTIFY A NOUN	DETERMINERS THAT MEASURE/QUANTIFY A NOUN
Articles: a, an, the	some, any, no
Possessive adjectives: my, your, his, her, its, our, your, their	each, every, either, neither much, many, more, most, enough,
Demonstrative pronouns: this, that, these, those	several, (a) little, (a) few all, both, half one, two, one hundred other, another

We use *most* and *most of the* similarly. Let's take a look.

MOST	MOST OF THE
Most employees work hard.	*Most of the employees* work hard.

> **Caution:** We do not use *most of* without *the* (for example, ~~Most of~~ *employees work hard.*).

Adverbs: *Just* and *Only*

When we talk about quantities and amounts, *just* and *only* have similar meanings, as shown here.

JUST	EXAMPLE	ONLY	EXAMPLE
Meaning: Not very much	How much soup do you want? *Just* a little, please.	**Meaning:** Limited to	How much soup do you want? *Only* a little, please.

Note

Little and *a little* (uncountable) have different meanings. *Little* has a negative meaning: "almost none; not enough." However, *a little* has a positive meaning: "some but not much." For example, *They have **little** food in their refrigerator* (they have almost no food or not enough food). *They have **a little** food in their refrigerator* (they have some food but not much; their refrigerator is not empty).

Few and *a few* (countable) also have different meanings. **Few** is negative: "almost none; less than expected." However, *a few* is positive: "some but not many." For example, *There were **few** people at the cookout* (there were almost no people or fewer people than expected). *There were **a few** people at the restaurant* (there were some people but not many).

Look at some example sentences with determiners. The determiners are in bold.

***Your** children are playing in **the** garden.*   ***Two** restaurants in **my** neighborhood have patios.*

***These** cookbooks have **many** recipes.*   ***His** sister is working at **that** grocery store.*

Exercise 3.16

Read the following sentences, and identify as many determiners as you can. Follow the preceding example sentences for help.

1. Several eggs from my chickens are blue.
2. Five cars are waiting in line at the drive-through restaurant.
3. Three cookies are on her plate.

4. Every customer in this restaurant is eating with two chopsticks.

5. My sister is ordering five combination platters for the family.

6. That chef is slicing many onions simultaneously.

Exercise 3.17

Create two sentences using identifying determiners and two sentences using quantifying determiners. Review the determiners in the previous table, and pay attention to count and noncount nouns.

Sentences with Identifying Determiners	Sentences with Quantifying Determiners
_____	_____
_____	_____

Asking *How Many/How Much*

When we want to know the quantity of something, we use the WH question words *How many* and *How much*. Use *How many* to ask about count nouns. Use *How much* to ask about noncount nouns. Let's look at a few example sentences.

How Many + Count Nouns	*How Much* + Noncount Nouns
How many tomatoes do you need?	*How much* tomato soup do you want?
How many people are eating dinner in the restaurant?	*How much* cheese is in the refrigerator?
How many egg rolls should I order?	*How much* Chinese food should I order?
How many bottles of water do you have?	*How much* water do you have?

Exercise 3.18

Read the following sentences. Decide whether each should begin with How many *or* How much.

EXAMPLE   *How much* milk would you like?

1. _____ cereal should I pour into the bowl?

2. _____ cherries do you have?

3. _____ fruit should I buy?

4. _____ rice does the recipe require?

5. _____ varieties of peppers are you growing?

6. _____ herbs do I need?

7. _____ kinds of music do you like?

8. _____ coconut water does he want?

Exercise 3.19

Construct two questions using How many *and two questions using* How much. *Use vocabulary about food, cooking, and restaurants, and follow the spelling rules for plural count nouns.*

How Many

_____

_____

How Much

_____

_____

Grammar: Definite and Indefinite Articles

In English, we use articles with both count nouns and noncount nouns. The **definite article** *the* can be used for count, noncount, singular, and plural nouns. The **indefinite articles** are *a, an, some,* and *any. A* and *an* are used for singular count nouns. *Some* is used for both plural count nouns and noncount nouns. *Any* is used in questions and negatives. You can omit the article if the noun is plural or noncount. You can *never* omit the article with singular count nouns. The following table helps you see how the articles work.

	COUNT NOUNS	*NONCOUNT NOUNS*
Singular	Definite article: *the* Indefinite articles: *a, an* Article required	
Plural	Definite article: *the* Indefinite articles: *some, any* No article	
Unchanging form		Definite article: *the* Indefinite articles: *some, any* No article

We use *a* before a noun or an adjective that begins with a consonant sound. We use *an* before a noun or an adjective that begins with a vowel sound. Details are given in the following table.

Note: A singular count noun *must* have an article.

EXAMPLE SENTENCES USING A OR AN	EXPLANATION
She is eating at a restaurant.	The word *restaurant* begins with the consonant *r* with the sound /r/, so the indefinite article used is *a*.
She is eating at an excellent restaurant.	The word *excellent* begins with the vowel *e* with the sound /ɛ/, so the indefinite article used is *an*.
He is studying at a university.	Although the word *university* begins with the vowel *u*, it has the consonant sound /y/, so the indefinite article used is *a*.
He is studying at an Ivy League university.	The word *Ivy* begins with the vowel *i* and the sound /ay/, so the indefinite article used is *an*.

We use definite articles when we are talking about specific things and to refer to something we already know. We use indefinite articles to talk about general or nonspecific things. Here are some examples.

	INDEFINITE ARTICLE	DEFINITE ARTICLE
Count noun, singular	I would like *an* orange. (Which orange? Any orange—not a specific orange.)	I would like *the* orange, please. (There is only one orange.)
	I would like *a* plum. (Which plum? Any plum—not a specific plum.)	I would like *the* plum you bought at the farmers' market. (Which plum? A specific plum—the plum from the market.)
Count noun, plural	I am eating *some* cookies. (Which cookies? Nonspecific cookies.)	I am eating *the* cookies you baked. (Which cookies? Specific cookies—the ones you baked.)
Noncount noun	Let's have *some* wine. (Nonspecific wine)	Let's have *the* wine we bought in Italy. (Specific wine—the wine from Italy)

We can use an indefinite article when we first talk about a noun, then use a definite article for the same noun the second time it is mentioned. See the examples sentences here.

EXAMPLE 1:   I am reading ***a*** *good book*. I bought ***the*** *book* yesterday.

Sentence	**Reason for Using a Definite or an Indefinite Article**
I am reading ***a*** *good book*.	This is the first time talking about the book.
I bought ***the*** *book* yesterday.	We know which book.

EXAMPLE 2:   I am trying *a* new recipe. I found ***the*** recipe in my new cookbook.

Sentence	Reason for Using a Definite or an Indefinite Article
I am trying *a* new recipe.	This is the first time talking about the recipe.
I found ***the*** recipe in my new cookbook.	We know which recipe.

Exercise 3.20

Read the following sentences. Complete each sentence with an indefinite article (a, an, or some) or the definite article the.

EXAMPLE   I am trying <u>a</u> new Indian restaurant. <u>The</u> restaurant is downtown.

1. They received _____ invitation to a dinner party. They accepted _____ invitation.

2. Her graduation party was at _____ Vietnamese restaurant. _____ restaurant is new.

3. She is shopping for _____ birthday cake. She wants _____ cake to be chocolate.

4. Oscar wants _____ big party. _____ party is for his daughter's *quinceañera*.

5. She is buying _____ orange energy drink. She read about _____ energy drink in a magazine.

Exercise 3.21

Read the following sentences. Choose the correct article for each sentence. The symbol Ø means no article.

EXAMPLE   I am trying <u>a</u> new Indian restaurant.   a   any

1. Do you like _____ red wine we made?   the   Ø

2. We are all eating _____ pork you bought.   any   the

3. I don't want _____ sauce on my pasta, thank you.   any   some

4. Is she enjoying _____ restaurant?   the   some

5. My father is buying _____ new stove.   a   Ø

Exercise 3.22

Construct one sentence for each category. Use the correct definite or indefinite article for count or noncount nouns. Use the vocabulary you've learned for food, cooking, and restaurants. Be sure to follow the spelling rules for plural count nouns.

	INDEFINITE ARTICLE	DEFINITE ARTICLE
Count noun singular	1. _____	2. _____
Count noun plural	3. _____	4. _____
Noncount noun	5. _____	6. _____

Eating at a Restaurant

Sometimes, we cook and eat dinner at home. Other times, we eat a meal at a restaurant. Let's learn some common expressions used when eating at a restaurant.

Vocabulary: Phrasal Verbs for Eating, Food, and Restaurants

In this section, we will learn more phrasal verbs. Let's look at some phrasal verbs related to eating, food, and restaurants.

Exercise 3.23

Read the phrasal verbs on the left. Then read the definitions on the right. You may know some of these verbs. Match the verbs with the appropriate definitions. For the phrasal verbs you do not know, take a guess. Some of these verbs can be separated with a noun or pronoun; they are shown in **bold**.

1. To eat out
2. To chip in
3. To clean **something** up
4. To tidy **something** up
5. To fill **something** up
6. To add **something** up

a. To wash an area that is dirty
b. To supply completely
c. To give some money for a bill
d. To put items in their proper places
e. To calculate
f. To dine at a restaurant

Exercise 3.24

Complete the sentences with the correct phrasal verb. Be sure to use the present progressive verb form, and use the third person singular verb form when necessary.

EXAMPLE   The waiter *is cleaning up* the spill.

1. The busboy _____ the table.

2. The server _____ the water glass _____.

3. Sean _____ the bill to make sure it is correct.

4. Dr. Marsden and his wife _____ tonight at a special restaurant. It's their wedding anniversary.

5. Dee Dee and Sylvie _____ $25 each for lunch.

Conversation: Making Polite Requests at a Restaurant

When we eat at a restaurant and order food, we use polite language. We make requests using expressions such as *May I, Could I*, and *Can I*. We also use expressions such as *I'd like the* and *I'll have the* to order food. Now let's study a conversation involving Derek, Nora, and a server at the restaurant where they are having dinner.

CONVERSATION AT A RESTAURANT	CONVERSATION GUIDE
SERVER: Welcome to Charlie's Seafood. My name is Ian. I'll be your server this evening. Would you like[1] some water?	1. To offer something, we use different expressions. Another one is *Can I get you* + noun.
NORA: Yes, please. And could I[2] also get an iced tea?	2. To order food, you can also use these expressions: *May I* + verb and *Can I* + verb such as *May I have* + noun and *Can I get* + noun, and *I'll have the* + noun.
SERVER: Of course. Anything for you,[3] sir?	3. This is another way of asking if a customer wants something.
DEREK: Water is fine for me, thanks.	
SERVER: Okay. Our specials tonight are[4] the halibut and the catfish. The halibut is grilled and comes with garlic mashed potatoes and green beans. The catfish is breaded and fried and comes with roasted potatoes and broccoli. I'll be back in just a moment with your drinks.	4. The waitperson usually tells the customers about special meals of the day.

CONVERSATION AT A RESTAURANT

DEREK AND NORA: Thank you.

Five minutes later

SERVER: Here is[5] your water and iced tea, and your water. Do you have any questions about the menu?

NORA: I am looking at the[6] fisherman's stew. What do you think? Is it good?[7]

SERVER: It's very popular, and it's one of our house specialties. It's a good-sized serving, so some of our guests split it[8] between two people.

NORA: Oh. Derek, if we split it, we could get something else and split that too.

DEREK: I am thinking of getting the[9] scallop dish. Would you want to[10] split that?

NORA: Where is that on the menu? Oh, I see it. That looks delicious. Let's do it.

DEREK: Okay, good. We'll take the[11] fisherman's stew and the scallop dish.

SERVER: Perfect. I'll bring extra plates so you can split them. And I'll be back with bread.

DEREK AND NORA: Thank you.

Five minutes later

SERVER: And here's your bread. Can I get you anything else[12] to drink?

DEREK: Can I get[13] a glass of white wine?

SERVER: We have[14] a house white or a chardonnay from California.

CONVERSATION GUIDE

5. We use *here is* + noun to present something.

6. *I am looking at the* is an expression to indicate the food we are considering ordering.

7. Sometimes we ask the waitperson for his or her recommendation.

8. To **split a meal** means to divide it so two people can enjoy it.

9. *I am thinking of getting the* + noun is another expression we use to indicate what we are considering.

10. *Would you want to* is an expression for asking someone to do something.

11. To order food, you can also use these expressions: *Can I get the* + noun and *I'll have the* + noun.

12. A different expression for offering something is *Would you like* + noun.

13. To order food, you can also use this expression: *I'll take the* + noun.

14. *We have* is used to offer options.

(continued)

CONVERSATION AT A RESTAURANT

DEREK: I'll have the[2] chardonnay.

SERVER: Coming right up.[15]

DEREK AND NORA: Thank you.

Five minutes later

SERVER: Your California chardonnay. (Places wine in front of Derek)

DEREK: Thank you.

Twenty minutes later

SERVER: Here you go.[16] Your fisherman's stew (placing dish in front of Nora) and your scallops (placing dish in front of Derek).

NORA: Ooh. It looks delicious. Thank you. And may I get a[2] glass of that white. It's very good.

SERVER: Absolutely. Would you like another,[18] sir?

DEREK: Yes, please.

SERVER: Okay. Is there anything else you need?[19]

NORA: No. I think we're good[20] for now.

SERVER (smiling): I'll be right back with more wine.

SERVER: Here is your wine. Enjoy your meal.

DEREK AND NORA: Thank you.

Ten minutes later

SERVER: How is everything?[21]

NORA: Mm. Very good, thank you. The fisherman's stew is excellent. I can see why it's popular.

SERVER (smiling): Wonderful!

CONVERSATION GUIDE

15. This expression means "I will come back with that quickly."

16. This expression is used to present something.

18. This is a way to ask if a customer wants more.

19. This is another way to ask if a customer wants something additional.

20. **We're good** means "Everything is okay," or "We have what we need."

21. This expression is used to check the situation.

Fifteen minutes later

(Derek gets the server's attention.[22])

SERVER: May I[23] take your plates? Thank you. Would you like to[23] see a dessert menu? The tiramisu is especially good.

DEREK: I think we'll pass on[24] dessert tonight. That was a lot of food!

SERVER (smiling): Very good. I will bring your check.[25]

Five minutes later

WAITER (smiling): I'll take care of that whenever you're ready.[26]

DEREK: Here you go.[17] (Hands waiter a credit card with the check)

SERVER: Thank you. I'll be right back[16] with that.

Three minutes later

SERVER (smiling): Thank you so much. Please come again.

NORA (smiling): Thank you. It was wonderful.

DEREK (smiling): Thank you.

22. To get a server's attention, make eye contact. When he or she sees you, indicate that you would like him or her to come to your table by raising your hand to eye level. You can raise your whole hand (palm facing the person) or just your index finger. Sometimes we just nod and raise our eyebrows to show that we want the server to come over. You want to get his or her attention discreetly. If the server is busy, you may need to wait until he or she walks by your table and then say, "Excuse me," or "Pardon me." Do not yell.

23. *May I* + verb and *Would you like to* + verb are also used to offer things.

24. To **pass on something** means to decline it.

25. The **check** is the bill.

26. **Whenever you're ready** is an expression that means "Don't rush," or "Take your time."

Exercise 3.25

Sara and Joan are at a restaurant. They want to order something to drink and something to eat. Create a conversation between Sara and Joan and the server. Use the preceding conversation as a guide. The conversation has been started for you.

SERVER: Welcome to Quince. My name is Josh. I'll be your server this afternoon. Would you like to start with some water?

SARA: Yes. No ice, please.

JOAN: I'd like a cup of coffee, please.

SERVER: _____

_____

_____

_____

_____

_____

_____

_____

_____

_____

Reading About It

In this section, we'll review how to identify the topic and main idea of a passage while pre-reading. We will also learn how to discover the meaning of vocabulary through context.

Topics and Main Ideas

As you learned in Chapter 2, we pre-read to find the topic and main idea of a passage. Remember, the **topic** is the large category of the passage. The **main idea** is a specific idea in that category. To find the topic, ask the question *What is this story about?* Or *What is the subject of this passage?* To find the main idea, ask the question *What about the topic?* Let's practice finding the topic and main idea.

Exercise 3.26

Spend one or two minutes pre-reading the following article. Look for the topic and the main idea of the passage. To pre-read, read the title, the first sentence, and the last sentence of the paragraph. Underline the topic and highlight the main idea.

 **Sally Grows Her Food**

Sally likes to grow her own food. She has a vegetable garden in her backyard. She is growing different types of green leafy vegetables such as spinach, arugula, and dandelion greens. It is summer, so she is also growing sugar snap peas, fennel, and cherry tomatoes. She makes fresh salads every day for lunch with her homegrown vegetables. Her backyard gets a lot of sun, so she is growing blackberries, raspberries, and blueberries in her garden too. For breakfast, Sally eats cereal with berries from her garden. This garden makes Sally very happy. She enjoys eating food she has grown herself.

Now, answer these two questions:

What is the topic? _____

What is the main idea? _____

Discovering Meaning Through Context

When you see a vocabulary word you don't know, what do you do?

1. Ignore the word.

2. Look the word up in the dictionary.

3. Try to guess the meaning.

4. Ask someone for the meaning.

You can do all of these things, depending on the situation. If the word is repeated often, you may want to look it up in the dictionary or ask a native speaker for the definition. If the word is not repeated, you may be able to ignore it.

In this section, we'll discuss how to discover the definition of a new word by guessing its meaning from the **context**, or the words around it. Many clues can help you. Let's learn five of these definition context clues.

DEFINITION CONTEXT CLUES	EXAMPLE SENTENCES
1. *Or* **, or** _____ , A comma after the new word or phrase is followed by the word *or* + a definition or synonym and another comma.	The stems and leaves of Florence fennel, *or finocchio*, can be sliced and put in salads.
2. Commas , _____ , A comma appears after the new word or phrase and another comma after the definition or synonym.	Greens, *leaf vegetables*, are very healthy for you.
3. Dashes — _____ — A dash comes after the new word or phrase and another dash after the definition or synonym.	Greens—*leaf vegetables*—are very healthy for you.
4. Parentheses (_____) Parentheses enclose the definition or synonym that directly follows the new word or phrase.	Greens *(leaf vegetables)* are very healthy for you.
5. Also called, also known as, aka , also called _____ , , also known as _____ , , aka _____ , A comma appears after the new word or phrase, then one of the phrases shown here + the definition or synonym followed by another comma.	Arugula, *also called roquette*, has a peppery flavor. Arugula, *also known as roquette*, has a peppery flavor. Arugula, *aka roquette*, has a peppery flavor.

Note

If the definition comes at the end of the sentence, do not use a comma. Use the appropriate end-of-sentence punctuation, such as a period or a question mark.

Exercise 3.27

Look at the following sentences and find the definition of the boldface words.

EXAMPLE   **Dandelion greens**—the leaves of the dandelion plant—are rich in calcium and iron. *the leaves of the dandelion plant*

1. **The farmers' market** (an outdoor market where farmers sell directly to consumers) offers organic foods, fresh meat, and local art.

   _____

2. I am growing squash and cucumbers on my fence. These are **climbing vegetables**, or vegetables that grow on a vine and climb.

   _____

3. **Lacinato kale**, also called dino kale and Tuscan kale, is high in vitamins A, C, and K. _____

4. Nutritionists recommend eating **superfoods**, or foods with many nutrients.

   _____

5. **Phytonutrients**, natural chemicals in plants, help people fight diseases.

   _____

Writing About It

In writing, we sometimes want to provide a list of items. You may read lists of ingredients in recipes, grocery lists, and descriptions of food on a menu. In this section, you will learn how to use commas in a list.

Using Commas in a List

In English, we use commas when we write a list, as shown. Find all the commas.

Summer Salad Recipe
This fresh salad is a quick and nutritious lunch on a

Summer Salad Recipe

This fresh salad is a quick and nutritious lunch on a hot summer day. You will need some kale leaves, a few leaves of fresh spearmint, a handful of cherry tomatoes, ½ cup of shredded parmesan cheese, ¼ cup of olive oil, the juice of one lemon, and 1 teaspoon of red wine vinegar. Chop the kale into thin strips, slice the tomatoes in half, and mince the mint. Place the dry ingredients in a bowl. Mix the oil, lemon, and vinegar with a whisk and add to the dry ingredients. Toss the salad and enjoy with friends!

Dinner Menu

Almond-encrusted roast chicken

Free-range chicken encrusted with organic almond meal, salt, pepper, and lemon zest and roasted until crisp on the outside and juicy and tender on the inside. Served with fingerling potatoes, French fries, or mashed potatoes.

Baked salmon with greens

Wild salmon from Alaska baked to retain its natural juices. Served on a bed of fresh baby greens—a combination of spinach, collards, rainbow chard, and mustard greens. Comes with roasted potatoes.

Note

In a list of more than two things, the comma before *and* and *or* with the last item is omitted in British English usage and required for North American usage. For example, these two sentences are both correct, depending on where you are: (with comma) *The chicken comes with roasted, French fried, or mashed potatoes.* / (without comma) *The chicken comes with roasted, French fried or mashed potatoes.*

Exercise 3.28

Think of your favorite meal. Now describe it. Construct a few sentences with a list of ingredients. Use commas in a list of three or more items.

_____

_____

_____

_____

_____

Quiz

You have finished Chapter 3. Great work! Now take the quiz to see what you remember. Choose the correct answers for each question.

1. When forming the present progressive verb tense, which structure do we use?

   BE + verb   BE + verb-**ing**

   BE + past tense verb   DO + verb-**ing**

2. For the present progressive verb tense, which is the correct spelling rule for verbs that end in a silent *e*?

Drop the *e* and add **-ing**.   Drop the *e* and add **-ed**.

Add **-ing**.   Change the *e* to an *i* and add **-ing**.

3. Which time word or phrase is *not* used with the present progressive verb tense?

Right now   Every day

This winter   Nowadays

4. Read this sentence: *She is eating dinner right now.* What is the *incorrect* negative form of the verb in that sentence?

isn't eating   is not eating

does not eating   's not eating

5. What is the correct short answer to this question: *Where is she eating?*

At the café.   She's eating in the café.

Yes.   No, she isn't.

6. What is the correct short answer to this question: *Is she having fun right now?*

No, she is.   Yes, is.

She, is.   Yes, she is.

7. Which of these words requires an extra syllable when it is pronounced?

Salads   Mixes

Herbs   Shakes

8. Which word is *always* noncount?

Salt   Chicken

Pie   Cherry

9. Which is the most appropriate quantifier to use with the noncount noun *oil*?

A handful of   A slice of

A teaspoon of   A few

10. Which of the following article + noun phrases is *incorrect*?

An apple   A orange

A banana   A ripe apple

Do It Out There!

Now that you have learned how to talk about activities you are doing right now and how to order food in a restaurant, try it out in the world. Review this chapter, and go out and use English! Put a checkmark next to each activity as you complete it.

To Do This Week

- ❑ Use the present progressive verb tense. Talk about the activities you are doing and *not* doing at the moment of speaking.
- ❑ Write a recipe for a friend. Use commas when giving a list of ingredients.
- ❑ Practice count and noncount nouns. In your recipe, use correct articles and determiners for each ingredient.
- ❑ Go out to dinner and practice using polite expressions to order food in a restaurant.
- ❑ Use a few new phrasal verbs that you learned in this chapter.
- ❑ Practice finding the meanings of new words from context clues while you read about food in a magazine or on the Internet.

Weekly Log

Keep a weekly log of your progress. Make notes on how your practice went. What happened? Was it successful? How do you know it was successful? Was it unsuccessful? How do you know? Review all the instructions, pronunciation tips, and culture notes in Chapter 3.

_____

_____

_____

_____

_____

_____

4

Getting Around Town

In this chapter you will learn about:

Speaking
- ✓ How to ask for directions
- ✓ How to ask for repetition of information
- ✓ How to check your understanding by paraphrasing
- ✓ How to give directions
- ✓ How to discuss schedules

Vocabulary, Reading, and Writing
- ✓ Prepositions of place
- ✓ Vocabulary for downtown
- ✓ Expressions for directions
- ✓ Expressions of time
- ✓ How to discover vocabulary from examples
- ✓ Phrasal verbs

Grammar
- ✓ How to use the imperative
- ✓ How to use *there is* and *there are*
- ✓ How to use the simple present verb tense for schedules

Body Language
- ✓ How to point to places and locations (giving directions)
- ✓ How to shrug your shoulders to indicate that you don't know

Walking Around Town: Giving and Getting Directions

When you need to find a place, you can ask for directions. Perhaps you are walking to a doctor's appointment, or maybe you are driving in a new city and need to find a restaurant. When you don't know where you're going, it's helpful to ask someone.

Conversation: Asking for Directions

Let's look at a sample conversation about directions.

CONVERSATION	CONVERSATION GUIDE
LEO: Excuse me.[1] How do I get to the post office?[2]	1. Other expressions to get someone's attention: Excuse me, please. / Pardon me. / Pardon me, please.
	2. Other expressions to ask a WH question about a location: Where can I find the _____? / Could you tell me where the _____is? / Do you know where the _____ is?
JOSIE (person on the street): Go straight on this street (pointing) and take a right on River Road. It'll be[3] on your left next to the bakery.	3. Alternative expressions: You'll see it / It's.
LEO: So,[4] I go straight down this street and go left on River Street?[5]	4. Other expressions to check understanding by paraphrasing: So, I need to / So you're saying that / In other words.
	5. Use rising pitch to show uncertainty.
JOSIE (pointing): No, go *right* onto River *Road*.[6] Right here.	6. Stress words to correct information.
LEO: Oh, okay.[7] I turn right on River Road.[8,9] Is the post office far from here?[10]	7. Use an interjection to show understanding of the correction: Ah! / Okay. / I think I've got it now.
	8. Repeat information to show understanding.
	9. Use falling pitch to show certainty.

CONVERSATION

JOSIE: It's only one block down.[11]

LEO (smiling[12]): Thank you for your help![13]

JOSIE: You're welcome.[14]

CONVERSATION GUIDE

10. Other expressions to ask for additional information: How far is that? / How long will it take me to walk there? / Can I walk from here, or should I take the bus?

11. Other directions might include: It's down the street / It's one block up / It's up the street.

12. Smile when you express gratitude.

13. Other ways to express gratitude: Thank you! / Thank you very much! / Thank you so much! / Thanks a lot!

14. Other expressions to respond to gratitude: Not at all. / It's nothing. / Don't mention it. / You bet. / Sure. / Of course.

Pointing and Shrugging Shoulders

It's helpful to point at locations when giving directions. We point using the index finger. It's not polite to point directly at people, but it's okay to point at places and things. When we point, we usually extend our arm fully and point with the index finger in the direction of the destination.

Sometimes, people don't know the destination you're looking for. They may not be able to give you directions. In this case, they may say, "I don't know." Sometimes, they will **shrug their shoulders**, which also means "I don't know." In either case, you can say, "Thank you," and ask someone else for directions.

Vocabulary: City Center

Let's learn some vocabulary related to a city center, also known as *downtown*. Look at the map of Porter City. A vocabulary list follows the map, and each word or phrase corresponds to something on the map. Read each vocabulary item. Identify the vocabulary that is new to you. Then find each item on the map.

Culture Note: In British English, a parking lot is called a car park and a pharmacy is called a chemist.

Key Vocabulary on the Map of Porter City

1. A pedestrian
2. A block
3. A crosswalk
4. A streetlight
5. A stop sign
6. A traffic light
7. An intersection
8. The post office
9. The bank
10. The bakery
11. A sidewalk
12. The café
13. The Italian restaurant
14. The Chinese restaurant
15. The grocery store
16. A parking lot
17. A street
18. A road
19. The office building
20. The pharmacy
21. The movie theater
22. The hospital
23. The department store
24. The library
25. City Hall
26. The police station
27. The fire station
28. The hotel
29. The hardware store

Exercise 4.1

Answer the questions about the vocabulary for a city center.

1. What two things stop cars? _____

2. What lights a street at night? _____

3. What do we call a person who is walking? _____

4. What is the area where cars park? _____

5. What's another word for drugstore? _____

6. Name the six places where people can get food. _____

7. What two words mean a surface on which cars drive? _____

8. What do we call the area where pedestrians walk? _____

9. What word means where two streets cross? _____

10. How many blocks are on the map of Porter City? _____

Exercise 4.2

Find Leo and Josie on the map of Porter City. They are standing in front of the Chinese restaurant. Read Josie's earlier directions to Leo again. Can you find the post office? Use the numbered vocabulary to help you.

Grammar: Using the Imperative

In English, we use the imperative to give directions and instructions. You can see the imperative in things like recipes and instruction manuals. When you ask for directions, you are asking for instructions to get somewhere. In this section, we will practice giving directions using the imperative. Let's look at some example sentences:

Take a left at the hospital.

When you get to the intersection, go right one block.

Turn right when you reach the traffic light.

Walk straight for two blocks and *take* a right.

Forming the Imperative

To form the imperative, use the base form of a verb. The **base form of the verb** is a verb with no verb endings. For example, we do not add **-s** or **-ing** or **-ed** to the verb. The subject is *you*, but we do not say or write the subject. Look at the following chart.

	(SUBJECT PRONOUN)	*BASE FORM OF THE MAIN VERB*	*REST OF SENTENCE*
	(You)	Take	a left at the hospital.
When you get to the intersection,	(you)	turn	right.
	(You)	Go	right when you reach the traffic light.
	(You)	Walk	straight for two blocks and
	(you)	take	a right.

Here are examples of correct and incorrect imperative sentences. Notice that the correct sentence does *not* add an ending to the verb.

CORRECT: *Take a left at the library.*

INCORRECT: *~~Taking~~ a left at the library.*

INCORRECT: *~~Takes~~ a left at the library.*

Let's practice the imperative. Look at the map of Porter City, and find the post office. This is your starting point. Now look at the following destinations. A **destination** is the place you want to go. Which direction (imperative sentence) matches each destination?

Exercise 4.3

> **Door** refers to a building or house when giving directions.

Match the destination with the correct direction.

Starting Point	Destination	Directions
1. The post office	City Hall	a. Cross the street.
2. The post office	The bank	b. Walk two doors down.
3. The post office	The bakery	c. Walk to the intersection and cross the street.
4. The post office	The Italian restaurant	d. Take a right, and cross both River Road and Main Street at the intersection.
5. The post office	The hardware store	e. Go next door.

> **Next door** means the next building or house.

Forming the Negative Imperative

When we want to stop someone from doing something, we use the negative imperative. The most common form is to use the contraction *don't*. Let's take a look at how we form it.

DO	NEGATIVE	BASE FORM OF VERB	REST OF SENTENCE	EXAMPLE SENTENCES
Do	not	take	a left at the hospital.	Do not take a left at the hospital.
Do	n't	take	a left at the hospital.	Don't take a left at the hospital.

Read these example sentences aloud:

Don't go left. Go right.

When you get to the intersection, don't cross the street.

Don't go that way. Go this way.

Make sure to go one block past the park. Don't take a left at the park.

Exercise 4.4

Look at the following words. Form imperative and negative imperative sentences from them.

EXAMPLE   turn / left / at the light

<u>Turn left at the light.</u>   <u>Don't turn left at the light.</u>

Imperatives	**Negative Imperatives**

1. cross / the street

   _____   _____

2. go / straight / for two blocks

   _____   _____

3. when you get to the hospital, / go / right

   _____   _____

4. at the intersection, / make / a left

   _____   _____

5. after you pass the movie theater, / turn right

   _____   _____

Vocabulary: Expressions Used in Directions

Here are some common expressions we use to give directions.

To take/make a right/left	To cross the street	To go through/past the intersection
To turn right/left	On the right/left	To go to the intersection
To go right/left	On your right/left	Just after/past the _____
To stay/go/keep straight	On the right/left side of the street	Just before the _____

 Exercise 4.5

Find the common expressions used with directions in the imperative sentences you formed in Exercise 4.4.

Vocabulary: Prepositions of Place

Here are prepositions used to describe location:

in

on

into

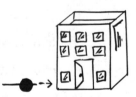

to/toward

from

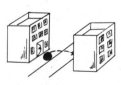

across (the street) from

next to

next door to

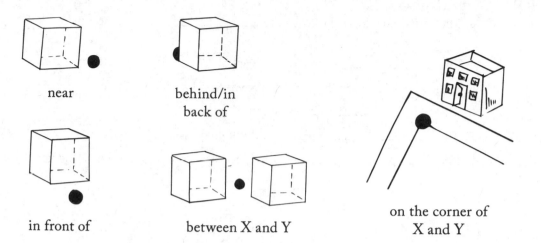

near   behind/in
                    back of

in front of   between X and Y   on the corner of
                                           X and Y

Let's look at some example sentences that use prepositions of place. These sentences refer to the map of Porter City.

*The fire station is **between** the hotel **and** the department store.*

*The bakery is **across the street from** the café.*

*The hospital is **on the corner of** Main Street **and** River Road.*

*The movie theater is **next to** the pharmacy.*

*The grocery store is **behind** the office building.*

*A parking lot is **in back of** the Italian restaurant and the café.*

Articles
Remember that when we know *which* bakery, fire station, department store, or café, we use the definite article *the*. We also use *the* to indicate that there is only *one* bakery, fire station, department store, or café; for example, *the* bakery, *the* fire station, *the* department store, and *the* café.

Now let's practice using prepositions. Study the prepositions and their meanings, then complete the following activity.

 Exercise 4.6

Look at the map of Porter City, and complete each sentence with the correct vocabulary. There may be more than one correct answer.

EXAMPLE   The *bank* is across from the hardware store.

1. The _____ is next door to the hardware store.

2. The Chinese restaurant is across the street from the _____.

3. The office building is between the _____ and the
_____.

4. The _____ is next to the hospital.

5. _____ is on the corner of River Road and Main Street.

6. The _____ is in back of the Chinese restaurant.

7. The _____ is across from the Italian restaurant.

8. The _____ is between the hardware store and the movie theater.

Exercise 4.7

*Look at the map of Porter City, and complete each sentence with the correct
prepositions of place. There may be more than one correct answer.*

EXAMPLE   The bank *is across from/across the street from* the hardware store.

1. The hospital is _____ Main Street _____ River Road.

2. The fire station is _____ the department store.

3. The movie theater is _____ the Chinese restaurant.

4. The café is _____ the hardware store _____ the Italian
restaurant.

5. A parking lot is _____ the hotel.

6. The police station is _____ the grocery store.

7. The doughnut shop is _____ the movie theater.

8. The park is _____ the library.

Now that you have practiced vocabulary referring to downtown and
prepositions of place, let's practice following directions.

Exercise 4.8

Use the map of Porter City. Look at the starting point, and follow the directions. Where do you end up? Indicate the destination.

EXAMPLE:

   STARTING POINT: The movie theater

   DIRECTIONS: Go up Main Street to the intersection. Take a left. It'll be on your right. It's across the street from the library.

   DESTINATION: *The park*

1. STARTING POINT: Office building

   DIRECTIONS: Take a left out of the office building. Walk to the intersection. Cross River Road. It's next to the hospital on Main Street.

   DESTINATION: _____

2. STARTING POINT: The café

   DIRECTIONS: Walk up to the intersection of Main Street. Then turn left. When you get to the movie theater, cross the street. It's a small building.

   DESTINATION: _____

3. STARTING POINT: The park

   DIRECTIONS: Start at River Road. Go to the intersection of Main Street and take a right. Walk down to the doughnut shop. Cross the street. It's behind the movie theater.

   DESTINATION: _____

You have practiced the imperative, expressions for directions, vocabulary for downtown, and prepositions of place. Now practice using all of this language together to give directions.

Exercise 4.9

Jack is asking you for directions to different places in Porter City. His starting point is the Chinese restaurant, and his destinations are indicated. Construct directions for each destination. Use the imperative, expressions for giving directions, and prepositions of place.

EXAMPLE

STARTING POINT: The Chinese restaurant

DIRECTIONS: *Take a right. Walk to the intersection and cross Main Street. Go down River Road until you reach the library. It's across the street from the library.*

DESTINATION: The park

1. STARTING POINT: The Chinese restaurant

   DIRECTIONS: _____

   DESTINATION: Hotel Casa

2. STARTING POINT: The Chinese restaurant

   DIRECTIONS: _____

   DESTINATION: The pharmacy

3. STARTING POINT: The Chinese restaurant

   DIRECTIONS: _____

   DESTINATION: The grocery store

Grammar: *There Is/There Are*

When we give directions, we describe the location of things. We also talk about how many things exist. To describe the location and the quantity of something, we often use the expressions *there is* and *there are*. When we are talking about one thing, we use *there is*. When we are talking about two or more things, we use *there are*. Let's look at some example sentences:

There is a gas station on the corner.

Down two blocks, **there is** an ice cream shop.

There are two office buildings at the end of the road.

In the middle of the block, **there are** two parking lots.

> *There are* is **not** the same as *they are*. *There are* is an expression we use to talk about the location or amount of something. *They are* is the subject and verb of a sentence. The two words are also pronounced differently. They do **not** sound the same. *There* rhymes with *air* and *hair*. *They* rhymes with *say* and *pay*. Do not pronounce these two words the same way.

There Is/There Are: How to Form the Affirmative

In sentences using *there is/there are*, the subject comes after the verb. The verb is a form of BE. Look at the following chart to see how to form *there is* and *there are*.

THERE	BE VERB	SUBJECT	LOCATION
There	is	a gas station	on the corner.
There	are	two office buildings	at the end of the road.

Sometimes, we form the sentences with the location first. Notice that we use a comma after the location.

LOCATION	THERE	BE VERB	SUBJECT
Down two blocks,	there	is	an ice cream shop.
In the middle of the block,	there	are	two parking lots.

Exercise 4.10

Let's see how there is *and* there are *work. Use the map of Porter City. Complete the sentences with the appropriate vocabulary about downtown Porter City.*

EXAMPLE   There is a <u>grocery store</u> behind the office building.

1. There is a _____ behind the pharmacy.

2. Next to Hotel Casa, there is a _____.

3. There is an _____ across the street from the post office.

4. Between the doughnut shop and the bank, there is an _____.

5. There are two large _____ in downtown Porter City.

6. In between the bakery and the fire station, there are many _____.

7. There are _____ places to get something to eat in Porter City.

8. Across from City Hall and next to the café, there is a _____.

Exercise 4.11

Use there is *and* there are *to complete the following sentences. Remember to begin each sentence with a capital letter.*

EXAMPLES   <u>*There is*</u> a doughnut shop at the end of River Road.

          At the end of River Road, <u>*there is*</u> a doughnut shop.

1. _____ two big parking lots downtown.

2. In Porter City, _____ several places to eat.

3. _____ a bank on the corner.

4. Behind the park, _____ a parking lot for bicycles.

5. _____ many trees in the alley between the bakery and the fire station.

6. Next to the police station, _____ a grocery store.

7. Behind the movie theater, _____ a large parking lot.

8. _____ many tall buildings downtown.

There Is/There Are: How to Form the Negative

Sometimes, we talk about what does *not* exist. In this case, we use *there is/there are* in the negative form. Let's see how to form the negative.

THERE	BE VERB	NEGATIVE	SUBJECT	LOCATION
There	is	not	a gas station	on the corner.
There	are	not	two office buildings	at the end of the road.

In English, we usually use the contraction of the negative *there is* and *there are*. Let's look at these contractions.

THERE	BE VERB	NEGATIVE	CONTRACTION	EXAMPLE SENTENCES
There	is	not	There isn't	There isn't a gas station on the corner.
There	are	not	There aren't	There aren't two cafes on the corner.

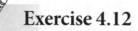

Exercise 4.12

Complete the sentences by writing the negative form of there is *or* there are. *Use the contraction. Refer to the map of Porter City to help you. Remember to begin each sentence with a capital letter.*

EXAMPLES   *There isn't* a fire station on Main Street.

On Main Street, *there isn't* a fire station.

1. _____ any parking lots on River Road.

2. Behind the post office, _____ a grocery store.

3. _____ an ice cream shop at the intersection of Main Street and River Road.

4. In the middle of the block, _____ any schools.

5. _____ a movie theater on River Road.

6. _____ two hotels downtown.

7. Next to the police station, _____ any parking lots.

8. _____ a library on Main Street.

Exercise 4.13

Look at the map of Porter City. Construct sentences using there is *or* there are *and prepositions of place about the words in parentheses. You may need to use the negative form of* there is/there are. *If so, use the contraction. Remember to use the correct article (a, an, or the) if there is only one.*

EXAMPLES   movie theater / pharmacy   *There is a movie theater next to the pharmacy.*

Italian restaurant /   *There isn't an Italian restaurant on*
Main Street   *Main Street.*

1. bakery / post office _____

2. parking lot / downtown Porter City _____

3. café / corner of Main Street and River Road _____

4. library / park _____

5. two Indian restaurants / downtown Porter City _____

6. hospital / bank _____

7. library / Main Street _____

8. trees / park _____

Yes/No Questions Using *There Is/There Are*

BE VERB	THERE	SUBJECT	LOCATION
Is	there	a gas station	on the corner?
Are	there	fast-food restaurants	downtown?

When you ask a yes/no question using *there is/there are*, the answer is usually short. See the answers that follow.

QUESTION	ANSWER
Excuse me. Is there a gas station on the corner?	Yes, there is. No, there isn't.
Pardon me. Are there fast-food restaurants downtown?	Yes, there are. No, there aren't.

Let's practice short answers with *there is/there are*.

 ## Exercise 4.14

Answer the following questions with an appropriate short answer. The answer may be affirmative or negative. Use the map of Porter City to help you.

EXAMPLE   Is there a movie theater downtown Porter City?   <u>Yes, there is.</u>

1. Is there an Italian restaurant on Main Street? _____

2. Is there a place to buy groceries downtown? _____

3. Are there any places to park my car? _____

4. Is there more than one bank downtown? _____

5. Is there a place where I can buy nice clothing? _____

When we give a short answer, we usually give more information, as in the following chart.

QUESTION	ANSWER + ADDITIONAL INFORMATION
Excuse me. Is there a gas station on the corner?	No, there isn't. But there is one up Main Street about five blocks.
Excuse me. Is there a gas station on the corner?	Yes, there is. You can see the sign there. (Points)
Pardon me. Are there any fast-food restaurants downtown?	No, there aren't. There are take-out restaurants but no fast-food places.
Pardon me. Are there any fast-food restaurants downtown?	Yes, there are. There's a burger place on River Road and a taco place on Main Street.

Now let's practice yes/no questions and short answers with *there is/there are*. Notice that more information is given to help you.

Exercise 4.15

Complete the sentences about Porter City. Use the preceding example questions and answers to guide you.

EXAMPLE   Excuse me. _Is there_ a church downtown?
           No, there isn't. But you can find one about five blocks down Main Street.

1. Pardon me. _____ any bookstores around here?
   _____. But there is a library on River Road.

2. Excuse me. On Main Street, _____ a place to get my car washed?

   _____. I don't know where you can get your car washed.

3. Excuse me. _____ any places to get some lunch?
   _____. There are a couple of restaurants and a café close by.

4. Pardon me. _____ a doughnut shop around here?
   _____. It's at the end of Main Street next to the office building.

5. Excuse me. _____ a hardware store downtown?
   _____. It's over there (pointing) on the corner of Main Street and River Road.

WH Questions with *There Is/There Are*

When you are looking for a particular place, you can ask using the WH question word *where*:

> Excuse me. **Where** is there a bookstore around here?
>
> Pardon me. **Where** is there an ice cream shop, please?

Look at the table to learn how to form these questions

WH WORD	BE VERB	THERE	SUBJECT	LOCATION
Where	is	there	a gas station, please?	
Where	are	there	fine dining restaurants	downtown?

Exercise 4.16

Complete the questions using the words given. Use the previous example questions to guide you. Be sure to end the sentence with a question mark. Add please *to the end of the question to be polite.*

EXAMPLE   Where / BE / there / a hospital?

Where is there a hospital, please?

1. Where / BE / there / a police station downtown?

   _____

2. Where / BE / there / a place to get breakfast?

   _____

3. Where / BE / there / a café with Wi-Fi?

   _____

4. Where / BE / there / a place to donate clothes?

   _____

Describing Your Town

We have talked about Porter City. Now it's time to talk about your own town.

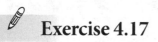

Exercise 4.17

Create a simple map of your city. Show the downtown with streets, shops, and other buildings. Use the map of Porter City as an example.

Exercise 4.18

Construct five sentences about where things are located in your town. Use prepositions, downtown vocabulary, and there is/there are. *Review the tables and exercises in this chapter to help you.*

1. _____

2. _____

3. _____

4. _____

5. _____

Exercise 4.19

Now create directions for five different destinations. Choose a starting point on your map. Begin at the same starting point for each destination. Use prepositions, downtown vocabulary, sentences with there is/there are, and expressions for directions. Review the tables and exercises in this chapter to help you.

Starting Point	Destination	Directions
1. _____	_____	_____
2. _____	_____	_____
3. _____	_____	_____
4. _____	_____	_____
5. _____	_____	_____

Communication Strategy: Understanding Directions

Sometimes, it's difficult to understand directions. Someone may speak too quickly or use vocabulary you don't know. When you want to be sure you understand directions, you can check in two ways. One way is to ask for repetition. Another way is to paraphrase, or confirm, what you have heard. To **paraphrase** means to **say in another way or in your own words**. Let's practice asking for repetition.

Asking for Repetition

There are many ways to ask for repetition. Here are a few expressions you can use:

> It's okay to say that you are learning English. When you don't understand someone, it's okay to ask for repetition. It's important that you understand information.

Could you please repeat that?

I'm sorry. I didn't catch that. Could you say that again, please?

I'm sorry. I didn't understand what you said. Could you please repeat that?

Sorry, what was that?

Pardon me. Could you speak more slowly, please? I'm learning English. (Smile)

Excuse me. Could you say that again, please?

Pronunciation Tip
When you ask for someone to repeat what they have said or when you paraphrase to check understanding, use rising pitch to show uncertainty. See the Appendix for more information.

Now let's see how questions for repetition can be used. In the two examples that follow, James is giving Isabel directions. She doesn't understand, so she asks for repetition.

GIVING DIRECTIONS	ASKING FOR REPETITION
JAMES: Once you get to the hardware store, take a right, and you'll see the cafe next to the Italian restaurant on the right.	ISABEL: I'm sorry, I didn't understand what you said. Could you repeat that, please?
JAMES: Go right at the department store, and it's on your left after the library.	ISABEL (smiling): I'm sorry. I'm learning English. Could you speak more slowly, please?

Exercise 4.20

Read the directions that James gives. Construct a different question that asks for repetition for each set of directions given.

GIVING DIRECTIONS	ASKING FOR REPETITION
JAMES: Take a left at the intersection. Go two blocks, and it's on your right.	1. _____
JAMES: Cross the street and walk behind the bank. It's next to the police station.	2. _____

Paraphrasing to Check Understanding

When you need to be sure you understand something like directions, you can paraphrase what you have heard. There are several ways to begin a paraphrase:

So, . . . ? / Do you mean . . . ? / So, I should (base form of verb) . . . ?

What you mean is . . . ? / I need to (base form of verb) . . . ? / You're saying . . . ?

Now let's see how to use these expressions. James is giving Isabel directions. She checks her understanding of the directions by paraphrasing.

GIVING DIRECTIONS	PARAPHRASING FOR UNDERSTANDING
JAMES: Once you get to the hardware store, take a right, and you'll see the café next to the Italian restaurant on the right.	ISABEL: *What you mean is* after I take a right at the hardware store, the café will be on the right side of the street?
JAMES: Once you get to the hardware store, take a right, and you'll see the café next to the Italian restaurant on the right.	ISABEL: *So,* after I take a right at the hardware store, the café will be on the right side of the street?
JAMES: Once you get to the hardware store, take a right, and you'll see the café next to the Italian restaurant on the right.	ISABEL: *I need to* take a right at the hardware store, and the café will be on the right side of the street?

Pronunciation Tip
Remember to use rising pitch to show uncertainty. See the Appendix for more information.

Exercise 4.21

Read the directions that James gives. Paraphrase to check understanding. Create a different paraphrase for each using different expressions. Review the previous examples to help you.

DIRECTIONS	PARAPHRASE FOR UNDERSTANDING
JAMES: Go right and walk to the intersection. Cross River Road. Walk half a block. Hotel Casa is on the right.	1. _____
JAMES: Walk up River Road. Take a right at the hardware store. The Italian restaurant is on the right just past the café.	2. _____

Exercise 4.22

Look at the following scrambled conversation. Jackie is asking how to get to the movie theater, and a pedestrian is giving her directions. Put the sentences in the correct order by numbering them. The first one and the last one are done for you.

    1   Pardon me. Do you know where the movie theater is?

_____ Okay, great! Thank you very much!

_____ So, I should take a right, and it will be on my right?

_____ Yes. Walk down this street, and take a left at the traffic light. You'll see it on the right.

_____ No. Actually, you take a *left*, and it's on the right.

_____ Just half a block.

_____ Ah, okay. I take a left, and it's on the right. How far down is it on the right?

    8   Sure.

Exercise 4.23

Now that you have learned about giving and getting directions, try it yourself. Maria's starting point is the post office in Porter City, and her destination is the Chinese restaurant. She asks a passerby, Eric, for directions to the restaurant. Eric gives her directions. Complete the conversation between Maria and Eric using the map of Porter City. For help, review the conversation at the beginning of this chapter. To complete the conversation, use the vocabulary, prepositions, imperatives, and repetition/paraphrasing expressions you have learned.

1. Get someone's attention politely. / Maria: _____

2. Use a WH question to ask for directions to the Chinese restaurant. / Maria:

   _____

3. Give directions using the imperative. / Eric: _____

4. Ask for repetition. / Maria: _____

5. Repeat instructions. / Eric: _____

6. Paraphrase for understanding. / Maria: _____

7. Reply *yes* or *no*. If incorrect, give correct directions and capitalize stressed words. / Eric: _____

8. Repeat information to show understanding. / Maria: _____

9. Ask for additional information. / Maria: _____

10. Give answer. / Eric: _____

11. Express gratitude. / Maria: _____

12. Respond to gratitude. / Eric: _____

Taking Public Transportation

Sometimes you need to take public transportation. You can take a bus or a train to get to work or go shopping. In this section, we will learn about expressions of time, the verb tense, and the verbs we usually use for public transportation schedules.

Conversation: Public Transportation Schedules

First, let's look at a conversation about schedules. In this conversation, Sebastian is in Porter City and needs to get to Emeryville. He doesn't know the bus schedule, so he walks to the bus station. When he gets there, he goes to the ticket counter. Here is his conversation with the customer service agent.

CONVERSATION

SEBASTIAN: Excuse me.[1] Which bus goes to Emeryville?[2]

CUSTOMER SERVICE AGENT: Where do you want to go in Emeryville—downtown or to the beach?[3]

SEBASTIAN: I need to get to[4] the shopping district.

CUSTOMER SERVICE AGENT: Then you'll want to[5] take the bus that goes downtown. It's the Emeryville 26 bus.

CONVERSATION GUIDE

1. Expressions to get someone's attention: Excuse me, please. / Pardon me. / Pardon me, please.

2. Expressions to ask a WH question about the bus or train schedule: How can I get to _____? / What train should I take to get to _____? / Do you know which bus I need to get to _____?

3. Ask a question to get more information. You can ask yes/no questions or WH questions.

4. Alternative expressions: I'd like to go to / I want to go to / I'm trying to get to _____.

5. Alternative expressions: Then you should / Then you'll need to / You should take _____.

CONVERSATION

SEBASTIAN: Oh, okay. Where do I catch the Emeryville 26?[3]

CUSTOMER SERVICE AGENT: You can catch it right here at the station. Go to terminal 2 and wait there.[6]

SEBASTIAN: And terminal 2 is over there[7]? (Points)

CUSTOMER SERVICE AGENT: It's on the side of this building. (Points[8]) Look for the sign.

SEBASTIAN: Thank you! And when's[9] the next one?[10]

CUSTOMER SERVICE AGENT: In the mornings, it runs[11] every 10 minutes. But now that it's afternoon, it comes[11] every 30 minutes. Here's[12] the schedule for all the bus routes.

SEBASTIAN: And where do I buy a bus ticket?[13]

CUSTOMER SERVICE AGENT: You can buy[14] individual tickets or bus passes at the kiosk near the terminals. Information about tickets and passes is on the bus schedule I gave you.

SEBASTIAN: So, I can buy a ticket or pass at the kiosk over there (pointing) near the terminal I leave from?[15]

CUSTOMER SERVICE AGENT: That's right.[16]

CONVERSATION GUIDE

6. As we learned earlier in this chapter, you can use the imperative to give directions.

7. Use rising pitch to show uncertainty. Rising pitch shows that Sebastian needs an answer.

8. Pointing helps show people locations.

9. *When's* is a contraction for *when + is.*

10. *One* is a pronoun. We use *one* when we are talking about something and we know what the thing is. Here, Sebastian is referring to the next bus.

11. Use the simple present verb tense for schedules.

12. *Here's* is a contraction for *here + is.*

We use this term when we are showing someone something or offering someone something.

13. Ask a WH question to get more information, and use falling pitch.

14. Use *you can* + the base form of the verb to show ability.

15. Check understanding by paraphrasing.

16. Confirm or correct. To confirm, you can also use other expressions: Yes. / That's correct. / Mm hm. (Nod)

To correct, say, "No" or "Actually" and give correct information.

(continued)

CONVERSATION	CONVERSATION GUIDE
SEBASTIAN: Thank you very much.[17] Have a nice day![18] (Smiles[19])	17. Showing gratitude is polite.
	18. We say, "Have a nice day," to be courteous to people. We can also say, "Have a good day," "Have a good one," or "Have a great day!"
	19. Smiling is always polite and friendly.
CUSTOMER SERVICE AGENT: You're welcome. You have a good day too, sir.[20]	20. It is common for customer service personnel to refer to men as *sir* and women as *ma'am*. The term used depends on the region.

Grammar: The Simple Present Verb Tense for Schedules

You learned in Chapter 2 to use the simple present verb tense to talk about habits, customs, and traditions. We also use the simple present to talk about set schedules, such as bus or train schedules or store hours. When you take public transportation, you need to be able to read a schedule. In this section, you will learn how to talk about schedules using the simple present verb tense. The following tables will remind you how to form the simple present. (For a complete review, see Chapter 2.) Read the example sentences aloud as you go.

The Simple Present: Forming the Affirmative

SUBJECT OR SUBJECT PRONOUN	VERB IN SIMPLE PRESENT FORM	EXAMPLE SENTENCES
I/You/We/They	take	They *take* the bus to work. / Jim and Cindy *take* the bus to work.
He/She/It	takes	She *takes* the bus to work. / Cindy *takes* the bus to work.

The Simple Present: Forming the Negative

SUBJECT OR SUBJECT PRONOUN	DO OR DOES	NEGATIVE	VERB IN SIMPLE PRESENT FORM	EXAMPLE SENTENCES
I/You/We/They	do don't	not	take	I *do not take* the bus to work. I *don't take* the bus to work.
He/She/It	does doesn't	not	take	He *does not take* the bus to work. He *doesn't take* the bus to work.

Here are verbs we usually use to discuss schedules.

to come	to arrive	to open	to start	to begin
to leave	to depart	to close	to end	to finish
to run (to operate)				

Let's look at some example sentences that express schedules using the simple present and these verbs:

*The bus **comes** every 10 minutes.*

*The bus **leaves** at 7:15 A.M.*

*The train usually **arrives** on time.*

*The train **departs** every hour on the hour.*

*The store **opens** at 8 A.M. and **closes** at 8 P.M.*

Vocabulary: Public Transportation

Let's look at some vocabulary related to public transportation. Look at the illustrations of a bus station and a train station. You'll see numbers next to the images in the illustrations. Now look at the following vocabulary. Identify the ones you know.

1 Bus station   6 Train station

Here is some vocabulary we use for public transportation:

NOUNS: THINGS	NOUNS: PEOPLE	VERBS
A bus station	A bus driver	To catch a bus/train
A bus stop	A customer service agent	To miss a bus/train
A ticket counter	A conductor	To get on a bus/train
A terminal		To get off a bus/train
A kiosk		To embark
A train station		To disembark
A ticket		
A schedule		
A bus/train line		
A bus route		

Exercise 4.24

Choose the vocabulary words that describe the numbered images in the illustrations. The first one is done for you. Include the appropriate indefinite article (a or an).

1. *A bus station*
2. _____
3. _____
4. _____
5. _____
6. _____
7. _____
8. _____
9. _____
10. _____
11. _____

Vocabulary: Expressions of Time

We often use expressions of time when we talk about schedules. Here are some of the most common expressions.

To be on time / to not be on time / to be late (These expressions are always used with the BE verb.)

At _____ (Use a specific time, such as 8:15 A.M.)

Every hour / every hour on the hour / on the hour / every half-hour / every 15 minutes

Until / till _____ (Use a specific time, such as 8:15 A.M.)

The first bus/train / the last bus/train

Let's look at some example sentences that describe schedules using the simple present verb tense and expressions of time:

*The bus runs **every half hour**.*

*The bus leaves **at 6:30** A.M.*

*The bus **is** often **late**.*

*The train **is** always **on time**.*

*The train departs **every 15 minutes**.*

Exercise 4.25

Look at the following bus schedule, then complete the sentences with the name of the correct bus route.

BUS / ROUTE	ARRIVAL TIMES						
	Morning Schedule						
Alameda 8	6:00	6:10	6:20	6:30	6:40	6:50	7:00
Alameda 31	5:30	6:00	6:30	7:00	7:30	8:00	8:30
Berkeley 5	4:00	4:15	4:30	4:45	5:00	5:15	5:30
Berkeley 29	6:00	6:10	6:20	6:30	6:40	6:50	7:00
Emeryville 3	4:00	5:00	6:00	7:00	8:00	9:00	—
Emeryville 26	5:30	5:40	5:50	6:00	6:10	6:20	6:30
Oakland 11	6:30	7:00	7:30	8:00	8:30	9:00	9:30
Oakland 27	5:00	5:15	5:30	5:45	6:00	6:15	6:30

EXAMPLE   The *Emeryville 3* comes every hour on the hour.

> Remember that when there is only *one* of something, we use the article *the*.

1. The last bus on the _____ runs at 9:30 A.M.

2. The _____ comes every 10 minutes until 7:00 A.M.

3. The bus that runs every 15 minutes till 5:30 A.M. is the _____.

4. The _____ comes every half hour starting at 5:30 A.M.

5. The _____ runs every 15 minutes till 6:30 A.M.

6. The last bus you can catch in the morning is the _____ at 9:30 A.M.

Exercise 4.26

Look at the bus schedule again. Now complete sentences about the bus routes. Use expressions of time and vocabulary.

EXAMPLE   The Oakland 27 *runs every 15 minutes until 6:30 A.M.*

1. The Oakland 11 _____.

2. The Emeryville 3 _____.

3. The Berkeley 29 _____.

4. The Alameda 31 _____.

Exercise 4.27

Now that you have learned how to use the simple present to talk about schedules and practiced expressions of time, put it all together and compose a conversation. In this conversation, you are at the train station in Porter City. You need to get to downtown Oakland. Create a conversation between you and a customer service agent. For help, review the conversation at the beginning of this section. Use the vocabulary, time expressions, and the simple present verb tense you have learned. Also, use the imperative and repetition/paraphrasing expressions. Be sure to follow the sample conversation, expressions, and grammar structures correctly.

1. Get the customer service agent's attention politely. Use a WH question to ask about which train goes to downtown Oakland. / You: _____
   _____

2. Ask a WH question to get more information. / Customer service agent:
   _____

3. Answer question. / You: _____

4. Give information about which train goes to downtown Oakland. /
   Customer service agent: _____

5. Ask for more information about the train's schedule using a clarification question. / You: _____

6. Answer the question about the train schedule using the simple present. /
   Customer service agent: _____

7. Ask for additional information about where to catch the train. / You:

_____

8. Answer the question. Point. / Customer service agent:

_____

9. Paraphrase information to check your understanding. / You:

_____

10. Give confirmation or correction. / Customer service agent:

_____

11. Express gratitude. Show courtesy. / You: _____

12. Respond to gratitude. / Customer service agent:

_____

Vocabulary: Phrasal Verbs for Getting Around Town

We use phrasal verbs when getting around town. Let's look at some common ones.

Exercise 4.28

Read the phrasal verbs on the left, and then read the definitions on the right. You may know some of these phrasal verbs. Match the verbs with their appropriate definitions. For the phrasal verbs you do not know, take a guess. Some of these verbs can be separated with a noun or pronoun; they are shown in **bold**.

1. to top **something** off	a. to investigate and discover
2. to pick **something/someone** up	b. to add an amount to fill completely
3. to drop **something/someone** off	c. to investigate by asking many people
4. to ask around	d. to retrieve
5. to get around	e. to leave at a location
6. to look **something** up	f. to travel
7. to figure **something** out	g. to find in a schedule or guide

✎ Exercise 4.29

Complete the sentences with the correct phrasal verb. Use the base form of the verb for each.

EXAMPLE   The bus driver *will pick* 10 people *up* at the bus stop.

1. The print was so small, Leo needed his glasses to _____ which train to take on the train schedule.

2. Can you _____ me _____ after school?

3. Josie's car had some gas, but the gas station was very close. She decided to _____ the gas tank.

4. I need to _____ which bus is the fastest in the morning.

5. Josie loves how easy it is to _____ Porter City. There are many buses, trains, and walking paths.

6. Isabel didn't know what bus to take, so she had to _____.

Reading About It

Do you remember the three steps to reading effectively? They are: (1) pre-read; (2) read actively; and (3) check your understanding. Review this information in more detail in Chapter 1.

Let's Read Together

In this chapter, we're focusing on getting around town. Let's practice the three steps to reading effectively with the following passage. The first step is to pre-read.

Review Pre-Reading
Let's review how to pre-read:

1. Read the title of the passage.

2. Read the first sentence of the paragraph.

3. Read the last sentence of the paragraph.

Exercise 4.30

First, pre-read the passage quickly *and answer these two questions:*

1. What is the topic? _____

2. What is the main idea? _____

 Josie Gets around Porter City

Josie enjoys living and working in Porter City. She lives on the outskirts, or the outer area, of the city. She works downtown in the financial district. The public transportation system is very convenient. Every weekday, she takes the bus to work because it is too far to walk. She catches the bus at 8:00 A.M. At 6:15 P.M., she takes the bus back home, where she arrives at 7:00 P.M. Every Saturday, Josie walks to the grocery store to buy food for the week. On Sundays, she rides her bicycle to the park. Her neighborhood park is five blocks from her house. There are many activities to do in the park such as exercising, barbecuing, and relaxing. Right now, Josie is playing tennis in the park with her friend. Porter City is a nice place to live, and Josie likes it because it is easy to get around.

Read Actively

When you read, remember to read actively by circling words you do not know and highlighting important ideas. Follow these steps:

1. Underline the topic.

2. Circle new vocabulary.

3. Put a question mark (?) next to unclear parts.

4. Take notes.

5. Highlight the main idea and key words.

6. Mark examples with "Ex."

7. Number main points, lists, or ideas.

8. Make a list of comments or questions.

Exercise 4.31

Actively read the passage about Josie. After you mark up the passage, see an example of active reading in the Answer Key.

Understand What You Read

Did you understand the passage? After you have actively read it, check your understanding of the details.

Exercise 4.32

Review the passage and your annotations. Then answer these questions about the passage.

1. What time does Josie catch the bus to work every weekday? _____

2. What time does she arrive home from work? _____

3. Where does Josie play tennis? _____

4. Does she like living in Porter City? _____

5. Why does she like living in Porter City? _____

Discovering Meaning Through Context

Sometimes when we read, we find words we don't know. In Chapter 3, we discovered how to find the meaning of a new word from definition context clues. In this chapter, we will learn another way to find the meaning of a word—from example context clues. **Example context clues** provide examples or details to help you understand the meaning of new words. There are many example clues that can help you. We'll learn five of them. Examples are usually introduced with phrases such as *for example*, *for instance*, *including*, *such as*, and *like*. Look at the following example sentences. The underlined word is the new vocabulary. The phrase that introduces an example is in bold, and the examples that help us understand the meaning of the new word are in italics.

EXAMPLE CONTEXT CLUES	*EXAMPLE SENTENCES*
1. For example, Place a comma after *For example* at the beginning of a sentence.	There are many ways to <u>commute</u>. **For example,** you can *walk, bike, drive, or take the train to work.*

2. For instance,
Place a comma after *For instance* at the beginning of a sentence.

There are many ways to <u>commute</u>. **For instance,** you can *walk, bike, drive, or take the train to work.*

3. including
Sometimes we use a comma before *including*.

There are many ways to <u>commute</u>, **including** *walking, biking, driving, taking the train, taking the bus, and carpooling to work.*

4. such as
Sometimes we use a comma before *such as*.

There are many ways to <u>commute</u>, **such as** *walking, biking, driving, taking the train, taking the bus, and carpooling to work.*

5. like
Sometimes we use a comma before *like*.

There are many ways to <u>commute,</u> **like** *walking, biking, driving, taking the train, taking the bus, and carpooling to work.*

From these sentences, we can see that driving, walking, biking, taking the bus, taking the train, and carpooling are all ways to travel to work. Therefore, to **commute** means to travel to work.

Let's practice understanding the meaning of words from examples.

Exercise 4.33

Look at the following sentences. The new word is in bold. Identify the examples in the sentence that describe the new word.

EXAMPLE   ***High Occupancy Vehicles (HOVs)****, such as vans, shuttles, and cars carrying multiple people, save people money on tolls.* <u>vans, shuttles, and cars carrying multiple people</u>

1. Some cities promote **commute rewards,** such as tax benefits and discounted tolls. _____

2. One way to get downtown is to **carpool.** For instance, you can drive to work with a family member, a friend, or a coworker. _____

3. Using public transportation is **environmentally friendly.** For example, taking the bus and the train saves gas and decreases air pollution.

   _____

4. **Rideshare programs** like the vanpool and company shuttles save fuel.

   _____

5. Many cities have designated **bicycle lanes.** For instance, most Montclair Village streets leave space for cyclists to ride alongside cars.

   _____

Writing About It

In English, we use a subject-verb-object (SVO) sentence structure. Most sentences follow this structure: (S) the subject usually comes at the beginning of a sentence; (V) the action verb follows the subject; and (O) an object follows the verb. Let's look at some examples from the reading about Josie. In each sentence the subject is bold, the verb is underlined, and the object is italicized.

Every week day, **she** <u>takes</u> the *bus* to work.

She <u>catches</u> the *bus* at 8:00 A.M.

At 6:15 P.M., **she** <u>takes</u> the *bus* back home.

On Sundays, **she** <u>rides</u> her *bicycle* to the park.

Right now, **Josie** <u>is playing</u> *tennis* in the park with her friend.

Josie <u>likes</u> *Porter City* because it is easy to get around.

Identifying the SVO Sentence Structure

There are three steps to finding the S, V, and O of a sentence.

1. **Step 1:** Find the verb. The verb is the action of the sentence. You can ask the question *What is the action?*

2. **Step 2:** Find the subject. The subject is the noun that usually comes before the verb in a simple sentence. You can ask the question *Who/what is doing the action?*

3. **Step 3:** Find the object. The object of the verb usually follows the verb. You can ask a question using the verb + *what/whom?*

Let's look at an example using this sentence:

On Sundays, she rides her bicycle to the park.

1. Find the verb. What is the action of the sentence? Answer: *rides*. So the verb is <u>rides</u>.

2. Find the subject. Who/what rides? Answer: *she*. The subject is **she**.

3. Find the object. Rides what? (verb + what/whom) Answer: *her bicycle*. The object of the verb is *her bicycle*.

On Sundays, she rides her bicycle to the park.
                  S   V   O

Look at the other example sentences given previously. Do steps 1 through 3 to identify the subject, verb, and object in each sentence. Now let's practice finding the subjects, verbs, and objects in other sentences.

Exercise 4.34

Read the following sentences. Find the SVO in each sentence. Use the previous steps to help you.

EXAMPLE   *Henry takes the train to work every day.*

Subject: Henry / Verb: takes / Object: the train

1. Jacob gets a paycheck every two weeks. _____

2. Right now, Sandra is walking her dog. _____

3. Geraldo likes movies. _____

4. Every day, the bus takes Audrey to school. _____

5. Joseph plays baseball. _____

6. Mike is taking a taxi to work. _____

7. This semester, Tanaka is studying economics. _____

8. The Williams family plans a vacation every year. _____

Exercise 4.35

Construct sentences about the city you live in and your activities. Think about how you commute to work. Consider the public transportation system. Use the reading passage about Josie to guide you. Use the simple present verb tense (see Chapter 2) to talk about habits, regular activities, and customs. Use the present progressive verb tense (see Chapter 3) to talk about temporary actions happening now. Use the vocabulary from this chapter and earlier chapters. Practice everything you are learning. Be sure that every sentence follows the SVO sentence structure. After you create each sentence, use the three steps to check that you have a subject, a verb, and an object. Use the words given to guide you.

Writing Tips
Remember to start every sentence with a capital letter and end every sentence with a period, question mark, or exclamation point. For this activity, you will end every sentence with a period.

EXAMPLE   Weekly activity / simple present *Every Friday night, I see a movie.*

                                                            S V   O

1. Daily activity / simple present _____

2. How you commute to work / simple present _____

3. What you are doing right now / present progressive _____

4. Bus or train schedule information / simple present _____

5. A custom in your city / simple present _____

Writing Tips: Abbreviations

We often use abbreviations in addresses; however, we usually do not use them in formal writing. When writing your mailing address, use abbreviations. Here are some common abbreviations for streets:

Street = St.   Avenue = Ave.   Road = Rd.
Boulevard = Blvd.   Terrace = Ter.   Circle = Cir.
Place = Pl.

This is the format we use when writing a mailing address:

Name
Street address
City, State Zip code

Here is an example of a mailing address:

Josie Ferem
2652 Lincoln St.
Porter City, CA 95499

 Exercise 4.36

Write your name and mailing address using this format.

_____

_____

_____

Quiz

You have finished Chapter 4. Great work! Now take the quiz to see what you remember. Choose the correct answers for each question. There may be multiple correct answers for some of the questions.

1. What kind of verb do we use to give directions?

Simple present   Present progressive

Simple past   Imperative

2. Which expression do we use for a plural?

There is

There are

3. What is a preposition that means the same as *in back of*?

Near   Across from

Behind   In front of

4. Which is *not* a preposition we use in English?

Next to   Near to

In between   In

5. We can ask for repetition when we don't understand information.
True or False?

6. Which verb tense do we use to talk about schedules?

Simple present   Present progressive

Simple past   Imperative

7. When we don't know the meaning of a word, which expressions do we
use to find examples in a passage?

Such as   For example

Like   Including

8. What is the sentence structure used in English?

VOS   SOV

SVO   OSV

9. Which answers mean the same as *take a right*?

Make a right.   Turn right.

Go right.   Be right.

10. When we want to check our understanding, what do we do?

Ask for repetition   Say thank you

Paraphrase   Shake hands

Do It Out There!

Now that you have learned how to talk about schedules and how to ask for public transportation information, try it out in the world. Review this chapter and go out and use English! Put a check mark next to each activity as you complete it.

To Do This Week

☐ Use the affirmative and negative simple present verb tense to talk about schedules.
☐ Practice using new vocabulary and expressions of time.
☐ Ask people about bus, train, and store schedules. Be sure to use rising pitch.
☐ Ask people to repeat what they've said. Be sure to use rising pitch.
☐ Check your understanding by paraphrasing. Be sure to use rising pitch..
☐ Give people directions using the imperative.
☐ Use prepositions of place when giving directions.
☐ Tell people where things are or how many there are using *there is* and *there are*.

Weekly Log

Keep a weekly log of your progress. Make notes on how your practice went. What happened? Was it successful? How do you know it was successful? Was it unsuccessful? How do you know? Review all the instructions, pronunciation tips, and culture notes in Chapter 4.

_____

_____

_____

_____

_____

_____

_____

5

Recreation and Hobbies

In this chapter you will learn about:

Speaking
✓ How to talk about what you did last weekend
✓ How to ask about someone else's weekend
✓ How to talk about hobbies and recreation
✓ How to express likes and dislikes
✓ How to encourage someone
✓ How to express disbelief

Vocabulary, Reading, and Writing
✓ Vocabulary for recreation and hobbies
✓ Time expressions for the simple past
✓ How to discover vocabulary using contrast
✓ How to write about past actions
✓ How to use the exclamation point

Grammar
✓ How to use the simple past verb tense
✓ How to use gerunds and infinitives with the verbs *like*, *love*, *hate*, and *prefer*
✓ How to use go + verb-**ing**
✓ Some irregular verbs
✓ How to use possessive adjectives

Body Language
✓ The meaning of "thumbs-up" and the "fist bump"
✓ The meaning of "high five" and "giving ten"

Talking About Last Weekend

Let's talk about last weekend. Usually, the weekend is a time for recreation. We spend time with our family and friends and have fun. We participate in recreational activities and spend time on our hobbies.

Conversation: Talking About What You Did

To build relationships with people at work or to maintain relationships with friends, we often talk about what we did over the preceding weekend. Let's see a sample conversation.

CONVERSATION

MARISA: Hey there! How are you?[1]

ANGELITA: Wish it were still the weekend.[2]

MARISA: Really? What did you do?[3]

ANGELITA: Oh, we had such[4] a great weekend! We went camping[5] all weekend and went white-water rafting[5] on the Russian River. It was so much fun!

MARISA: Wow![6] That sounds like fun! How was the weather?[7]

ANGELITA: Just beautiful.[8] Sunny all day with a cool breeze and cool at night.[8] We had such[4] a great time.[9] It was so relaxing.[9] We really enjoyed it.[9]

CONVERSATION GUIDE

1. You can also use other expressions from Ch 1. Other questions to ask about the weekend: What did you do this weekend? / How was your weekend?

2. In conversation, we often omit the "I" at the beginning of the sentence. For example: I wish it were still the weekend.

3. **Pronunciation note:** *What did you do?* is pronounced *Whadidja do?*

4. *Such* is used as an intensifier here. Other intensifiers are *very, so, really, totally,* and *too.* They are usually used before a verb or an adjective. *Such* is usually used before an adjective and a noun.

5. Some activities are used with *go.* The structure is go + verb-**ing**. You will find more about this in the "Activities with the Word *Go*" section later in this chapter.

6. Interjections are words we use to express emotion. They usually comprise a word or phrase and are followed by an exclamation point. *Wow!* shows enthusiasm. Alternative expressions: Fun! / Really? / Nice! / Cool!

7. Asking WH questions keeps the conversation going. This is a great way to build and nurture relationships.

8. In casual conversation, we often omit *It is* or *It was*. Just beautiful. = It was just beautiful. / Sunny all day with a cool breeze and cool at night. = It was sunny all day with a cool breeze and cool at night.

9. It's common to repeat a sentiment in different ways to emphasize and show enthusiasm.

MARISA: I've never been white-water rafting. Is it hard?[10] It seems so scary![11]

ANGELITA: Well, I was a little nervous. And I did have[12] to pay attention. But my adrenaline kicked in[13] and it was really exhilarating! What about you? What did *you*[14] do over the weekend?[15]

MARISA: Nothing as fun as you.[16] We went food shopping[5] and cleaned the house. Mostly, we relaxed, watched TV, and rented a movie. But next weekend, I'll do something fun outdoors![17]

10. Asking yes/no questions is another good strategy to show interest and keep the conversation going.

11. Giving your opinion politely elicits further conversation.

12. *Did have* is used instead of *had* for emphasis.

13. **Kicked in** is a phrasal verb for initiated, started, or began.

14. *You* is stressed here to show the shift in subject. Because *you* is stressed, *what did you* does **not** sound like *whadidja*.

15. Over the weekend = during the weekend.

16. As + adjective + as = a comparison. Other expressions: as short as / as cool as / as strange as / as fun as / as enjoyable as.

17. End the conversation on a positive note.

Grammar: Using the Simple Past Verb Tense

In English, we use the simple past verb tense to talk about actions and events in the past. The past is any time before this moment. In the following examples, *now* means the moment of speaking. Let's look at some example sentences. The verb is in bold. Time expressions for the past tense are italicized. The word in parentheses is the base form of the verb used.

EXAMPLE 1:   Shauna **read** a mystery novel *last weekend.* (read)

Note: The past tense of *read* has the same spelling as the simple present form for *I, you, we,* and *they.*

Shauna read a book from Friday to Sunday. She did other things also. But most of the weekend, she read a novel.

EXAMPLE 2:   Mason **went** clothes **shopping** *on Saturday.* (go shopping)

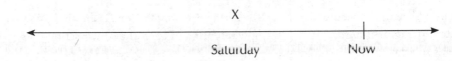

For a few hours on Saturday, Mason went shopping for clothes. He bought a few shirts and some pants.

EXAMPLE 3:   We **drove** to Lake Tahoe *for the weekend.* (drive)

The Williams family went to Lake Tahoe for the weekend. They drove there on Friday and returned on Sunday. They stayed in a cottage on the lake. They played games, went swimming, and relaxed around the lake.

The Simple Past: Forming the Affirmative

How do we form the simple past verb tense? We usually add **-d** or **-ed** to the base form of a verb. Study the following table; be sure to read the example sentences aloud.

SUBJECT OR SUBJECT PRONOUN	VERB IN SIMPLE PAST FORM	EXAMPLE SENTENCES
I/You/We/They/ He/She/It	played	I played soccer on Saturday and Sunday. They played soccer on Saturday and Sunday. She played soccer on Saturday and Sunday.

Spelling Rules for the Simple Past Verb Tense

To form the simple past tense with regular verbs, there are four rules to remember:

1. If the word ends in *-e*, add **-d**.

   exercise → exercise**d**
   like → like**d**
   rake → rake**d**

2. If the word ends in one vowel + one consonant, double the consonant and add **-ed**.

   shop → shop**ped**
   plan → plan**ned**
   jog → jog**ged**

3. If the word ends in a consonant + *y*,   study → stud**ied**
   change the *y* to an *i* and add **-ed**.   cry → cr**ied**
                                                supply → suppl**ied**
4. In all other cases, add **-ed**.   play → play**ed**
                                                look → look**ed**
                                                mow → mow**ed**

Let's practice using the simple past verb tense.

Exercise 5.1

Complete the sentences with the simple past form of the verb given in parentheses.

EXAMPLE   (enjoy) Ashish really *enjoyed* the weekend at the beach.

1. (cook) Tad _____ dinner for six people on Friday night.

2. (exercise) On Sunday, Cheryl _____ at the gym.

3. (rake) Nathan _____ the front and back yards this past weekend.

4. (walk) The whole class _____ five miles on Saturday to raise money.

5. (bike) Marilyn and Michelle _____ 30 miles last weekend.

6. (work) Unfortunately, we _____ all day Sunday.

7. (grill) This past weekend, my father _____ on the barbecue.

8. (carry) My brother _____ my luggage for me.

Pronunciation Tip: Three Different -ed Ending Sounds for Regular Verbs

In English, we make three different sounds for the **-ed** ending. The sound is determined by the last consonant sound in the word.

- For example, let's look at the word *walk*. The last consonant sound is /k/. The /k/ sound is voiceless, so the sound of the **-ed** ending will be /t/.

- Another example is the word *love*. The last consonant sound here is /v/. Because the /v/ sound is voiced, the **-ed** ending will sound like /d/.

- The word *want* ends in the /t/ sound, so we need to add a syllable to pronounce it correctly in the simple past form. *Want* has one syllable; *wanted* has two.

See the table for a list of the sounds and rules.

SOUND	/t/	/d/	/ɪd/
Examples	worked, stopped, raced, laughed, watched, fished	played, exercised, lived, studied, judged, mowed	started, decided, wanted, created
Final consonant sounds	/s/, /f/, /p/, /k/, /θ/, /tʃ/, /ʃ/	/b/, /g/, /v/, /z/, /ð/, /m/; /l/; /w/; /y/; /ŋ/; /dʒ/; all vowel sounds	/t/, /d/
Rules and notes	When the final consonant sound in a regular verb is voiceless, the -ed ending is pronounced as the /t/ in *time*. It is a voiceless sound because it does not engage the vocal cords; only air is used to make the sound. Put your hand on your throat as you make this sound; there is no vibration.	When the final consonant sound in a regular verb is voiced, the -ed ending is pronounced like a /d/. It is a voiced sound because it engages the vocal cords, meaning the vocal cords vibrate. Put your hand on your throat and feel the vibration as you make the sound /d/ as in *dog*.	When the final consonant sound in a regular verb is either the /t/ or the /d/ sound, use this -ed ending sound. This ending adds a syllable to the word. It is a voiced sound and is pronounced like /ɪd/, as in *did*.

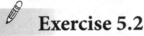

Exercise 5.2

Look at the simple past tense verbs given. Identify the last consonant sound it has before the -ed ending. Then check the previous table. Does the ending sound like /t/, /d/, or /ɪd/? Choose the correct sound for each verb.

1. divided   /t/   /d/   /ɪd/   5. counted   /t/   /d/   /ɪd/
2. missed   /t/   /d/   /ɪd/   6. picked   /t/   /d/   /ɪd/
3. danced   /t/   /d/   /ɪd/   7. jogged   /t/   /d/   /ɪd/
4. moved   /t/   /d/   /ɪd/   8. mailed   /t/   /d/   /ɪd/

Exercise 5.3

Think of two different verbs for each -ed ending sound shown. To help you, think of the activities you did last weekend, and use the preceding chart to guide you.

/t/   /d/   /ɪd/

_____   _____   _____

_____   _____   _____

Irregular Verbs in the Past

In English, we usually form the simple past tense with the -ed ending. Verbs that take this ending are called **regular verbs**. **Irregular verbs**, however, do not take the -ed ending. Rather, the past tense of these verbs take different forms. Study the following table; be sure to read the example sentences aloud.

SUBJECT OR SUBJECT PRONOUN	IRREGULAR VERB IN SIMPLE PAST FORM	EXAMPLE SENTENCES
I/You/We/ They/He/She/It	drove	The Williams family drove to Lake Tahoe for the weekend. They drove to Lake Tahoe for the weekend.

Here is a list of common irregular verbs:

BASE FORM	SIMPLE PAST FORM	BASE FORM	SIMPLE PAST FORM
Go	Went	Buy	Bought
See	Saw	Do	Did
Drive	Drove	Make	Made
Put	Put	Have	Had
Sing	Sang	Give	Gave
Forget	Forgot	Come	Came
Read	Read	Ride	Rode
Drink	Drank	Eat	Ate
Understand	Understood	Stand	Stood
Sit	Sat	Feel	Felt
Is	Was/were	Tell	Told
Say	Said	Catch	Caught
Get	Got	Sleep	Slept
Write	Wrote	Think	Thought
Run	Ran	Teach	Taught
Swim	Swam	Find	Found
Shake	Shook	Lose	Lost
Break	Broke	Win	Won

Now let's practice using the simple past tense with irregular verbs.

Exercise 5.4

Complete the sentences with the simple past form of the verb given in parentheses.

EXAMPLE   (come) Lois *came* to my house for the weekend.

1. (swim) My aunt _____ in the pool last week.

2. (run) I _____ six miles yesterday.

3. (drink) On Saturday afternoon, we _____ homemade iced tea.

4. (buy) Cole _____ a new car last weekend.

5. (sleep) My husband _____ terribly last night.

6. (sing) Julie _____ in the church choir on Sunday.

7. (forget) He _____ his keys on the kitchen counter this morning.

8. (make) His sister _____ a delicious dinner Tuesday night.

Time Expressions for the Past Tense

Here are some time expressions commonly used with the past tense. Study the expressions and read the example sentences aloud.

TIME EXPRESSION	EXAMPLE SENTENCES
On + day	On Saturday, we watched the football game.
For + time period	John was in Las Vegas for the weekend.
Over + time period	They relaxed over the weekend.
All + time period	She attended art school all summer.
Yesterday / yesterday morning / yesterday afternoon / last night	Last night, Mary went to dance class.
Last Monday/Tuesday/etc.	We won the game last Thursday.
Last week/weekend/month/year	Last year, I played on the baseball team.
This past weekend (use this phrase when it is soon after the weekend, such as on Monday or Tuesday)	This past weekend, I tried water skiing.
Amount of time + *ago*	Three years ago, I broke my leg.
This morning (It's later than morning.)	I lost my car keys this morning.
Earlier today / this week / this month	Earlier this month, I was sick.

Now practice using different time expressions for the simple past verb tense.

Exercise 5.5

Create sentences using the words given, and put the verb in the simple past tense. Don't forget to put a period at the end of the sentence.

EXAMPLE   Celina / walk / five miles / last weekend.
           Celina walked five miles last weekend.

1. Denise and Kerry / dance / all night / at the party.

2. Jeremy and his friends / ride / their motorcycles / last weekend.

_____

3. On Friday, / she / drive / to the country.

_____

4. Earlier this week, / Matt / move / to a new apartment.

_____

5. I / hike / the mountain / yesterday afternoon.

_____

6. They / enjoy / the weather / this past weekend.

_____

The Simple Past: Forming the Negative

When we form the negative simple past verb tense, we need to use *did* + *not* + the base form of the verb. As you study the following table, read the example sentences aloud.

SUBJECT OR SUBJECT PRONOUN	DID	NEGATIVE	VERB IN SIMPLE PAST FORM	EXAMPLE SENTENCE
I/You/We/They/ He/She/It	did	not	play	We did not play basketball last weekend.

Important: With negatives, do *not* put the main verb in the past tense form. The word *did* shows the past tense, so the main verb does not need to. See the example sentences.

INCORRECT: *He **did not played** tennis on Sunday.*

CORRECT: *He **did not play** tennis on Sunday.*

Exercise 5.6

Complete the sentences with the correct negative form of the simple past tense verb.

EXAMPLE   (play) Marvin *did not play* with his friends yesterday.

1. (cook) Faith _____ the meal by herself on Friday night.

2. (run) The track team _____ after school on Tuesday.

3. (come) Mrs. Oberman _____ to the celebration last weekend.

4. (have) Last night, Judy _____ fun at the party.

5. (win) The team _____ the game yesterday.

6. (hike) Harry and I _____ the long trail on Sunday.

The Simple Past: Forming Negative Contractions

In English, we usually speak using contractions. It's less formal. Look at how we form contractions for the negative form of the simple past tense. Read the example sentences aloud.

SUBJECT OR SUBJECT PRONOUN	DID	NEGATIVE	CONTRACTION OF DID AND NEGATIVE	VERB IN SIMPLE PAST FORM	EXAMPLE SENTENCES
I/You/We/They/ He/She/It	did	not	didn't	find	She didn't find her car keys.

 Exercise 5.7

Create sentences using the words given. First, use the negative simple past verb form, then use the negative contraction.

EXAMPLE   Nan / NEGATIVE / go / to the graduation ceremony.

Nan did not go to the graduation ceremony.

Nan didn't go to the graduation ceremony.

1. Vera / NEGATIVE / like / the movie.

_____

_____

2. Hilal and her mother / NEGATIVE / go / to the store.

_____

_____

3. He / NEGATIVE / understand / the math class.

_____

_____

4. I / NEGATIVE / forget / the concert tickets.

_____

_____

Vocabulary: Recreation and Hobbies

What is recreation? **Recreation** is what people do for fun, entertainment, amusement, and refreshment. There are many types of recreation. For example, some people like to go to history museums. Others enjoy attending plays at the theater. **Hobbies** are also activities people enjoy doing outside of work, but they are usually done repeatedly. Most people spend a lot of time on their hobby and take a great interest in learning all about the activity. For example, some people like to paint portraits, and they do it often. Others enjoy collecting old coins and know all about them. See the following short list of different types of recreation and hobbies.

RECREATION	HOBBIES
Go to the museum, the movies, the park, the library, the amusement park, the circus, the theater, poetry readings, comedy shows, and musical plays	Collect things such as baseball cards, stamps, coins, and antique furniture
	Take lessons in dancing, music, singing, and art
Play sports such as baseball, basketball, soccer, football, tennis, or volleyball	Create art—paint, color, draw, illustrate, take photographs, and make scrapbooks and collages
Do yoga, meditate, and volunteer	Play a musical instrument, sing in a band or choir, write song lyrics
Go to concerts and other live-music events	Make candles, soap, jewelry, or pottery
	Sew, quilt, knit, and crochet
	Cooking and gardening

Culture Note: In the United States, **American football** is played with a brown, oval ball and the players wear protective clothing. The game called **soccer** in the United States is called **football** in other parts of the world.

Exercise 5.8

Match the illustration of a type of recreation or hobby with the vocabulary.

1. Attending a concert   a.

2. Doing yoga   b.

3. Playing the guitar   c.

4. Taking photographs   d.

5. Playing tennis   e.

Activities with the Verb *Go*

In English, some verbs are often used with the verb *go*. The form is *go* + verb-**ing**. Look at the following list of activities commonly used with the verb *go*:

Shopping	Hiking	Camping
Skiing/waterskiing	Hunting	Running/walking/jogging
White-water rafting	Bungee jumping	Swimming
Sailing/parasailing	Rock climbing	Golfing
Dancing	Gambling	Skydiving
Bike riding/cycling	Hang gliding	Scuba diving
Snorkeling	Horseback riding	Snowboarding
Snowshoeing	Fishing	Boating/canoeing/rowing/kayaking

Let's look at some example sentences that use this form. These examples are in the simple past tense:

Affirmative	**Negative**
She *went swimming* yesterday.	She *didn't go swimming* yesterday.
They *went shopping* on Thursday night.	They *didn't go shopping* on Thursday night.
This past weekend, I *went bungee jumping*.	This past weekend, I *didn't go bungee jumping*.

 ## Exercise 5.9

*Complete the following sentences with an activity from the previous list. Use the go + verb-**ing** structure in the simple past tense. Some are negative. Don't forget to put a period at the end of each sentence.*

EXAMPLE 1   Darcy / go / ACTIVITY / all summer.

Darcy went swimming all summer.

EXAMPLE 2   Bo / NEGATIVE / go / ACTIVITY / yesterday.

Bo didn't go bungee jumping yesterday.

1. Raman / go / ACTIVITY / over the weekend.

_____

2. Tamara / NEGATIVE / go / ACTIVITY / last week.

_____

3. This morning, my mom / go / ACTIVITY.

_____

4. Last weekend, he / NEGATIVE / go / ACTIVITY.

_____

5. Gretel / NEGATIVE / go / ACTIVITY / on Saturday.

_____

6. Ulya / go / ACTIVITY / all winter.

_____

Grammar: Asking Questions with the Simple Past Verb Tense

We use the simple past to ask questions about activities that happened in the past.

The Simple Past: Forming Yes/No Questions

In conversation, we ask questions about what people did, for example, over the weekend. We use yes/no questions to start or maintain a conversation. As you know from previous chapters, we answer these questions with either *yes* or *no*. For yes/no questions in the simple past, we use *did*. As you review the table, be sure to read the example sentences aloud.

DID	SUBJECT OR SUBJECT PRONOUN	BASE FORM OF MAIN VERB	REST OF SENTENCE	EXAMPLE SENTENCES
Did	you	enjoy	your weekend?	Did you enjoy your weekend?
Did	he	go	on vacation yesterday?	Did he go on vacation yesterday?
Did	your sister	have	a good time at the party?	Did your sister have a good time at the party?

Pronunciation Tip

Remember to use rising pitch at the end of yes/no questions to indicate uncertainty. See the pitch chart in the Appendix for more information.

You can answer yes/no questions with long answers, using the complete verb tense and including all parts of the sentence. Or you can give a short answer that includes only part of the verb tense. You can also give a quick answer consisting of only *yes* or *no*. All of these types of answers are acceptable. Note that long answers use the simple past tense form of the verb and that the short answer uses only *did*.

Yes/no question: Did she have a good time at the party?

Affirmative Answers

LONG ANSWER: Yes, she *did* have a good time at the party. / Yes, she had a *great* time at the party!

SHORT ANSWER: Yes, she did.

QUICK ANSWER: Yes. (You can also use an alternative expression for *yes*. See Chapter 1 for more information.)

Negative Answers

LONG ANSWER: No, she *didn't* have a good time at the party.

SHORT ANSWER: No, she didn't.

> When the answer is negative, we often provide a reason or cause for the negative answer. For example, we might say, "No, she didn't. She wasn't feeling very well."

QUICK ANSWER: No. (You can also use an alternative expression for *no*. See Chapter 1 for more information.)

Pronunciation Tip

For long affirmative answers, stress *did* when it's used: *Yes, she **did** have a good time at the party*. When the simple past is used without *did*, stress the main idea: *Yes, she had a **great** time at the party!* For short affirmative answers, stress *did*: *Yes, she **did***. For both long and short negative answers, stress the negative contraction or *not*: *No, she **didn't** have a good time at the party*. / *No, she **didn't***. / *No, she did **not***.

Note: Do not stress quick answers.

The Simple Past: Short Answers to Yes/No Questions

There are a couple of rules to giving short answers to yes/no questions in the simple past tense.

- We usually omit the main verb in short answers.

- We do not contract the affirmative short answer.

YES OR NO + COMMA	SUBJECT OR SUBJECT PRONOUN	DID	NEGATIVE	NEGATIVE CONTRACTION*
Yes,	I/you/we/	did.		Yes, they did.
No,	they/he/she/it	did	n't.	No, she didn't.

*There are no contractions for affirmative answers.

Exercise 5.10

Form yes/no questions with the simple past verb tense using the words given. Then create long, short, and quick answers to the question. Answer the questions affirmatively (Yes) or negatively (No) as indicated.

EXAMPLE 1   Did / Heidi / attend / the meeting / yesterday? (Yes)

QUESTION: *Did Heidi attend the meeting yesterday?*

LONG ANSWER: *Yes, she did attend the meeting yesterday.*

SHORT ANSWER: *Yes, she did.*

QUICK ANSWER: *Yes.*

EXAMPLE 2   Did / Thurston / go golfing / last Sunday? (No)

QUESTION: _Did Thurston go golfing last Sunday?_

LONG ANSWER: _No, he didn't go golfing last Sunday._

SHORT ANSWER: _No, he didn't._

QUICK ANSWER: _No._

1. Did / Felicia / go / to the museum / on Saturday? (Yes)

QUESTION: _____

LONG ANSWER: _____

SHORT ANSWER: _____ QUICK ANSWER: _____

2. Did / Manny / catch / his flight to Hong Kong this morning? (Yes)

QUESTION: _____

LONG ANSWER: _____

SHORT ANSWER: _____ QUICK ANSWER: _____

3. Did / Dr. Lane / run / the marathon / last week? (No)

QUESTION: _____

LONG ANSWER: _____

SHORT ANSWER: _____ QUICK ANSWER: _____

4. Did / you / get / the tickets / for the musical? (Yes)

QUESTION: _____

LONG ANSWER: _____

SHORT ANSWER: _____ QUICK ANSWER: _____

5. Did / Salvatore / register / for ballroom dancing lessons? (No)

QUESTION: _____

LONG ANSWER: _____

SHORT ANSWER: _____ QUICK ANSWER: _____

The Simple Past: Forming WH Questions

In conversation, we ask people about actions in the past. We use WH questions, or information questions, to ask about the time, location, manner of, and reason for an action. These questions begin with WH question words or phrases such as *who, what, when, where, why, how, what kind, which one, how long, how many,* and *how much.* (For a list of WH question words, refer to the Appendix.) Review the following examples and how to form these questions; be sure to read the example sentences aloud.

WH QUESTION WORD OR PHRASE	DID	SUBJECT OR SUBJECT PRONOUN	BASE FORM OF MAIN VERB	REST OF SENTENCE	EXAMPLE SENTENCES
When	did	you	go skiing	?	When did you go skiing?
Where	did	they	take	singing lessons?	Where did they take singing lessons?
How long	did	the band	play	in the park?	How long did the band play in the park?
How much	did	the tickets	cost	?	How much did the tickets cost?
Who/whom (object of verb)	did	she	call	yesterday?	Who/whom did she call yesterday?

When *who* is the subject of the sentence, we do not add another subject. We do not add *I, you, we, they, he, she,* or *it.* In these questions, we do **not** use *did.* As you review the following examples, read the example sentences aloud.

WHO (SUBJECT OF SENTENCE)	MAIN VERB IN SIMPLE PAST FORM	REST OF SENTENCE	EXAMPLE SENTENCES
Who	went scuba diving	in Mexico?	Who went scuba diving in Mexico?
Who	saw	the movie last night?	Who saw the movie last night?

Pronunciation Tip

We usually use falling pitch at the end of WH questions. However, if you need the speaker to repeat something, use rising pitch. For the questions in Exercise 5.11, use rising pitch. See the pitch chart in the Appendix for more information.

Just like yes/no answers, we can answer WH questions in different ways. We give a long answer, which is a complete sentence. Although a long answer can be shortened, it must be a complete sentence. We also may give a short answer with only the essential information that answers the question. See the following examples.

Exercise 5.11

Form WH questions with the simple past verb tense using the statements given. Form long and short answers using the information in parentheses. Notice that the questions and long answers can usually be shortened.

EXAMPLE 1   Jessie and Paula went bungee jumping off a bridge last weekend. (Where)

QUESTION: *Where did Jessie and Paula go bungee jumping? / Where did they go bungee jumping? / Where did they go?*

LONG ANSWER: *They went bungee jumping off a bridge.* (complete sentence)

SHORT ANSWER: *Off a bridge.* (essential information only)

EXAMPLE 2   Ned and Tara went snorkeling in the Red Sea last summer. (When)

QUESTION: *When did Ned and Tara go snorkeling in the Red Sea? / When did they go snorkeling in the Red Sea? / When did they go snorkeling? / When did they go?*

LONG ANSWER: *They went snorkeling in the Red Sea last summer. / They went snorkeling last summer. / They went last summer.*

SHORT ANSWER: *Last summer.*

EXAMPLE 3   Sue and Cathy went to the zoo yesterday afternoon. (Who)

QUESTION: *Who went to the zoo yesterday afternoon? / Who went to the zoo? / Who went?*

LONG ANSWER: *Sue and Cathy went to the zoo yesterday afternoon. / Sue and Cathy went.*

SHORT ANSWER: *Sue and Cathy.*

> Reminder: When you ask a question about *who*, do not use *did*. Use only the simple past form of the main verb. This is because *who* is in the subject position of the sentence. Compare the question in example 3 with the questions in examples 1 and 2. Examples 1 and 2 have *did* in the question, but example 3 does not. (Refer to the table in the "The Simple Past: Forming WH Questions" section earlier.)

1. Eveline and Jack went to the symphony on Sunday evening. (When)

   QUESTION: _____

   LONG ANSWER: _____

   SHORT ANSWER: _____

2. Ingrid and her mother quilted a beautiful blanket for the raffle. (Who)

QUESTION: _____

LONG ANSWER: _____

SHORT ANSWER: _____

3. Her aunt baked three delicious berry pies for the picnic. (What)

QUESTION: _____

LONG ANSWER: _____

SHORT ANSWER: _____

4. Paul and Martin walked in Spain last spring. (Where)

QUESTION: _____

LONG ANSWER: _____

SHORT ANSWER: _____

5. The mediation group lived in the Himalayas for one month. (How long)

QUESTION: _____

LONG ANSWER: _____

SHORT ANSWER: _____

Grammar: The Simple Past BE Verb

In English, we often use the BE verb to describe people, places, and things in the past. In this section, we will practice using the BE verb in the simple past form. As you review the example sentences, read them aloud.

*I **was** a student last year.*   *They **were** excited yesterday.*
*Sue and Bob **were** at work an hour ago.*   *It **was** broken a week ago.*
*We **were** happy last night!*   *Lonnie **was** late this morning.*

The Simple Past of BE: The Affirmative Form
To write the BE verb in the affirmative simple past form, use the following chart. Read the example sentences aloud.

SUBJECT PRONOUN	SIMPLE PAST FORM OF BE VERB	EXAMPLE SENTENCES
I	was	I was sad yesterday.
You/We/They	were	You were happy. / We were happy. / They were happy.
He/She/It	was	He was okay. / She was okay. / It was okay.

Exercise 5.12

Choose the correct form of the simple past BE verb in the sentences. Use the preceding chart for guidance.

EXAMPLE   The little boy was/were brave.   *was*

1. At lunch, the cafeteria was/were noisy. _____

2. Guadalupe was/were a nurse 10 years ago. _____

3. I was/were hungry for ice cream! _____

4. Julian and Joselyn was/were good students. _____

5. Ms. Wyler was/were our teacher last year. _____

6. We was/were sad about the rain. _____

7. She was/were here earlier. _____

8. It was/were red before. Now it's blue. _____

9. The books was/were heavy last semester. _____

10. That was/were a useful lesson. _____

Exercise 5.13

Complete the sentences with the correct affirmative BE verb in the simple past form.

EXAMPLE   Sandra *was* my neighbor two years ago.

1. I _____ angry this morning.

2. Suzy _____ my coworker before.

3. We _____ friends growing up.

4. Juan and Tyler _____ neighbors earlier this year.

5. Myron _____ an employee there a few years ago.

6. Zhou and I _____ classmates last semester.

7. He _____ fine this morning.

8. It _____ rainy yesterday.

9. Jesus and Daphne _____ at school an hour ago.

10. I _____ busy last weekend.

Note: We do *not* contract the simple past form of the BE verb. We always use the full form of the simple past tense.

The Simple Past of BE: The Negative Form

To write the BE verb in the negative simple past form, use the BE verb + *not*. Read the example sentences aloud.

SUBJECT PRONOUN	SIMPLE PAST FORM OF BE VERB	NEGATIVE	CONTRACTION (BE + NEGATIVE)	EXAMPLE SENTENCES
I	was	not	wasn't	I wasn't at school.
You/We/They	were	not	weren't	You weren't at work. / We weren't at work. / They weren't at work.
He/She/It	was	not	wasn't	He wasn't at the movies. / She wasn't at the movies. / It wasn't a problem.

Exercise 5.14

Read the sentences and choose the correct negative BE verb contraction in the simple past form.

EXAMPLES Moe wasn't/weren't an engineer last year.   *wasn't*

They wasn't/weren't coworkers.   *weren't*

1. Linda wasn't/weren't a theater actor. _____

2. We wasn't/weren't in that class. _____

3. Juana wasn't/weren't there. _____

4. My parents wasn't/weren't happy with my grades. _____

5. Kisa and Morgan wasn't/weren't friends. _____

6. You wasn't/weren't at the party. _____

7. I wasn't/weren't an accountant. _____

8. She wasn't/weren't angry with you. _____

9. We wasn't/weren't tired last night. _____

10. He wasn't/weren't serious. _____

Exercise 5.15

Construct sentences using the words given and a negative past tense BE verb. Contract the BE verb with not. Refer to the preceding chart for help.

EXAMPLE   Margit and Tina / BE / not / at school. *Margit and Tina weren't at school.*

1. Marion and Trudy / BE / not / at the café this morning. _____
   _____

2. They / BE / not / happy yesterday. _____

3. Cheyenne and I / BE / not / bad students last year. _____
   _____

4. Lucy / BE / not / worried. _____

5. My computer / BE / not / broken. _____

6. We / BE / not / hungry at lunch. _____

Exercise 5.16

Create sentences about yourself, your friends, and your family. Construct two sentences using the affirmative BE verb and two sentences using the negative BE verb. Use contractions for the negative sentences.

Simple Past Form of BE: Affirmative

1. _____
2. _____

Simple Past Form of BE: Negative

3. _____
4. _____

Exercise 5.17

Create affirmative sentences using subject pronouns and time expressions for the past. Do not use contractions.

EXAMPLE   (They) *They were coworkers last year.*

Affirmative BE Verb (No Contraction)

1. (She) _____
2. (He) _____

3. (It) _____

4. (You) _____

5. (We) _____

6. (They) _____

Exercise 5.18

Create negative sentences using subject pronouns and time expressions for the past. Contract the BE verb with not.

EXAMPLE   (They) *They were not coworkers last year.* / (They) *They weren't coworkers last year.*

Negative BE Verb (No Contraction)   **Negative BE Verb (with Contraction)**

1. (She) _____   7. (She) _____

2. (He) _____   8. (He) _____

3. (It) _____   9. (It) _____

4. (You) _____   10. (You) _____

5. (We) _____   11. (We) _____

6. (They) _____   12. (They) _____

The Simple Past of BE: Forming Yes/No Questions

When we talk to people, we ask questions about events and activities in the past. When we use yes/no questions, we use the simple past tense of BE. As you review the following chart, be sure to read the example sentences aloud.

SIMPLE PAST OF BE VERB	SUBJECT OR SUBJECT PRONOUN	REST OF SENTENCE	EXAMPLE SENTENCES
Was	I	a student last year?	Was I a student last year?
Were	you/we/they	there last week?	Were you there last week? / Were we there last week? / Were they there last week?
Was	he/she/it	fun at the party?	Was he fun at the party? / Was she fun at the party? / Was it fun at the party?

Pronunciation Tip
Use rising pitch at the end of yes/no questions. These questions indicate uncertainty, so we use rising pitch to show that we would like an answer. See the pitch chart in the Appendix for more information.

You can answer a yes/no question with a long answer, using the complete verb tense and all parts of the sentence. Or you can give a short answer that includes only part of the verb tense. You can also give a quick answer of only *yes* or *no*. All of these types of answers are acceptable. The most common is the short answer. See the following examples.

Yes/no question: Was he fun at the party?

Affirmative Answers

> LONG ANSWER: Yes, he *was* fun at the party.
>
> SHORT ANSWER: Yes, he was.
>
> QUICK ANSWER: Yes.

Negative Answers

> LONG ANSWER: No, he was *not* at the party. / No, he *wasn't* fun at the party.
>
> SHORT ANSWER: No, he was not. / No, he wasn't.
>
> QUICK ANSWER: No.

> **Pronunciation Tip:** For long affirmative answers, stress the BE verb: *Yes, he **was** fun at the party*. For short affirmative answers, stress the BE verb: *Yes, he **was***. For both long and short negative answers, stress the negative contraction or *not*: *No, he was **not** fun at the party. / No, he **wasn't***. **Note:** Do not stress quick answers.

The Simple Past of BE: Short Answers to Yes/No Questions

YES OR NO + COMMA	SUBJECT OR SUBJECT PRONOUN	SIMPLE PAST FORM OF BE VERB	NEGATIVE	NEGATIVE CONTRACTION*
Yes,	I	was.		
No,	I	was	not.	No, I wasn't.
Yes,	you/we/they	were.		
No,	you/we/they	were	not.	No, they weren't.
Yes,	he/she/it	was.		
No,	he/she/it	was	not.	No, she wasn't.

*There are no contractions for affirmative answers.

Caution
A quick answer can sometimes be perceived as abrupt and rude. Give quick answers in a polite tone. When giving a negative answer, we often offer more information, such as an explanation. For example, we might say, "No, he wasn't fun at the party. He was angry with me." When the answer is negative, we sometimes omit the negative answer and instead correct with the word *actually*. For example, we might say, "Actually, he was angry with me."

Exercise 5.19

Form yes/no questions with the simple past form of the BE verb using the words given. Then create long, short, and quick answers to the question. Answer the questions affirmatively (Yes) or negatively (No) as indicated. Use a subject pronoun and contractions for the short answers.

EXAMPLE 1   BE / you / tired? (Yes)

QUESTION: *Were you tired?*

LONG ANSWER: *Yes, I was tired.*

SHORT ANSWER: *Yes, I was.*   QUICK ANSWER: *Yes.*

EXAMPLE 2   BE / they / happy about it? (No)

QUESTION: *Were they happy about it?*

LONG ANSWER: *No, they were not happy about it. / No, they weren't happy about it*

SHORT ANSWER: *No, they were not. / No, they weren't.*   QUICK ANSWER: *No.*

1. BE / they / the owners of the store? (Yes)

   QUESTION: _____

   LONG ANSWER: _____

   SHORT ANSWER: _____   QUICK ANSWER: _____

2. BE / it / a good movie? (No)

   QUESTION: _____

   LONG ANSWER: _____

   SHORT ANSWER: _____   QUICK ANSWER: _____

3. BE / we / at school / at that time? (Yes)

QUESTION: _____

LONG ANSWER: _____

SHORT ANSWER: _____ QUICK ANSWER: _____

4. BE / she / a student / at the art school / last semester? (Yes)

QUESTION: _____

LONG ANSWER: _____

SHORT ANSWER: _____ QUICK ANSWER: _____

5. BE / you / happy / yesterday afternoon? (Yes)

QUESTION: _____

LONG ANSWER: _____

SHORT ANSWER: _____ QUICK ANSWER: _____

The Simple Past of BE: Forming WH Questions

To get information or to maintain a conversation, we can use WH questions with the BE verb. Review the following chart to see how to form these questions. Read the example sentences aloud.

WH QUESTION WORD OR PHRASE	SIMPLE PAST FORM OF BE VERB	SUBJECT OR SUBJECT PRONOUN	REST OF SENTENCE	EXAMPLE SENTENCES
When	was	I	a student?	When was I a student?
Where	were	you/we/they	over the summer?	Where were they over the summer?
Why	was	he/she/it	so bad?	Why was it so bad?

Pronunciation Tip
We usually use falling pitch at the end of WH questions. However, if you didn't hear or understand some information and you need the speaker to repeat it, use rising pitch. See the pitch chart in the Appendix for more information.

You can answer WH questions using the BE verb in different ways. You can give a long answer, which is a complete sentence and usually uses subject pronouns and contractions with the BE verb. You can also give a short answer with only the essential information that answers the question.

Exercise 5.20

Form WH questions with the BE verb in the simple past tense using the words given. Form long and short answers using the information given.

EXAMPLE 1   Where / BE / Sonja / last weekend? (at a jazz festival)

QUESTION: *Where was Sonja last weekend?*

LONG ANSWER: *She was at a jazz festival.* (complete sentence)

SHORT ANSWER: *At a jazz festival.* (not a complete sentence)

EXAMPLE 2   Why / BE / Amanda / at home / during the party? (She was sick.)

QUESTION: *Why was Amanda at home during the party?*

LONG ANSWER: *She was at home during the party because she was sick.*

SHORT ANSWER: *Because she was sick.*

> When we use the WH question word *why*, we usually use *because* in the answer.

1. When / BE / Vivian and Marcelle / there? (in the afternoon)

   QUESTION: _____

   LONG ANSWER: _____

   SHORT ANSWER: _____

2. Why / BE / the car / dead? (It ran out of gas.)

   QUESTION: _____

   LONG ANSWER: _____

   SHORT ANSWER: _____

3. How often / BE / you / at the beach? (every weekend)

   QUESTION: _____

   LONG ANSWER: _____

   SHORT ANSWER: _____

4. Where / BE / he / last week? (on vacation)

   QUESTION: _____

   LONG ANSWER: _____

   SHORT ANSWER: _____

5. How / BE / she? (okay)

QUESTION: _____

LONG ANSWER: _____

SHORT ANSWER: _____

6. What / BE / the problem? (The printer ran out of paper.)

QUESTION: _____

LONG ANSWER: _____

SHORT ANSWER: _____

Expressing Attitudes for Recreation and Hobbies

When we talk about our hobbies and the activities we do for fun, we often discuss our attitudes toward them. We talk about activities we like, love, hate, and prefer. We use the simple present verb tense for this because it is how we feel now. Review the grammar rules for the simple present verb tense in Chapter 2, and see the following example sentences using the verbs *like*, *love*, *hate*, and *prefer*:

Jenny loves hiking every Sunday morning.

Emily prefers jogging in the evening.

Paul likes to walk five miles every day.

Jeremy hates exercising.

I like going to free concerts in the park.

You hate watching plays!

We prefer to see early shows.

She loves to dance the tango.

In English, we use two specific grammar structures to express our attitudes toward activities: gerunds and infinitives. Let's learn about both of them.

Grammar: Gerunds and Infinitives

The verbs *like*, *love*, *hate*, and *prefer* can be followed by both gerunds and infinitives. The meaning is similar. Let's look at how to form these structures.

GERUND	INFINITIVE
verb + **-ing**	*to* + base form of verb
Example: snowboarding	**Example:** to snowboard

These structures follow the verbs *like*, *love*, *hate*, and *prefer*, as shown in the following example sentences:

Gerunds	**Infinitives**
Jenny loves *hiking* every Sunday morning.	Paul likes *to walk* five miles every day.
Emily prefers *jogging* in the evening.	We prefer *to see* early shows.
You hate *watching* plays!	Joey hates *to go* to the movies early.
Jeremy hates *exercising*.	She loves *to dance* the tango.
I like *going* to free concerts in the park.	They like *to buy* tickets online.

Let's practice identifying these structures in sentences.

Exercise 5.21

Read the following sentences with like, love, hate, *and* prefer. *Find the main verb in the sentence, then identify which structure follows the verb—a gerund or an infinitive.*

EXAMPLE   Vivian loves watching movies at home.

verb = loves / watching = <u>Gerund</u>

1. Sia prefers to go to art museums.   Gerund   Infinitive

2. Christina hates going to museums.   Gerund   Infinitive

3. Don and Ed like listening to live music.   Gerund   Infinitive

4. Adele and her friends love bungee jumping.   Gerund   Infinitive

5. Aunt Alice prefers to take guided tours of historic places. Gerund   Infinitive

6. They hate to wait in line for tickets.   Gerund   Infinitive

Exercise 5.22

Complete each sentence with both a gerund and an infinitive.

EXAMPLES   Shelly likes <u>knitting</u> sweaters for her children. (knit / gerund)

Shelly likes <u>to knit</u> sweaters for her children. (knit / infinitive)

1. a. Mike loves _____ in the Pacific Ocean. (fish / infinitive)

   b. Mike loves _____ in the Pacific Ocean. (fish / gerund)

2. a. Tammy prefers _____ in Baja, California. (scuba dive / gerund)

   b. Tammy prefers _____ in Baja, California. (scuba dive / infinitive)

3. a. Elise and Daniel like _____ in the Cayman Islands. (snorkel / infinitive)

   b. Elise and Daniel like _____ in the Cayman Islands. (snorkel / gerund)

4. a. They hate _____ in the bay. (waterski / gerund)

   b. They hate _____ in the bay. (waterski / infinitive)

Exercise 5.23

Form four different sentences expressing activities you like, love, hate, and prefer. Use two gerund forms and two infinitive forms. Use each verb once. Review and use the previous examples as a guide.

1. (like) _____

2. (love) _____

3. (hate) _____

4. (prefer) _____

Now that you have practiced expressing attitudes toward recreational activities and hobbies, let's learn about possessive adjectives.

Grammar: Possessive Adjectives

In English, we use possessive adjectives to talk about ownership—things we have and people and things that belong to us. The following example sentences use possessive adjectives:

> **My** mother likes to cook large meals for the family.
> **His** brother went skydiving.
> **Her** dog prefers to chew on raw bones. **Its** teeth are so white and clean.
> Did **your** class go to the opera?
> We love going to **their** parties.
> Uncle Hank loves to read **my** poetry.
> **Our** coworkers hate going to meetings.
> Mandy and Regina love to grow flowers in **their** garden.

The following table gives a list of possessive adjectives.

	SINGULAR	PLURAL
First person	My	Our
Second person	Your	Your
Third person	His (male)	
	Her (female)	Their
	Its	

PEOPLE ONLY	THINGS ONLY	PEOPLE AND THINGS
My	Its	Their
Your		
His (male)		
Her (female)		
Our		

Tip: *His* refers to a male, and *her* refers to a female. These are the only gender-specific pronouns. All other possessive adjectives are not gender-specific. *Its* refers to things and animals. *Their* can refer to things or people. When *their* refers to people, it can refer to males, females, or both together. *Their* can also refer to things, which are not gender-specific.

Culture Note: In the United States, *his*, *her*, and *their* are also used to refer to pets.

Possessive adjectives always precede a noun: possessive adjective + noun. We can see this in the preceding example sentences:

My mother	His brother	Her dog	Your class
Their parties	My poetry	Our coworkers	Their garden

Now let's practice identifying possessive adjectives in sentences.

Exercise 5.24

Identify the possessive adjectives in the following sentences. There may be more than one in each sentence.

EXAMPLE   He went hiking on the trails in my backyard yesterday. <u>my</u>

1. Their friends went dancing all night. _____

2. My brothers love to go camping in the mountains. _____

3. His cat went hunting for birds and mice. _____

4. My children like eating watermelon at your summer parties. _____

5. Her friends didn't like singing in the choir. _____

6. Her son came to my house. _____

7. They picnicked in the park at the end of my street. _____

8. Our kids went sailing on the lake behind our house. _____

Now let's practice writing sentences using possessive adjectives and the simple past verb tense.

Exercise 5.25

Create sentences using the words given. Use subject pronouns (see Chapter 1) to replace the subjects. Use the verb in the simple past tense form, and check for irregular verbs. Use possessive adjectives that match the subject pronouns.

EXAMPLE 1   Sarah and Ana / hike / in the Redwoods / behind / POSSESSIVE ADJECTIVE / house.

They hiked in the Redwoods behind their house.

EXAMPLE 2   Sam / write / short stories / in / POSSESSIVE ADJECTIVE / bedroom.

He wrote short stories in his bedroom.

1. Dionne and Rich / take / POSSESSIVE ADJECTIVE / daughter / to the park / last Saturday.

   _____

2. Michelle / swim / for one hour / yesterday afternoon / in / POSSESSIVE ADJECTIVE / pool.

   _____

3. Janet and Kyla / bring / POSSESSIVE ADJECTIVE / guitars / to the beach.

   _____

4. Charlie / paint / a mural / on / POSSESSIVE ADJECTIVE / front yard fence.

   _____

Exercise 5.26

Form four sentences about the recreational activities and hobbies you, your friends, and your family do. Use subject pronouns, the past tense, and possessive adjectives. Review and use the earlier example sentences as a guide.

1. _____

2. _____

3. _____

4. _____

Communication Strategy: Encouraging Someone

In conversation with people we know well, such as friends and family, we show encouragement. We also encourage new friends and people we want to know better. To **encourage** someone is to give support. Encouragement makes people feel good. We often use interjections when we give encouragement. **Interjections** are words or short phrases said with enthusiasm:

Wow!

That's amazing/fantastic/great/cool/wild/excellent/awesome!

Nice!

Yay!

Woohoo!

Good for you!

Yes!

Right on!

Rock on!

> **Culture Note:** *Brilliant* is a common word for *great* or *wonderful* in the United Kingdom.

Culture Note

In the United States, when we encourage someone, we sometimes use body language. Usually, friends use these gestures. They are *not* usually used at work or with a superior. See the different ways we express encouragement with friends using body language.

Give a Thumbs-Up

When we give a thumbs up, we make a fist and point our thumb up toward the sky like this:

High-Five Someone

To give someone a high five, we raise one hand with the palm facing our friend. That person responds by raising his or her hand, and we clap the two hands like this:

We sometimes say, "Give me five!"
Five = five fingers.
High five is both a noun and a verb.

Fist-Bump Someone

When we fist-bump someone, we make a fist with the knuckles facing our friend. He or she makes the same kind of fist, and we bump the two fists together.

Give Someone Ten

To give someone ten, we raise both hands with the palms facing our friend. That person responds by raising both of his or her hands, and we clap the four hands:

We usually say, "Give me ten (meaning 10 fingers)!"

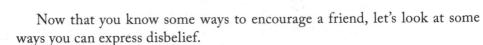

Now that you know some ways to encourage a friend, let's look at some ways you can express disbelief.

Communication Strategy: Expressing Disbelief

Sometimes it's difficult to believe what someone says. When this happens, we can express disbelief. Perhaps your friend did something unusual, scary, dangerous, exciting, or unexpected. We usually use interjections to express disbelief. The following are some examples of interjections used for disbelief:

Really?   Get out!

No way!   Are you kidding me?

You did?   What?

 Pronunciation Tip

When we ask a question to express disbelief, we raise our voice to the highest pitch (level 4) very quickly.

1. Really? / Are you kidding me? / You did?!
   When we make a statement (with an exclamation point), we begin at a high pitch level and drop our voice down.
2. No way! / Get out!

Conversation: Talking About the Weekend

Let's look at a sample conversation about events of the past weekend. The conversation uses the simple past with regular and irregular verbs, typical expressions in conversations, and the interjections you have learned. On the left is a conversation between two friends, Doris and Lloyd. On the right are explanations, alternative expressions, and other notes about the conversation. First, read the whole conversation between Doris and Lloyd. Then read it again along with the Conversation Guide on the right.

CONVERSATION	CONVERSATION GUIDE
DORIS: Hey, Lloyd![1]	1. This is a greeting. (See Chapter 1 for more greetings and responses.)
LLOYD: Hi, Doris. What's up?[1]	
DORIS: Nothing much.[1] What did you[2] do this weekend?	2. *What did you* is often pronounced *Whadidja.*
LLOYD: Oh, I just relaxed and took it easy.[3, 4] What about you?[5]	3. This uses the simple past tense. Check for regular and irregular verbs.
	4. *To take it easy* means to relax.
	5. This question turns the attention back to the other speaker. Rather than repeating the question, "What did you do this weekend?" Lloyd can ask, "What about you?"
DORIS: You'll never believe[6] what I tried this weekend.	6. *You'll never believe* is a common way to begin a story, especially to deliver unexpected news.
LLOYD: What did you try?[7]	7. WH questions continue the conversation, get more information, and build the relationship.
DORIS: Bungee jumping![8]	8. Short answer to the WH question, giving just essential information.
LLOYD: No way![9] How was it?[7] You obviously survived.	9. Expression of disbelief.
DORIS: It was crazy, Lloyd.[10] I never thought[3] I'd do something like that. I'm afraid of heights!	10. Saying the other person's name further builds the relationship.
LLOYD: Rock on![11] So, what was it like?[7]	11. Expression to show encouragement.
DORIS: It was *so*[12] scary at first. To jump off a cliff like that. I thought[3] I was going to die.	12. Italicized words indicate word stress. The speaker is making these words stronger, longer, and louder than the other words.

(continued)

LLOYD: Well, some people have died bungee jumping. How did you feel after?[7]

DORIS: I felt *so exhilarated*![12] My heart was beating so fast. I felt so *alive*![12] My adrenaline is *still* flowing.[12] It was amazing.

LLOYD: Wow! That's really great. Good for you![13] High five! (Lloyd puts his hand up for a high five.[14])

13. It's common to show encouragement by using a couple of different expressions to emphasize the sentiment.

14. A common gesture for encouragement is a high five. See the earlier Culture Note about ways to show encouragement using body language.

DORIS: Yeah. (Responds to high five by raising her hand and clapping Lloyd's.) Now I have to try to concentrate at work today.[15] My mind is still on the weekend.

15. Doris begins talking about work. Turning attention away from the topic (bungee jumping/weekend activities) is a way to signal the end of the conversation.

LLOYD: Well, hang in there![16] I've got to[17] go. I'll talk to you later.[18]

16. Lloyd understands the signal about changing the focus to work. He begins his good-bye with "Well, hang in there," which is similar in meaning to "Take care."

17. *Got to* is often pronounced *gotta*.

18. See Chapter 1 for alternative expressions for good-bye.

DORIS: I'll try.[19] Bye.[18]

19. Typical response to "Hang in there."

In this chapter, you have learned:

1. How to use the simple past verb tense to talk about what you did last weekend

2. How to express attitudes toward activities

3. Vocabulary for recreational activities and hobbies

4. How to use possessive adjectives

5. How to show encouragement and express disbelief

In the following exercises, you can put it all together.

Exercise 5.27

To complete the following conversation, use the simple past verb tense, communication strategies, time expressions for the past, possessive adjectives, and the vocabulary you learned in this chapter. In this situation, Jack and Kareem are friends. They also work together. It is Monday morning, and they are getting coffee in the cafeteria at work and talking about their weekend activities. Jack begins the conversation.

1. Greet friend. / Jack: _____

2. Greet friend. / Kareem: _____

3. Ask about weekend. / Jack: _____

4. Describe an exciting recreational activity. / Kareem: _____

   _____

5. Ask for clarification. / Jack: _____

6. Clarify. / Kareem: _____

7. Express disbelief. / Jack: _____

8. Ask for more information about the activity using a WH question. / Jack:

   _____

9. Answer question. / Kareem: _____

10. Show encouragement. / Jack: _____

11. Close the conversation by changing the focus to work. / Kareem:

    _____

12. Say good-bye. / Jack: _____

Vocabulary: Phrasal Verbs for Recreation and Hobbies

We use some common phrasal verbs when we talk about recreation and hobbies. Let's look at what they mean.

Exercise 5.28

*Read the phrasal verbs on the left, then read the definitions on the right. You may know some of these terms. Match the verbs with their appropriate definitions. For the phrasal verbs you do not know, take a guess. Some can be separated with a noun or pronoun; these are shown in **bold**.*

1. To look forward to **something**
2. To come down
3. To warm **something** up
4. To cool **something** down
5. To check in
6. To show up
7. To let **someone** down

a. To increase the heart rate and heat the body
b. To disappoint
c. To decrease a feeling of euphoria
d. To be excited about
e. To appear, arrive
f. To register for an event
g. To decrease heart rate and cool the body

Exercise 5.29

Complete the sentences with the correct phrasal verb. Be sure to use the correct verb tense and form. Use the third person singular verb form when necessary.

EXAMPLE　　When Abel arrived at the five-kilometer race, he <u>checked in</u> and got his race number. (simple past)

1. Before he works out, Moe _____ so he doesn't hurt his muscles. (simple present)

2. Mary was very happy that her friends _____ to watch her perform in the music concert last night. (simple past)

3. Bart _____ after every bicycle ride so that he doesn't get muscle cramps. (simple present)

4. Natasha's boyfriend _____ her _____ when he didn't show up for her performance. (simple past)

5. Mack always _____ the annual family reunion picnic. He loves to see his whole family and play games. (simple present)

6. It is difficult for Orlando to _____ after running in a marathon. After running for many hours, he experiences a feeling of euphoria. (simple present)

Reading About It

In this section, you will learn how to discover meaning from context using contrast clues. We will also review pre-reading and active reading.

Discovering Meaning Through Context: Contrast

Sometimes when we read, we find new vocabulary. In Chapter 3, we learned how to discover the meaning of a new word from definition context clues, and in Chapter 4, we learned how to use example context clues. In this chapter, we will learn another way to find the meaning of a word: from contrast context clues. **Contrast context clues** provide contrast, or differences, to help you understand the meaning of new words.

There are many contrast clues: *but, however, although, though, even though, instead of,* and *on the other hand.* Read the following example sentences. The underlined word is the new vocabulary word. The phrase that introduces contrast is in bold, and the contrasting word(s) that helps us understand the new vocabulary is in italics. Remember: contrast context clues introduce you to the opposite or different definition from your new word. Once you find the contrast clue, think about the opposite meaning. This will help you discover the definition of the new word.

CONTRAST CONTEXT CLUES

1. But
, but
Place a comma and a space before *but* when it's in the middle of the sentence.

2. However
However, / ; however,
Place a comma after *however* when it begins a sentence. Place a semicolon and a space before *however* and a comma after it when it's in the middle of a sentence.

3. Although / though / even though
, although / , though / , even though
Place a comma and space before *although, though,* and *even though* when they are in the middle of the sentence.
Although _____,

_____

Place a comma after the clause that begins with *although, though,* and *even though.*

EXAMPLE SENTENCES

He really liked the underlined exhilaration of hang-gliding, **but** it also made him *very tired.*
Explanation: *Very tired* is the opposite of exhilaration, so it must mean something similar to high energy.

She loves to do tai chi because it is meditative. **However,** sometimes she *can't focus or be silent and peaceful.* / She loves to do tai chi because it is meditative; **however,** sometimes she *can't focus or be silent and peaceful.*
Explanation: Being unable to *focus or be silent* is the opposite of being meditative, so meditative must mean something similar to focused, silent, and peaceful.

Most of the magic show was mesmerizing, **though** some parts were *too boring to watch.* / **Though** some parts of the magic show were *too boring to watch,* most of it was mesmerizing.
Explanation: Mesmerizing is different than *too boring to watch,* so it must mean something similar to attractive and exciting to watch.

(continued)

CONTRAST CONTEXT CLUES	EXAMPLE SENTENCES
4. Instead of **Instead of** _____, _____ Place a comma after the clause that begins with *instead of.* No punctuation is necessary when *instead of* is in the middle of the sentence.	**Instead of** being <u>frustrated</u> when they didn't catch any fish, they were *patient and looked for better strategies.* / When they didn't catch any fish, they were *patient and looked for better strategies* **instead of** being <u>frustrated</u>. Explanation: *Being patient and looking for better strategies* is different from being <u>frustrated</u>, so this word must mean something similar to upset and stuck.
5. On the other hand **On the other hand, / ; on the other hand,** Place a comma after *on the other hand* when it begins a sentence. Place a semicolon and space before *on the other hand* and a comma after it when it's in the middle of a sentence.	Some kinds of yoga are <u>invigorating</u>. **On the other hand,** some yoga styles are *very relaxing.* / Some kinds of yoga are <u>invigorating</u>; **on the other hand,** some yoga styles are *very relaxing.* Explanation: *Relaxing* is contrasted with <u>invigorating</u>, so <u>invigorating</u> must mean something similar to energizing.

Let's practice discovering the meanings of words from contrast context clues.

Exercise 5.30

*Look at the following sentences. The new word is in **bold**. Identify the contrast in the sentence that describes the opposite of that word. Then look at the vocabulary list and indicate the letter of the vocabulary item that best defines the new word in each sentence, which is opposite to the contrast given.*

EXAMPLE   Golfing can be extremely **relaxing**. On the other hand, if you compete, it can be stressful. *stressful / f*

1. Although exercising can be **therapeutic**, it can be damaging if you overexercise. _____

2. Sally likes to take dance lessons because it's **rejuvenating**. On the other hand, sometimes it makes her very tired. _____

3. Jared loves singing in a choir because it's **cathartic**, but if he doesn't release his negative feelings while singing, it isn't cathartic. _____

4. The light show at the concert was **captivating**. However, after 30 minutes of the bright lights, it wasn't exciting to look at anymore. _____

5. Though a few of the comedians were not funny, most of the comedy show was **hilarious**. _____

a. attention-grabbing   d. very funny

b. healing/purifying   e. getting energy back

c. releasing/purging   f. calming

Let's Read Together

Now that we have discussed another way to discover the meaning of new vocabulary, let's practice all the strategies for effective reading you have learned.

How do you pre-read?

1. Read the title of the passage.

2. Read the first sentence of the first paragraph.

3. Read the last sentence of the last paragraph.

After you pre-read, what do you do? You read actively by circling words you do not know and highlighting important ideas.

To Read Actively

1. Underline the topic.
2. Circle new vocabulary.
3. Put a question mark (?) next to parts that are unclear.
4. Take notes.
5. Highlight the main idea and key words.
6. Mark examples with "Ex."
7. Number main points, lists, or ideas.
8. Write down comments or questions.

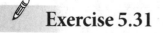

Exercise 5.31

First, pre-read the passage quickly and answer these two questions:

1. What is the topic? _____

2. What is the main idea? _____

Khaled's First Adventure

On his first adventure, Khaled jumped out of an airplane. He graduated from college a month ago, and he is celebrating by doing new recreational activities. He works full time, so he planned exciting weekends for the summer. Last weekend, he went skydiving. He jumped out of an airplane and free-fell until he opened the parachute. His parachute worked perfectly, and Khaled landed safely. After he landed, he yelled, "Woohoo!" He loved it. It was scary but also exhilarating. He is very excited about his adventure next weekend—parasailing. But he won't forget his first skydiving adventure.

Now that you have pre-read the passage, go back and read it actively.

Exercise 5.32

Read the preceding passage again. Follow the steps for active reading.

Understand What You Read
Active reading helps you understand the information in the passage. Did you understand what you read?

Exercise 5.33

Check your understanding of the passage details by answering the following questions. Use your active reading notes to help you.

1. Why did Khaled plan adventures? _____

2. When did he graduate from college? _____

3. What was his first adventure? _____

4. Did he like his first adventure? _____

5. What adventure does he plan to take next? _____

Writing About It

Let's practice writing! In this section, you will review the exclamation point and practice writing it. You will also practice writing sentences in the simple past tense using the SVO sentence structure.

Interjections: Using the Exclamation Point and Question Mark

As you learned earlier in this chapter, interjections are short phrases or single words spoken enthusiastically. They are usually responses to a situation or information. Some interjections require exclamation points, and some require question marks. You learned about these end-of-sentence punctuation marks in Chapter 1. Let's practice writing the exclamation point.

Exercise 5.34

Go back to the lists of expressions we use to show encouragement and express disbelief. Make a list of the expressions that use an exclamation point and another for the expressions that use a question mark.

Exclamation Point Interjections (!)

_____

_____

_____

_____

_____

_____

_____

_____

_____

_____

Question Mark Interjections (?)

_____

_____

_____

_____

_____

_____

_____

_____

_____

_____

Writing About Past Actions

Before you begin writing about past actions, let's review the sentence-verb-object sentence structure that you learned in Chapter 4. Go back to the reading in the previous section. Use the steps you learned in Chapter 4: (1) Find the verb; (2) find the subject; and (3) find the object. Label the verb with a V; label the subject with an S; and label the object with an O. If you need a guide, turn to Chapter 4 and review the SVO structure.

Now, let's practice writing sentences. Create sentences about the recreational activities and hobbies you did last weekend or any time in the past. Use the reading passage about Khaled to guide you. Use the SVO sentence structure, the simple past verb tense, time expressions and other vocabulary from this chapter, and special expressions we use for some activities such as *went swimming*. Practice everything you are learning. Be sure that every sentence begins with a capital letter and ends with a period if it is a statement, a question mark if it is a question, and an exclamation point if it's an interjection.

Exercise 5.35

Create sentences about your past weekend activities. Use the prompts to help you.

EXAMPLE   Fun activity: <u>On Saturday, I played soccer in the park with my friends</u>.
                              S   V   O

1. Fun activity or hobby: _____

2. Group activity with friends, family, or coworkers: _____

   _____

3. Exciting activity or hobby: _____

4. Invigorating activity: _____

5. Relaxing activity: _____

6. Meditative activity: _____

Quiz

You have finished Chapter 5. Great work! Now take the quiz to see what you remember. Choose the correct answers for each question. There may be multiple correct answers for some of the questions.

1. Gloria _____ last weekend with some friends.

   camping   go camping

   went camping   camp

2. Lori and Rob went white-water rafting _____.

   yesterday   last summer

   all summer   on Friday

3. What is the simple past tense form of the verb *buy*?

   buyed   bought

   boughted   buy

4. What is the simple past tense form of the verb *see*?

   seed   said

   sow   saw

5. You form a gerund like this: *to* + base form of verb. True or False?

6. Which questions are formed correctly?

   a. Did Anne-Marie have a   c. Who had a good weekend?
      good weekend?

   b. Where did Anne-Marie go   d. What did Anne-Marie do last
      last weekend?   weekend?

7. When we express attitudes toward recreation and hobbies, which verbs can we use with a gerund and infinitive?

   Like   Love

   Hate   Prefer

8. Which possessive adjective can we use for *things only*?

   Its   Their

   His   Your

9. Read the following sentence. Then guess the meaning of the italicized word from the contrast context clue.

   Playing basketball is *stimulating*, but it can also be tiring.

   Relaxing   Exciting

   Peaceful   Exhausting

10. We use exclamation points to express disbelief and show encouragement. True or False?

Do It Out There!

Now that you have learned how to talk about recreation and hobbies, try it out in the world. Review this chapter, and go out and use English! Put a checkmark next to each activity as you complete it.

To Do This Week

☐ Use the affirmative and negative simple past verb tense to talk about activities in the past.

☐ Use time expressions for the past.

☐ Ask people yes/no questions about their weekend, recreational activities, or hobbies. Use rising pitch.

☐ Ask people WH questions to keep the conversation going. Use falling pitch.

☐ Listen for interjections (expressions of disbelief and encouragement).

☐ Use interjections in conversation. See the Pronunciation Tip in the Communication Strategy: Expressing Disbelief section in this chapter for the correct pitch changes.

☐ Talk about recreational activities and hobbies using the vocabulary you have learned.

☐ Talk about your attitudes toward activities. Use *like*, *love*, *hate*, and *prefer*.

☐ Use possessive adjectives to talk about the people in your family and your friends.

Weekly Log

Keep a weekly log of your progress. Make notes on how your practice went. What happened? Was it successful? How do you know it was successful? Was it unsuccessful? How do you know? Review all the instructions, pronunciation tips, and culture notes in Chapter 5.

_____

_____

_____

_____

_____

_____

_____

6

Making Friends

In this chapter you will learn about:

Speaking
- ✓ Small talk, including compliments and questions
- ✓ How to form invitations
- ✓ How to accept and decline invitations
- ✓ How to share information
- ✓ How to give a phone number clearly

Vocabulary, Reading, and Writing
- ✓ Modal auxiliary verbs: *have to, have got to, must, be supposed to, will, might, may, can,* and *be able to*
- ✓ Phrasal verbs
- ✓ How to write sentences using the SVC sentence structure

Grammar
- ✓ How to use possessive pronouns
- ✓ How to use demonstrative adjectives with pronouns
- ✓ Modals of obligation and necessity
- ✓ Modals of possibility
- ✓ Modals of ability

Body Language
- ✓ How to point at things and people

Talking to New Friends

When you move to a new country, it's good to make new friends. How can you make new friends in an English-speaking country? The easiest way is to **have something in common**. This means that there is something people have, do, or believe that is similar, such as recreational activities, hobbies, work, or school. For example, if two people enjoy science fiction movies, they have science fiction movies in common. If two people swim at the same pool every day, they have this activity in common. If two people work at the same company or go to the same school, they have that place in common. In this chapter, we will learn expressions and ways to make new friends.

Exercise 6.1

Read the following situations. Identify which situations show people who have something in common.

1. Paula and Johanna eat lunch in the same cafeteria every weekday.

2. Jasmina, Nan, and Gilbert all own vintage bicycles.

3. Maximilian and Jake take the same economics class.

4. Gloria and Roshana live in the same apartment building. They do not know this, and they never see each other.

5. Farrah and Josh take the same bus every morning. They do not know this. Farrah always reads her book on the bus, while Josh wears his headphones and closes his eyes.

6. Sal, Marie, and Tony show up to play volleyball every Saturday afternoon in the same park.

7. Mick and Sally square-dance at the same hall every Tuesday and Saturday night.

8. Sofie and her boss both work at the same company.

In every situation in the previous exercise, people have something in common. However, some situations are better for making friends. Let's look at some cultural rules for making friends. Remember: although these are generally accepted rules, there are exceptions. **Exceptions** are situations that do not follow the rules.

1. To make friends, people have to notice each other. For example, in situations 4 and 5, the people don't notice each other, so they don't know they have something in common. These situations are not good for making friends.

2. In North America, when there are only two people involved, it's more common for two women to make friends and two men to make friends. So situations 1 and 3 are good situations for making friends.

3. When three or more people are involved, men and women make friends. In situations 2 and 6, the men and women become friendly because they share something in common.

4. In situation 7, Sally and Mick may meet for romance rather than friendship.

5. Usually, people of equal level—peers, colleagues, and coworkers—make friends. In situation 8, Sofie is subordinate to her boss, meaning they are not equal. Sofie and her boss would probably *not* become friends.

The best situations for making friends are 1, 2, 3, and 6. Now, let's look at an example conversation in which Emeline makes a new friend.

Conversation: Making a New Friend

Emeline and Cassandra both love to knit. They belong to a knitting club, where people gather to socialize and knit. Emeline has just started knitting. Cassandra has been knitting for a long time. They are both sitting on the couch and knitting.

> To **knit** is to weave yarn with knitting needles to make clothes.

Review the "Greeting People" section in Chapter 1 for tips on how to begin a conversation.

CONVERSATION	CONVERSATION GUIDE
EMELINE: Oh, those are pretty colors.[1] What are you making?[2] (Smiles[3])	1. It is common to begin a conversation with a compliment.
	2. Asking a simple WH question is a great way to start a conversation because it requires more than a yes or no answer.
	3. Smile when you meet someone. It is warm and welcoming.
CASSANDRA (smiling[3]): It's a scarf and hat set for my sister.[4]	4. Cassandra answers the question.

(continued)

CONVERSATION

EMELINE: What stitch are you using?[5] It's beautiful.[6]

CASSANDRA: It's the stockinette stitch. It's pretty[7] common, but I'm using this colorful yarn, which makes it look more fancy.[8]

EMELINE: It *does* look more complicated than the stockinette.[9] I finally mastered the basic stitch.[10] But that yarn you're using makes it look like an advanced stitch.

CASSANDRA: Yeah, that's the trick to looking like a good knitter: use colorful yarn![11] Seriously though,[12] this yarn really is great. I got it at that new yarn store on Lincoln Road. Have you been there?[13]

EMELINE: No, I haven't.[14] It sounds great.[15] Is it near downtown or at the other end of Lincoln?[16]

CASSANDRA: It's near the other end, over by the park. It's next to a coffee shop. You can take the 56 bus. But it's also close enough to ride your bike from here.[17]

CONVERSATION GUIDE

5. Asking WH questions keeps the conversation going.

6. Genuine compliments help build a relationship.

7. *Pretty* has several meanings. In this case, Cassandra means "fairly." It can also mean "very."

8. Cassandra wants to keep the conversation going, so she gives more information about the yarn.

9. **Pronunciation tip:** Stress the word *does* or other auxiliary verbs to show agreement.

10. Emeline gives information to indicate that she is a beginner at knitting. Sharing information about yourself is great for making friends. It builds trust.

11. Cassandra responds to Emeline's comments. She has a good sense of humor.

12. *Seriously though* is often used in North America to get serious about a topic after joking. Another expression is *but seriously*.

13. She gives information related to the topic and asks a question to keep the conversation going.

14. Answers question.

15. Other possible expressions: sounds good / sounds like a great place.

16. After a few initial WH questions, it's common to ask yes/no questions, because the dialogue is going back and forth more quickly.

17. Emeline is clearly interested in knitting and yarn, so Cassandra gives her all the information she can.

EMELINE: Wow, that's right near my house! Like a block away![18] I should definitely go there and check out[19] the yarn.[20] I don't know a lot about the different kinds yet.[21] I'm still figuring it out.[22] I'm Emeline, by the way.[23]

Inviting

CASSANDRA: I'm Cassandra.[24] It's nice to meet a yarn enthusiast! Do you wanna[25] go together sometime?[26] I'd be happy to show you around and give you some tips on the best yarns.[27]

EMELINE: I would love to![28] Thanks. I could learn so much.[29] That would be really fun.[30] When's good for you?[31,32]

Making a plan

CASSANDRA: Are Wednesdays good for you?[33]

EMELINE: Wednesday evenings are good. Would 6:00 P.M. be too late?[34] What are the store's hours?[35]

18. Emeline exclaims how close she lives to the yarn store because she's excited.

19. To **check out** means to look at, examine.

20. She expresses her interest.

21. Admits her beginner status in knitting

22. To **figure out** means to discover, learn.

23. Emeline introduces herself. She might also say, "My name is."

24. See Chapter 1 for more information on introducing yourself.

25. *Wanna* = want to.

26. Inviting Emeline to get together outside of the knitting club promotes friendship.

27. Cassandra tells how Emeline could benefit from the event.

28. *I would love to* usually means *yes*. Other possible expressions: That would be great! / Absolutely! / Yes, let's do it!

29. Emeline expresses gratitude.

30. Emeline reiterates her excitement.

31. *When's* is a contraction for *when + is*.

32. Asking for a schedule indicates the beginning of a plan.

33. Cassandra asks about Wednesdays in general—not a specific Wednesday. Other expressions: Do Wednesdays work for you? / How about a Wednesday?

34. Alternative expression: Is 6:00 P.M. too late?

35. Alternative expression: What time does the yarn store close?

(continued)

CASSANDRA: It closes at 7:00 P.M., I think.[36] So 6:00 P.M. works. How is next Wednesday?[37]

EMELINE: Next Wednesday is perfect.[38] Let's do it.[39]

CASSANDRA: Great![40] Should we just meet at the shop?[41]

EMELINE: Yes. I'll meet you there at 6:00 P.M. next Wednesday. Let me give you my cell phone number.[42]

CASSANDRA: Yeah, that's a good idea. We can text each other to confirm. My cell is 510-555-9031.[43]

EMELINE: Let me call you so you have my cell number.

CASSANDRA: Great. Thanks. Your number is 510-555-4825?[44]

EMELINE: Yup,[45] that's it.

Continue conversation or say good-bye

CASSANDRA: Now what are you knitting over there?[46]

36. Alternative expressions for *I think*: I believe / as far as I know.

37. Now Cassandra asks about a specific Wednesday. Alternative expressions: What about next Wednesday? / Does next Wednesday work? / Are you free next Wednesday?

38. Alternative expressions: Next Wednesday works for me. / Next Wednesday it is.

39. Alternative expressions: It's a plan. / Great, it's on my calendar. / It's a date!

40. Alternative expressions: Okay! / Perfect! / Yay! / Woohoo!

41. Alternative expressions for confirming the meeting place: Why don't we / Let's. (See the "Communication Strategy: Suggesting Activities" section later in this chapter for more information on this.)

42. Emeline wants to be sure they have a way to contact each other. She can offer her number or ask Cassandra for hers. Other possible expressions: Shall I give you my cell phone number? / What's your cell? / Should we exchange phone numbers?

43. It's important to be able to contact each other in case the situation changes. If Emeline has to cancel, she can call or text Cassandra. They can plan an alternative date or time to go to the yarn store.

44. **Pronunciation tip:** "Sing" the phone number song. You will learn about this later in the chapter.

45. Alternative informal expressions for *yes*: Yeah / Yessiree.

46. The conversation about knitting continues while they work on their projects.

Now that we have reviewed an example conversation, let's focus on starting a conversation with two types of small talk.

Communication Strategy: Small Talk

In Chapter 1, you learned many ways to make small talk, such as talking about the weather. In this section, you will learn two new ways. How did Emeline start a conversation with Cassandra? What strategies did she use? See points 1 and 2 in the conversation. Emeline used a compliment and a simple question. Compliments and simple questions open a conversation easily. Let's talk about compliments.

Compliments

A **compliment** is a positive comment about something. Let's look at some examples:

Those are beautiful shoes!	That antique car runs well.	That boat is beautiful.
That scarf is lovely.	Your dog is well trained.	That was a great presentation.

Notice that we comment on *something* and not *someone*. To be polite, do *not* compliment a person's hair or body. That is too private. The best compliments are about clothes or things connected to the person, such as a pet or a car. What was Emeline's compliment to Cassandra?

Simple Questions

A **simple question** is a yes/no or WH question that is easy to answer. Simple questions often follow compliments. Let's look at some examples of simple questions:

Those are beautiful shoes! Where did you get them?

That antique car runs well. What year is it?

That boat is beautiful. What kind is it?

That scarf is lovely. Is it silk?

Your dog is well trained. Did you train him?

That was a great presentation. Can I see it again online?

Notice that the question in each situation is related to the compliment. What was Emeline's simple question to Cassandra?

How to Make Friends

When we make a friend, certain things happen during the exchange:

- We find something we have in common.
- We decide we want to learn more about each other.

- There is a dialogue.
- We share personal information such as names, phone numbers, or e-mail addresses.
- We may plan another meeting.

In the preceding situation, Emeline and Cassandra are becoming friends. People usually join a club to meet people and make friends, because it's easy to find something in common. What are some other ways to make friends? List the ways *you* make new friends.

_____

_____

_____

As we have seen, the easiest way to make friends is to find something in common. Here is a list of ten ways you can meet people and make friends. As a bonus, you can also practice your English in each of these situations!

1. Join a club. Do activities you enjoy such as photography, cooking, or knitting. There are clubs at school, online, and in the community. What activities do *you* enjoy? Make a list.

   _____   _____   _____

   _____   _____   _____

2. Play individual sports such as running, hiking, swimming, and rock climbing, and meet others who like the same sport. Or you can play team sports like soccer, tennis, volleyball, and basketball, and meet your team members. Perhaps you like to watch live sporting events or watch sporting events on television. You could meet others who like to watch the same events or like the same team. What sports do *you* play or watch? Make a list.

   _____   _____   _____

   _____   _____   _____

3. If you are a student, make friends at school. You can create study groups, participate in extracurricular activities, join academic clubs, or take classes you enjoy such as art or movie production. How can *you* meet people at school? Make a list.

   _____   _____   _____

   _____   _____   _____

4. If you are employed, make friends at work. Join committees to help with social projects. For example, you could be on the holiday party organizing committee. How can *you* meet people at work? Make a list.

_____   _____   _____

_____   _____   _____

5. If you are a parent, get involved in your children's activities. Volunteer to help with school events such as sports, drama, and music. Help raise money for the school through bake sales and fairs. You can make friends with other parents. Do you have children in school in an English-speaking country? How can *you* volunteer to help? Make a list.

> A **bake sale** is a sale of baked goods such as cookies, brownies, pies, and cakes. Schools have bake sales to raise money for school programs. Parents usually bake the desserts at home and bring them to school to sell. A **fair** is a festival or outdoor party. It has food, music, and games.

_____   _____   _____

_____   _____   _____

6. Depending on your career, take part in professional development. For example, you can take classes such as public speaking. Attend industry conferences and meet other people in your field. What kind of professional development can *you* do? Make a list.

_____   _____   _____

_____   _____   _____

7. Meet people through your religion. For instance, you could meet people at church, the temple, or the mosque. Perhaps you can volunteer, join a club, or be on a committee. In what religious committees or projects can *you* participate? Make a list.

_____   _____   _____

_____   _____   _____

8. Volunteer. Volunteerism is very popular in North America. Volunteers help less fortunate people; for example, they serve food in soup kitchens or organize events to raise money for charities. Which charities would *you* like to help? Make a list.

> A **charity** is an organization that helps people in need.

_____   _____   _____

_____   _____   _____

9. Join a cause, which is similar to volunteering. For example, you can offer your help, expertise, or time to assist a program you believe in. Causes are similar to charities; they protect endangered species, help the poor, save animals, and fight for justice. Examples of some cause organizations are Habitat for Humanity, Save the Whales, and Amnesty International. Which causes do *you* believe in? Make a list.

_____   _____   _____

_____   _____   _____

10. Help with community and neighborhood activities. Does your neighborhood have block parties? Does your local library need volunteers? Get involved in your community center and offer to help. What programs and events are offered in *your* community? Make a list.

> A **block party** is a party given by a specific neighborhood. The street is closed off, and neighbors meet each other and have fun. Block parties usually have food, music, and games.

_____   _____   _____

_____   _____   _____

Culture Note

In North America, the two most common ways to make friends are (1) through shared activities, hobbies, and interests, and 2) through friends. It's uncommon to meet people or make friends in public places, such as at the bus stop or in the grocery store. However, it is possible to meet people and make friends in a public place where you go often. For example, if you go to a café every day at 8:00 A.M. to get coffee, you see the same people all the time. You can meet those people and maybe make friends.

Grammar: Possessive Pronouns

In English, we use possessive pronouns to talk about things that we have or own, as well as about people and things that belong to us. Here are a few rules for using them:

1. Possessive pronouns replace possessive nouns, such as *Mary's* and *Jim's*.

2. Possessive pronouns also replace a possessive adjective + a noun, such as *their children*.

> Remember: A **subject** usually comes before the verb in a sentence. An **object** usually comes after the verb. See Chapter 5 for a review of the subject-verb-object sentence structure.

3. Possessive pronouns can be a subject or an object.

4. Possessive pronouns can refer to singular or plural nouns.

5. Demonstrative pronouns are gender-neutral.

The following example sentences use possessive pronouns.

POSSESSIVE NOUN OR POSSESSIVE ADJECTIVE + NOUN	POSSESSIVE PRONOUN
That sweater is my sweater. (singular)	That sweater is *mine*.
Those sweaters are my sweaters. (plural)	Those sweaters are *mine*.
The blue car is our car. (singular)	The blue car is *ours*.
The blue cars are our cars. (plural)	The blue cars are *ours*.
Is this book your book? (singular)	Is this book *yours*?
Are these books your books? (plural)	Are these books *yours*?
The barking dog is Joseph's.	The barking dog is *his*.
Mary's is the white house with a red door.	*Hers* is the white house with a red door.
Mary and John's is the blue house on the corner.	*Theirs* is the blue house on the corner.

The following list shows the possessive pronouns.

Possessive Pronouns

	SINGULAR	PLURAL
First person	Mine	Ours
Second person	Yours	Yours
Third person	His	
	Hers	Theirs

> **Tip:** *His* refers to a male; *hers* refers to a female. These are the only gender-specific pronouns. None of the other possessive pronouns are gender-specific. *Theirs* can refer to things and people. When *theirs* refers to people, it can refer to males, females, or both together.

Now let's practice identifying possessive pronouns in context.

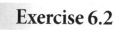

Exercise 6.2

Identify the possessive pronouns in the following sentences.

EXAMPLE   The book on the desk is hers. *hers*

1. Look at all the sweaters the knitting club made! His is the green one.

   _____

2. My brother has a beautiful flower garden. It's much prettier than mine.

   _____

3. See that shiny new car over there? It's hers. _____

4. Their nature photographs are in this gallery. Theirs are the pictures of mountains and lakes. _____

5. Is this pencil yours? _____

6. Here are two coats. Are the coats theirs? _____

Now let's practice writing sentences using possessive pronouns.

 ## Exercise 6.3

Create sentences using possessive pronouns to replace the underlined words.

EXAMPLE   The homework is <u>Steven's</u>. / *The homework is his.*

1. <u>Our house</u> was the red house on the right. It's not <u>our house</u> any longer. We sold it. / _____

2. Those shoes are <u>Sherry's</u>. / _____

3. The kids in the pool are <u>my kids</u>. / _____

4. The children eating popcorn are <u>Mary and Jim's kids</u>. / _____

Exercise 6.4

Use some possessive pronouns. Create six sentences about things you own or possess, or describe what your friends and family have. These sentences should be about things that people possess (like in sentences 1 and 2 in the previous exercise) and about people that belong to people (as in sentences 3 and 4). Use the example sentences in Exercise 6.3 to guide you.

1. (mine) _____

2. (ours) _____

3. (theirs) _____

4. (his) _____

5. (hers) _____

6. (yours) _____

Grammar: Demonstrative Adjectives

In English, we use demonstrative adjectives to talk about specific things and people. Let's look at the four demonstrative adjectives:

	SINGULAR	PLURAL
Near	This	These
Far	That	Those

We use *this* and *these* to talk about things and people that are near in distance or time. We use *that* and *those* to talk about things and people that are far in distance or time.

Now, let's review some example sentences with demonstrative adjectives.

	SINGULAR	PLURAL
Near	*This* person is my best friend.	*These* people are in my history class.
	My friend made *this* hat.	Do you like *these* pants?
Far	*That* story is wonderful!	*Those* flowers are colorful.
	Look at *that* bicycle!	She baked *those* chocolate chip cookies.

Demonstrative adjectives act just like possessive adjectives, which we talked about in Chapter 5. They always precede the noun: demonstrative adjective + noun. We use singular demonstrative adjectives with singular nouns and plural demonstrative adjectives with plural nouns, as shown in examples from the sentences in the preceding table:

This person (singular noun)

These people (plural noun)

That story (singular noun)

Those flowers (plural noun)

Exercise 6.5

Look at the examples of demonstrative adjectives and nouns in a *through* d *of the list, then answer the following questions.*

a. This hat

b. That bicycle

c. These pants

d. Those chocolate chip cookies

1. Which nouns are singular?_____

2. Which demonstrative adjectives are singular?_____

3. Which nouns are plural?_____

4. Which demonstrative adjectives are plural?_____

Here are some characteristics of demonstrative adjectives:

- Demonstrative adjectives act like possessive adjectives such as *my*, *her*, and *their*.

- Demonstrative adjectives talk about a specific noun or specific nouns.

- Demonstrative adjectives answer the question *Which one?* or *Which ones?*

- Demonstrative adjectives are gender-neutral.

 Note: We sometimes show what object we mean by pointing at it, holding it, touching it, or looking at it.

Let's look at two examples of things and people that are near and far in distance.

JACK: This person is Sally. That person is Tina. (Sally is near Jack. Tina is far from him.)

JACK: These trees are in my yard. Those trees are in the park. (The trees in Jack's yard are near him. The trees in the park are far from him.)

Although we sometimes point when we use demonstrative adjectives, you know from Chapter 1 that it's not polite to point at people with your finger. Instead, point at them with an open hand. See the following picture of Jack introducing Sally.

Jack is pointing at Sally using his whole hand, not his finger. Sally is one person (singular) near him, so he uses *this*. However, when we point at things, we can point with the index finger. See the following illustration where the boy points to a bike for an example.

Now practice using demonstrative adjectives.

Exercise 6.6

Look at the pictures that follow, and complete the sentences about them. Indicate whether this, that, these, *or* those *belongs in each blank space. Is the person or thing near or far? Is the noun singular or plural?*

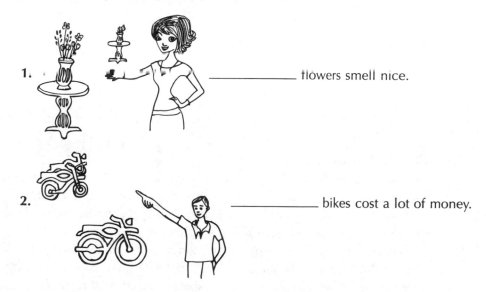

1. _____ flowers smell nice.

2. _____ bikes cost a lot of money.

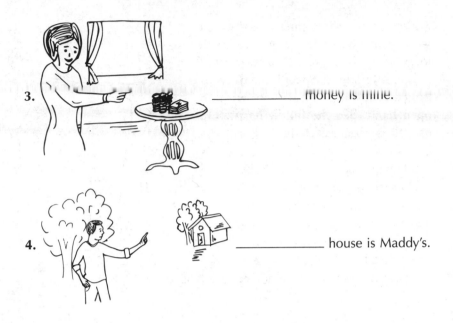

3. _____ money is mine.

4. _____ house is Maddy's.

Exercise 6.7

Create four sentences about things and people that are near and far. Use the demonstrative adjectives this, that, these, *and* those. *Use the example sentences in the preceding exercise to guide you.*

1. _____

2. _____

3. _____

4. _____

Places: *Here* and *There*

We talk about near and far places. We sometimes use *here* and *there* instead of *this place* and *that place*. When we talk about a place that is close, we say *this place*. We also say *this* + a specific place, such as *this house, this city, this street,* or *this field*. We can replace *this* + a specific place with *here*.

When we talk about a place that is far away, we say *that place*. We can also say *that* + a specific place, such as *that house, that city, that street,* or *that field*. Sometimes we replace *that* + a specific place with *there*. *Here* and *there* replace the preposition + the demonstrative adjective + noun. Let's look at some examples.

PREPOSITION + DEMONSTRATIVE ADJECTIVE + NOUN	HERE AND THERE
I live in this house.	I live here.
Preposition = *in*	
Demonstrative adjective = *this*	
Noun = *house*	

Note: If there is *no* preposition, you cannot use *here* or *there*.

Exercise 6.8

Practice using here *and* there *instead of the demonstrative adjectives* this *and* that. *Create a sentence for each of the following using* here *or* there *in place of the under-lined phrase.*

EXAMPLE   I play tennis <u>at that club</u>.   *I play tennis there.*

1. We live <u>on this street</u>. _____

2. Penelope studies <u>at that college</u>. _____

3. Gwen sings <u>in that church</u>. _____

4. He works <u>in this hotel</u>. _____

5. They often eat dinner <u>at that restaurant</u>. _____

6. My parents live <u>in this country</u>. _____

Exercise 6.9

Create eight sentences about places near and far. First, create a sentence with the preposition + demonstrative adjective + noun. Be sure you have a preposition. Then form the same sentence using here *and* there. *Review the example sentences from the earlier exercises to guide you.*

Preposition + Demonstrative Adjective + Noun   *Here* and *There*

EXAMPLE   *My mother lives in that house.*   *My mother lives there.*

1. a. _____   b. _____

2. a. _____   b. _____

3. a. _____   b. _____

4. a. _____   b. _____

Another way we use *here* is to talk about people and things that are in the same place as us. Similarly, we use *there* to talk about people and things that are not in the same place as us. Let's look at some examples.

Example: *My parents live **in this country**.* → *My parents live **here**.*

SENTENCE WITH HERE	EXPLANATION
My parents live here.	The parents live in the same country as the speaker. For example, they all live in Australia.

Example: *My parents live **in that country**.* → *My parents live **there**.*

SENTENCE WITH THERE	EXPLANATION
My parents live there.	The parents live in a different country than the speaker. For example, the speaker lives in Australia, and his or her parents live in China.

Now that you learned ways to use demonstrative adjectives and *here* and *there*, let's talk about demonstrative pronouns.

Grammar: Demonstrative Pronouns

Just like with demonstrative adjectives, we use demonstrative pronouns to talk about specific things and people. Let's look at some example sentences that use demonstrative pronouns.

SINGULAR	PLURAL
This is my best friend.	*These* are my glasses.
My sister made *this*.	Do you like *these*?
That is a wonderful story!	*Those* are pretty flowers.
Look at *that*!	She baked *those*.

The difference between demonstrative adjectives and demonstrative pronouns is that demonstrative adjectives require nouns; demonstrative pronouns *are* the nouns in pronoun form. Let's look at the difference:

DEMONSTRATIVE ADJECTIVE	DEMONSTRATIVE PRONOUN
My friend made this hat.	My sister made this.
Demonstrative adjective = *this*	Pronoun = *this*
Noun = *hat*	
Do you like these pants?	Do you like these?
Demonstrative adjective = *these*	Pronoun = *these*
Noun = *pants*	
Look at that bicycle!	Look at that!
Demonstrative adjective = *that*	Pronoun = *that*
Noun = *bicycle*	
She baked those chocolate chip cookies.	She baked those.
Demonstrative adjective = *those*	Pronoun = *those*
Noun = *chocolate chip cookies*	

Here are the rules for using demonstrative pronouns:

- Demonstrative pronouns replace demonstrative adjectives + nouns such as *this car* and *those shoes*.

- Demonstrative pronouns can be subjects or objects.

- Demonstrative pronouns are gender-neutral.

	SINGULAR	PLURAL
Near	This	These
Far	That	Those

> **Note:** It's less common to use demonstrative pronouns for people and more common to use them for things. A list of demonstrative pronouns appears in this table. Notice that this table is the same as the one you saw earlier in the "Grammar: Demonstrative Adjectives" section.

The following example sentences use demonstrative pronouns as both subjects and objects. Notice that the demonstrative pronouns in the subject position come before the verb in the sentence, and the ones in the object position come after the verb.

DEMONSTRATIVE PRONOUN AS SUBJECT	DEMONSTRATIVE PRONOUN AS OBJECT
Hannah, *this* is Jade.*	Does she like *this*?
That smells delicious.	I didn't know *that*.
These are the right answers.	I sell *these* every day.
Those are hers.	Where did you get *those*?

*In Chapter 2, you learned how to introduce one person to another. We use *This is* to make an introduction.

Now let's practice identifying demonstrative pronouns in sentences.

Exercise 6.10

Identify the demonstrative pronouns in the following sentences.

EXAMPLE   Do you like these?   *these*

1. Those are the good Web sites. _____

2. I can't believe that! _____

3. Have you seen this? _____

4. This is fun! _____

5. You can't have these. _____

6. That is bad news. _____

7. These are very fashionable. _____

8. What is that? _____

Now, let's practice writing sentences using demonstrative pronouns.

Exercise 6.11

Create sentences by replacing the demonstrative adjectives and nouns given with demonstrative pronouns.

EXAMPLE   This eraser is Zoey's.   *This is Zoey's.*

1. We love these games! _____

2. Those shoes are Sherry's. _____

3. These kids are my kids. _____

4. Those kids are Jim's kids. _____

Exercise 6.12

Create four sentences using demonstrative pronouns. Describe things and people at home and at work. Use the example sentences in the preceding exercise to guide you.

1. this _____

2. that _____

3. these _____

4. those _____

Bonus Question: In each sentence you created, is the demonstrative pronoun a subject or an object? Remember: if it appears before the main verb, it's a subject. If it comes after the main verb, it's an object. Note *subject* or *object* after each sentence.

Spending Time with Friends

When we have friends, we do activities together. We spend time, or **hang out,** with them. In this section, you will learn how to give, accept, and decline invitations politely, as well as how to make suggestions and share information with friends. You will also learn two new ways to make small talk.

Communication Strategy: Making Invitations

At the beginning of this chapter, Emeline and Cassandra met and became friends. In the conversation, Cassandra invited Emeline to go to the yarn store. How did she do this? What did she say?

Exercise 6.13

Go to the conversation and find Cassandra's invitation to Emeline. Note the invitation.

Cassandra's invitation to Emeline: _____

_____

There are many ways to invite people to events or just to hang out. Let's look at some of the most common expressions. They are on a scale of informal to formal.

	EXPRESSIONS FOR INVITATIONS	EXAMPLE SENTENCES
Informal	Wanna (do something)?	Wanna have lunch today?
		Wanna go to the movies Sunday afternoon?
	Do you want (to do something)?	Do you want to study for the test together this weekend?
	Do you fancy* (doing something)?	Do you fancy studying for the test together this weekend?
	What are you doing (time/day)?	What are you doing Saturday night?
	Are you free (time/day)?	Are you free Saturday night?
	Are you busy (time/day)?	Are you busy Saturday night?

(continued)

EXPRESSIONS FOR INVITATIONS	EXAMPLE SENTENCES
Can you (do something)?	Can you come to the party Friday night?
Are you interested in (event/doing something)?	Are you interested in having pizza for lunch?
How do you fancy* (doing something)?	How do you fancy having pizza for lunch?
I'd/We'd love/be delighted to have you (come over, join me/us) for (an event/meal).	We'd love to have you come over for dinner Sunday evening. We'd be delighted to have you join us for dinner Sunday evening.
Would you like (to do something)?	Would you like to go for a hike this weekend?
Can you join me for (something)?	Can you join me for a drink after work?
I was just wondering if you'd like/want (to do something).	I was just wondering if you'd like to work on the project together this week.
Formal Would you be interested in (doing something)?	Would you be interested in going to the art museum on Saturday?

*Used in British English rather than American.

Notice that some of the expressions in the preceding table use gerunds (verb-**ing**) and some use infinitives (*to* + base form of verb). Gerunds are indicated with *doing something*. Infinitives are indicated with *to do something*. Review the use of gerunds and infinitives in Chapter 5.

Note: Sometimes we use two or three expressions to form an invitation. For example, we may say, "What are you doing Saturday night? Would you like to come to a dinner party at our house? We'd love to have you."

> **Pronunciation Note**:
> *Would you* sounds like *Wouldju* or *Wouldja*.

WHEN TO BE LESS FORMAL	WHEN TO BE MORE FORMAL
It's a casual situation.	It's a formal situation.
You are younger (a teenager, a young adult, or in school).	You are a professional or at work.
You have known someone for a long time.	You have known someone for a short time.

Let's practice making invitations.

Exercise 6.14

Look at the following situations. Then create an invitation using the words given. Is the situation informal or formal? Review the expressions in the preceding section if needed.

Example situation: Joe and Dan just met at an antique car show. They both like the same car. Joe invites Dan to lunch at the car show.

DAN: *Are you free now? Can you join me for lunch?*

Time and day: now

1. Danielle and Shradha are in the same class in college. They have a test soon. Shradha invites Danielle to study with her for the test.

   Time and day: Friday afternoon

   SHRADHA: _____

   _____

2. Christine and Julia are in the same hiking group. They have hiked together three times already. Christine invites Julia to hike on a new trail.

   Time and day: Sunday morning

   CHRISTINE: _____

   _____

3. Margie and Lynette both have boys in the first grade. They met at a bake sale. Margie invites Lynette and her son to the park.

   Time and day: Wednesday after school

   MARGIE: _____

   _____

4. Howard and Seth are both engineers. They met at an engineering conference. Seth invites Howard to join him for dinner.

   Time and day: that same evening

   SETH: _____

   _____

5. Henry and Rishi are in the same scuba diving club. They have been scuba diving together twice. Henry invites Rishi to a party at his house.

   Time and day: 7:00 P.M. next Saturday night

   HENRY: _____

   _____

Now that you have learned how to extend invitations, let's look at how to accept and decline them. We begin with accepting invitations.

Communication Strategy: Accepting Invitations

When you get an invitation, how do you accept it? What are different ways to say yes? Note these expressions.

_____   _____   _____

Let's look at ways to accept invitations.

	EXPRESSIONS FOR ACCEPTING INVITATIONS
Informal	Sure! / Yeah, sure. / Okay!
↑	Thanks, I'd love to! / Thanks, I'd like that.
	That sounds like fun!
	That sounds fun/great/wonderful.
	That'd/That would be fun/great/wonderful!
↓	Thank you, I would love to!
Formal	That's very kind of you, yes.

Now, let's look at ways to decline an invitation.

Communication Strategy: Declining Invitations

Maybe you can't accept an invitation. How do you decline it? Note different ways to say no to an invitation.

_____   _____   _____

When we decline an invitation, we usually give a reason to be polite. We are more direct with friends we know well and less direct with new friends or work mates. Here are ways to decline an invitation.

LESS DIRECT/MORE POLITE	EXAMPLE
1. Start with a courtesy statement.	I'd love to[1], but I can't.[2] I have plans that night.[3]
2. Say no.	
3. Give a general or specific reason.	
1. Start with a courtesy statement.	I'd love to[1], but I have plans that night.[3]
2. Skip step	
3. Give a general or specific reason.	

MORE DIRECT/LESS POLITE	EXAMPLE
1. Skip step	I can't.[2] I'm working that day.[3]
2. Say no.	
3. Give a general or specific reason.	

Let's look at some other expressions to decline invitations. In each case, a reason can be added at the end.

	EXPRESSIONS FOR DECLINING INVITATIONS
Informal	Bummer! I can't.
↑	Sorry, I can't.
	I would, but (this time/day/date) isn't good/ doesn't work.
	I'd love to, but I can't.
	That sounds like fun, but I can't.
	That sounds fun/great/wonderful, but I can't.
↓	Thank you. I wish I could, but I can't.
Formal	That's very kind of you, but I can't.

In North America, **bummer** means "This is a disappointment."

Let's look at examples of courtesy statements, expressions for declining invitations, and common reasons used.

A **courtesy statement** is a polite statement, or a nice thing to say. It makes an invitation refusal more acceptable. Examples of courtesy statements are *I'd love to* and *That sounds like fun.*

COURTESY STATEMENT	DECLINE INVITATION	REASON
Bummer!	I can't.	**Specific reasons:**
Oh,	I can't go,	I'm (doing something),
Sorry, but	I can't make it.	I have to (do something).
I'd love to, but	I won't be able to.	I've got to (do something).
I wish I could, but	I won't be able to go.	I'm supposed to (do something).
I'm afraid	I won't be able to make it.	I must (do something).
		General reasons:
		I'm busy.
		I'm doing something else.
		I already have plans (at time/on day/on date).
		I have plans.

Now let's practice declining invitations.

Exercise 6.15

Read the following situations. Use the steps and expressions in the preceding sections to decline each invitation politely. Remember to think about whether the situation is informal or formal.

EXAMPLE   Abdul and Hiro play on the same high school basketball team. Abdul invites Hiro to have pizza after the game. Hiro has other plans. He has to work at the mall.

ABDUL: Hey, do you wanna get pizza after the game?

HIRO: *Bummer! I can't. I have to work at the mall.*

1. Shauna and Sia take flute lessons together at school. Shauna invites Sia to hang out after school. Sia wants to hang out, but she can't. She has to babysit her brother after school.

    SHAUNA: Sia, do you wanna hang out after school today?

    SIA: (informal) _____

    _____

2. Jim and Ralph are at a business conference and just attended the same workshop. They were partners for role-playing. Jim wants to have lunch with Ralph after the workshop. Ralph must decline because he has a business meeting to attend during lunch.

    JIM: Are you free for lunch?

    RALPH: (more formal) _____

Pronunciation Note

It's important to say *can* and *can't* correctly. They do *not* sound the same in English. Let's look at how to say them differently.

FEATURES	CAN	CAN'T
1. Stress	*can* = Unstressed word	*can't* = Stressed word
2a. Vowel sound	Three possible vowel sounds: /ə/ as in **kən**; /ɛ/ as in **kɛn**; /ɪ/ as in **kɪn**	One vowel sound: American: /æ/ as in **kænʔ** British: /aː/ as in **kaːnt** or **kaːnʔ**
2b. Vowel length	The vowel sound is reduced or spoken very quickly. It sounds like **k'n.**	The vowel sound is full, so it is longer.

FEATURES	CAN	CAN'T
3. /t/ sound	No /t/ sound	American: You almost never hear the /t/ sound. You don't release the /t/ sound with air. It sounds like /ʔ/. British: You sometimes do not hear the /t/ sound. Sometimes, it is a clear /t/ sound released with puff of air. Sometimes, it sounds like /ʔ/.
4. Main verb Example	Main verb = stressed I can **go**. → IkIn **go**.	Main verb = stressed I can't **go**. → American: I **kænʔ go**. British: I **ka:nt go**. / I **ka:nʔ go**.

Grammar: Modals of Obligation and Necessity

When we give a reason for declining an invitation, we often use modals of obligation and necessity. Here are some examples:

I have to study for my marketing test.	We've got to work Friday afternoon.
She must finish her proposal.	I'm supposed to babysit my little sister.

Modal auxiliary verbs are used with main verbs. Always use the base form of the main verb, and be sure there is subject-verb agreement. Let's look at how to form modals.

SUBJECT OR SUBJECT PRONOUN	MODAL OF OBLIGATION	BASE FORM OF MAIN VERB (SAME FOR ALL SUBJECTS)	EXAMPLE SENTENCES	MEANING
I	have to	study	I have to study for my marketing test.	Necessity—there will be consequences if I don't do it.
We	have got to ('ve got to)	work	We have got to work Friday afternoon. We've got to work Friday afternoon.	Necessity.

(continued)

SUBJECT OR SUBJECT PRONOUN	MODAL OF OBLIGATION	BASE FORM OF MAIN VERB (SAME FOR ALL SUBJECTS)	EXAMPLE SENTENCES	MEANING
She	must*	finish	She must finish her proposal.	Strong necessity.
I	am supposed to (use correct form of BE verb)	babysit	I am supposed to babysit my little sister. I'm supposed to babysit my little sister.	Obligation— something that is planned or expected by others.

*The modal *must* does **not** take *to*.

The form of the main verb is the same for all subjects: the base form. However, the auxiliary verbs BE and HAVE must agree with the subject. For example, ***She has*** *got to work tonight* and ***They have*** *got to work tonight*. Think about which form of BE and HAVE to use with modals of obligation as you practice forming sentences with them.

✎ Exercise 6.16

Form sentences using the words given. Create four sentences for each question. Review how to form modals. Be sure to use the correct form of BE and HAVE. You can use contractions with BE in be supposed to *and with HAVE in* have got to.

EXAMPLE   I / MODAL OF OBLIGATION / see / my school counselor / on Tuesday afternoon.

> *I have to see my school counselor on Tuesday afternoon.*
> *I have/I've got to see my school counselor on Tuesday afternoon.*
> *I must see my school counselor on Tuesday afternoon.*
> *I am/I'm supposed to see my school counselor on Tuesday afternoon.*

1. We / MODAL OF OBLIGATION / have / dinner with my parents / Thursday evening.

   _____

   _____

   _____

   _____

2. I / MODAL OF OBLIGATION / walk / my dogs / after dinner.

_____

_____

_____

_____

3. He / MODAL OF OBLIGATION / finish / his research paper / this weekend.

_____

_____

_____

_____

4. They / MODAL OF OBLIGATION / visit / their sister / that day.

_____

_____

_____

_____

5. She / MODAL OF OBLIGATION / clean / her house / this afternoon.

_____

_____

_____

_____

6. I / MODAL OF OBLIGATION / work / on my résumé / Wednesday evening.

_____

_____

_____

_____

7. We / MODAL OF OBLIGATION / do / our homework / tonight.

_____

_____

_____

_____

8. I / MODAL OF OBLIGATION / meet / with my supervisor / that morning.

_____

_____

_____

_____

 ## Exercise 6.17

Create four sentences in which you state obligations you or others have. Does the obligation have consequences if you don't do it? If so, use have to. *Do others expect you to do something? If yes, use the correct form of BE* supposed to. *Use contractions where possible. Review how to form modals of obligation.*

1. have to _____

2. have got to _____

3. am supposed to _____

4. must _____

Pronunciation Note
In English, we often shorten and link sounds when speaking. With modals of obligation, *have to = hafta, has to = hasta,* and *got to = gotta.* Let's look at some examples.

She has to prepare for her big meeting. = She hasta prepare for her big meeting.

I have to practice my role in the play. = I hafta practice my role in the play.

I've got to spend time with my family. = I've gotta spend time with my family.

Mary's got to go to the doctor's office. = Mary's gotta go to the doctor's office.

Suggesting Another Time
Sometimes we want to accept an invitation, but we are busy, so we suggest a different time to do the activity. To make suggestions, we use these expressions:

	EXPRESSIONS FOR SUGGESTING A DIFFERENT TIME/DAY/DATE	EXAMPLE SENTENCES
Informal ↑↓ Formal	What about (time/day/date)?	What about tomorrow afternoon?
	How about (time/day/date)?	How about tomorrow afternoon?
	Can we do it (time/day/date)?	Can we do it on Wednesday?
	Could you do it (time/day/date)?	Could you do it this weekend?
	Would (time/day/date) work for you?	Would next Tuesday night work for you?

We can also ask for a rain check. A **rain check** postpones an activity. We usually say, "Can I take a rain check?" so we can make a new plan to spend time together.

Now that you know ways to accept and decline invitations, let's practice.

Exercise 6.18

Look at the following situations. You have already written invitations. Now create answers to the invitations. Is the situation formal or informal? What expressions do you use? Is it less direct and more polite, or more direct and less polite?

Example 1: Joe and Dan just met at an antique car show. They both like the same car. They are talking about the car. Joe invites Dan to lunch at the car show.
Time and day: now
Answer: yes

DAN: *Are you free right now? Can you join me for lunch?*

JOE: *Yeah, sure. I have time. Where do you want to eat?*

Example 2: Danielle and Shradha are in the same class in college. They have a test soon. Shradha invites Danielle to study with her for the test.
Time and day: Friday afternoon
Answer: no; suggestion for another time
Reason: working

SHRADHA: *Hey, would you like to study for the test together Friday afternoon?*

DANIELLE: *I'd like that, but I can't on Friday. I'm working. How about Saturday morning?*

1. Christine and Julia are in the same hiking group. They have hiked together three times already. Christine invites Julia to hike at a new trail.
Time and day: Sunday morning
Answer: no; rain check
Reason: general

CHRISTINE: _____

_____

JULIA: _____

_____

2. Margie and Lynette both have boys in first grade. They met at a bake sale. Margie invites Lynette and her son to the park.
   Time and day: Wednesday after school
   Answer: yes

   MARGIE: _____

   _____

   LYNETTE: _____

   _____

3. Howard and Seth are both engineers. They met at an engineering conference. Seth invites Howard to join him for dinner.
   Time and day: that same evening
   Answer: no
   Reason: finishing a work project

   SETH: _____

   _____

   HOWARD: _____

   _____

4. Henry and Rishi are in the same scuba diving club. They have been scuba diving together twice. Henry invites Rishi to a party at his house.
   Time and day: 7:00 P.M. next Saturday
   Answer: yes

   HENRY: _____

   _____

   RISHI: _____

   _____

Communication Strategy: Suggesting Activities

Another way to give an invitation is to make a suggestion. We usually use this kind of invitation with our established friends rather than with someone we have just met. There are a few expressions you can use to make a suggestion.

	EXPRESSIONS FOR SUGGESTING ACTIVITIES	EXAMPLE SENTENCES
Informal	Let's (do something).	Let's play soccer this Saturday.
	Why don't we (do something)?	Why don't we study for the test later today?
	Should we (do something)?	Should we finish this project tomorrow?
Formal	Shall we (do something)?	Shall we join the party?

Let's practice making suggestions.

Exercise 6.19

Suggest activities. Create sentences using the words provided. Remember to use the correct punctuation at the end of each sentence.

EXAMPLE   EXPRESSION FOR SUGGESTING ACTIVITY / rehearse / for the recital / on Sunday

Let's rehearse for the recital on Sunday.

1. EXPRESSION FOR SUGGESTING ACTIVITY / work on / the art project / Thursday evening

   _____

2. EXPRESSION FOR SUGGESTING ACTIVITY / play / the game / today

   _____

3. EXPRESSION FOR SUGGESTING ACTIVITY / get together / soon

   _____

> To **get together** means to spend time together in person; to hang out. It is informal.

4. EXPRESSION FOR SUGGESTING ACTIVITY / eat / lunch / today

   _____

Grammar: Modals of Possibility

We use modals to talk about possibility; for example, when we make plans with a friend. Let's look at some examples:

I *might* go to the movies.	The Johnsons *may* join us for the movie.
Jarrod *may* meet us at 5:00 P.M.	Damian and Fred *will* be there.

You learned modals of obligation earlier. Modals of possibility are similar. Modal auxiliary verbs are used with main verbs. Always use the base form of the main verb. Let's look at how to form modals of possibility.

SUBJECT OR SUBJECT PRONOUN	MODAL OF POSSIBILITY	NEGATIVE	BASE FORM OF MAIN VERB	REST OF SENTENCE	LEVEL OF POSSIBILITY
I	will	(not)	meet	you at 10:00 A.M.	100 percent certainty
She	might	(not)	eat	dinner with Noelle.	About 50 percent certainty: informal, more common in conversation

(continued)

SUBJECT OR SUBJECT PRONOUN	MODAL OF POSSIBILITY	NEGATIVE	BASE FORM OF MAIN VERB	REST OF SENTENCE	LEVEL OF POSSIBILITY
I	may	(not)	have	an appointment that day.	About 50 percent certainty: slightly more formal; less common in casual conversation

Note: Another modal of possibility is *can*. We use *can* to show that something is possible. More details about *can* are given in the next section on modals of ability.

Now, let's practice modals of possibility.

Exercise 6.20

Form sentences using the words provided. Review the preceding table if you need help forming modals.

EXAMPLE 1   I / MODAL OF POSSIBILITY / choose / the economics class / next term. (about 50 percent certainty)

I might choose the economics class next term. / I may choose the economics class next term.

EXAMPLE 2   I / MODAL OF POSSIBILITY / choose / the economics class / next term. (about 50 percent certainty of negative outcome)

I might not choose the economics class next term. / I may not choose the economics class next term.

1. We / MODAL OF POSSIBILITY / cook / brunch / for Leyla's birthday / on Sunday. (100 percent certainty)

A **brunch** is a late breakfast/ early lunch. It's a combination of breakfast and lunch foods. The word is formed from the *br* in breakfast and the *unch* in lunch.

2. Seamus / MODAL OF POSSIBILITY / do / his presentation / on Monday. (about 50 percent certainty of negative outcome)

3. I / MODAL OF POSSIBILITY / pass / the test / in math class. (about 50 percent certainty)

4. My boss / MODAL OF POSSIBILITY / give / me / a raise / next year.
   (100 percent certainty)

   _____

5. Professor Dunn / MODAL OF POSSIBILITY / give / a test / in computer
   class / next week. (about 50 percent certainty)

   _____

Exercise 6.21

Create three sentences about possible activities in your life. Review how to form modals of possibility.

1. will _____

2. might/might _____

3. may/might (negative outcome) _____

Grammar: Modals of Ability (*Can + Be Able To*)

We also use modals to talk about ability, such as when we make plans. Let's look at some examples:

Affirmative	Negative
1. I *can go* to the party.	4. She *can't* meet you at 3:00 P.M.
2. I *am able to* join you for dinner.	5. We're *not able to* attend the concert.
3. I *might be able to* come.	6. She *might not be able to* come.

Just like modals of obligation and possibility, modal auxiliary verbs of ability are used with the base form of the main verb. Notice we can use a modal of possibility with *BE able to* (see examples 3 and 6 in the list). We *cannot* use a modal of possibility with *can*. See the following examples:

CORRECT: *We might play tennis.* (possibility)

CORRECT: *We can play tennis.* (ability)

INCORRECT: *We ~~might can~~ play tennis.*

Now, let's see how to form modals of ability.

SUBJECT OR SUBJECT PRONOUN	MODAL AUXILIARY	NEGATIVE	BE ABLE TO	BASE FORM OF MAIN VERB	REST OF SENTENCE
I	can	(not)	—	meet	you at 10:00 A.M.

I can meet you at 10:00 A.M. / I can't meet you at 10:00 A.M.

| She | — | → | is* (not) able to | eat | dinner with Noelle. |

She is able to eat dinner with Noelle. / She isn't able to eat dinner with Noelle. / She's not able to eat dinner with Noelle.

| She | might/ may/will | → | be** (not) able to | eat | dinner with Noelle. |

She might be able to eat dinner with Noelle. / She might not be able to eat dinner with Noelle.

*The BE verb must agree with the subject. Here, third person singular BE = *is*. Be sure to use *is* with *he*, *she*, and *it*. See Chapter 1 for a review of BE verb tenses.

**We must use *be* in its base form with a modal of possibility in *BE able to*. Do not use *am*, *is*, or *are*.

Now let's practice modals of ability.

✎ Exercise 6.22

Create sentences using the words provided. Review how to form the modals of ability.

EXAMPLE 1   I / MODAL OF ABILITY/ win / the chess game / tomorrow. (can)

I can win the chess game tomorrow.

EXAMPLE 2   I / MODAL OF ABILITY / travel / to Thailand / for vacation. (BE able to—about 50 percent certainty)

I might be able to travel to Thailand for vacation.

1. He / MODAL OF ABILITY / understand / the math problem. (can—negative)

   _____

2. Janice / MODAL OF ABILITY / understand / the math problem. (BE able to)

   _____

3. Paul / MODAL OF ABILITY / understand / the math problem. (BE able to—negative)

_____

4. The Greggs family / MODAL OF ABILITY / go camping. (BE able to—50 percent certainty)

_____

5. Sheena and her daughter / MODAL OF ABILITY / go camping. (BE able to—50 percent certainty of negative outcome)

_____

6. Preston and his son / MODAL OF ABILITY / go camping. (BE able to—negative)

_____

Exercise 6.23

Create six sentences about things you can and can't do. Review how to form modals of ability, and use possibility in some of your sentences.

1. can _____

2. can (negative) _____

3. BE able to _____

4. BE able to (negative) _____

_____

5. BE able to (about 50 percent certainty) _____

6. BE able to (about 50 percent certainty of negative outcome) _____

_____

Communication Strategy: Sharing Contact Information

When we make friends, we usually share contact information. Examples of contact information are your name, phone number, and e-mail address. It is the information that people use to reach, or contact, you. In this section, we will learn how to ask for and give phone numbers clearly.

Saying Phone Numbers

There is a certain way we say our phone number. It's like a song, so we basically "sing" the numbers. How do we sing the phone number song?

Here are the rules. We will use 510-672-1194 as our example number.

RULE	FEATURE	EXAMPLE
1. We stress the last number of each group.	a. The vowel sound is longer. b. We say the number louder.	Five-one-*ooooh* Six-seven-*twooo* One-one-nine-*foouur*
2. We use different pitch changes for different groups of numbers.	a. The first two groups = slightly rising pitch. b. The last group = falling pitch.	Five-one-*ooooh* Six-seven-*twooo* One-one-nine-*foouur*
3. We pause between groups of numbers.	a. Pause before and after saying the whole phone number. b. Pause between groups. c. Pause slightly in the middle of the last group of for digits.	(pause) Five-one-*ooooh* (pause) Six-seven-*twooo* (pause) One-one (short pause) nine-*foouur* (pause)

So we say the sentence like this: "My phone number is five-one-*ooooh* . . . six-seven-*twooo* . . . one-one . . . nine-*foouur*."

Pronunciation Tips

1. Say "oh" instead of "zero." With an accent, *zero* can sound like *seven*.

2. Speak slowly. Don't say numbers quickly.

3. Be sure to pronounce the final consonant of a number. For example, say *fi**ve***, not *fi*.

4. Pronounce *one* correctly. It sounds like *won*. It has an /**n**/ sound at the end. It does *not* sound like /**wung**/. It does *not* have an /ŋ/ sound at the end.

5. Ask people to repeat your number to be sure they got it right. Expressions you can use: *Can you repeat that number, please? / Could you please say that back to me?*

Exercise 6.24

Now, practice saying these numbers.

1. 888-625-0048
2. 508-722-9546
3. 978-445-1105
4. 919-236-9815

Pronunciation Note

Now, let's practice pronouncing numbers correctly. Some numbers that are often confused are 13 through 19 and 30 through 90. We say these numbers differently. In the following table, the dots separate syllables and the (air) symbol indicates that the /t/ sound requires a big puff of air to make a strong /t/ sound as in *time*. Let's see how we say these numbers.

13–19	EXAMPLE	30–90	EXAMPLE
Stress at end on **teen**.	Four•teen	Stress at beginning of word.	**For**•ty
The /t/ sound is strong with a big puff of air. This is shown with the (air) symbol.	Four•t(air)een	The /t/ sound is like soft /d/ sound with no puff of air.	**For**•dy
The /n/ sound is at the end of the word.	Four•t(air)ee**n**	The /iy/ sound is at the end of the word.	**For**•diy

The numbers sound like this:

13–16	30–60	17–19	70–90
13: Thir•t(air)een	30: **Thir**•diy	17: Sev•en•t(air)een	70: **Sev**•en•diy
14: Four•t(air)een	40: **For**•diy	18: Eight•t(air)een	80: **Eight**•diy
15: Fif•t(air)een	50: **Fif**•diy	19: Nine•t(air)een	90: **Nine**•diy
16: Six•t(air)een	60: **Six**•diy		

Now, let's practice pronouncing numbers correctly.

Exercise 6.25

Practice saying the following numbers. First, practice all of the teens in order from 1a to 1g. Then practice the tens in order from 2a to 2g. Finally, practice the teens and tens together like this: 1a, 2a, 1b, 2b, and so on.

1. Teens   a. 13   b. 14   c. 15   d. 16   e. 17   f. 18   g. 19
2. Tens   a. 30   b. 40   c. 50   d. 60   e. 70   f. 80   g. 90

Vocabulary: Phrasal Verbs for Plans and Activities

We use some common phrasal verbs when we talk about plans and activities. Let's look at these verbs.

Exercise 6.26

Read the phrasal verbs on the left, then read the definitions on the right. You may know some of these verbs. Match the verbs with their appropriate definitions. For the verbs you do not know, take a guess. Some phrasal verbs can be separated with a noun or pronoun; these are shown in **bold**.

1. To hang out with **someone**

2. To call up **someone**/to call **someone** up

3. To call off **something**/to call **something** off

4. To call back **someone**/to call **someone** back

5. To back up **someone**/to back **someone** up

6. To get along (with **someone**)*/to get on (with **someone**)**

7. To cheer up **someone** / to cheer **someone** up

8. To bring **someone** down

9. To do **something** over

10. To leave out **something**/to leave **something** out

11. To end up **somewhere**

12. To pass up **something**/to pass **something** up

a. To cancel

b. To support

c. To spend time with

d. To call on the phone

e. To make happy

f. To omit

g. To forgive

h. To decline

i. To review

j. To arrive at a certain place, sometimes unexpectedly

k. To do something again

l. To make unhappy

*American usage.
**British usage.

13. To make up with **someone**

14. To go over **something**

m. To enjoy someone's company

n. To return someone's call; to call someone on the phone after they have called you

> **Culture Note:** In the United Kingdom, to **do someone over** means to ransack their home or office. This is different from to **do something over**.

Exercise 6.27

Complete the following sentences with the correct phrasal verb. Be sure to use the correct verb tense and form. Use the third person singular verb form when necessary.

EXAMPLE   Sara and Jenny *get along* very well. They always have fun together.

1. After they argued, Alice and her sister _____. They weren't angry with each other for long. (simple past)

2. Jules _____ the invitation to the musical play. She had other plans. (simple past)

3. Henry and Olivia _____ their friend Joline. Joline feels sad. (present progressive)

4. Nan called me, but I wasn't home. I have to _____ her _____ soon. (base form of verb)

5. Coach Quilici always _____ his players. He's a good coach. (simple present)

6. My parents _____ my birthday party because I failed my test. (simple past)

7. After hours of hiking in the woods, we _____ at the ranger station. (simple past)

8. The teacher lets the students _____ a test _____ when they fail. (simple present)

Conversation: Putting It All Together

In this chapter, you have learned the following:

1. How to make friends

2. How to make, accept, and decline invitations

3. How to use possessive pronouns and demonstrative adjectives and pronouns

4. How to use modals of obligation, possibility, and ability

5. Vocabulary for activities and plans

6. How to pronounce phone numbers

Now let's try to put it all together.

Exercise 6.28

To complete the following conversation, use all the verb tenses you know: simple present, present progressive, simple past, imperatives, gerunds and infinitives, and modals. Use communication strategies, possessive pronouns, and demonstrative adjectives and pronouns. Also use the vocabulary and expressions you learned in this chapter. In this situation, Nejoom and Junko are in the same photography class. Nejoom wants to make friends with Junko and take nature photographs with her. Nejoom begins the conversation. Add more dialogue.

Making Friends

1. Small talk: give Junko a compliment and ask a simple WH question (for example, talk about Junko's photographs). / Nejoom: _____
   _____

2. Answer question. / Junko: _____

3. Ask another WH question to keep conversation going. / Nejoom: _____
   _____

4. Answer question. / Junko: _____

5. Keep conversation going. / Nejoom: _____

6. Answer questions, make comments, and ask questions. / Junko: _____
   _____

7. Turn conversation to places to take nature photographs. / Nejoom: _____
   _____

8. Talk about places to take nature photos. / Junko: _____

9. Introduce self. / Nejoom: _____

10. Introduce self. / Junko: _____

Inviting

11. Turn conversation to a specific place to take nature photographs. / Nejoom:
    _____

12. Ask location of place. / Junko: _____

13. Answer questions; discuss place. / Nejoom: _____

14. Ask questions about place. / Junko: _____

15. Invite Junko to go to this place on Saturday morning. / Nejoom: _____
_____

16. Can't go Saturday morning; suggest Sunday morning. / Junko: _____
_____

Making a Plan

17. Say yes; Sunday morning and suggest a time. / Nejoom: _____

18. Agree to time; ask where to meet. / Junko: _____

19. Answer where to meet. / Nejoom: _____

Sharing Contact Information

20. Ask for phone number. / Nejoom: _____

21. Give phone number; ask Nejoom to repeat phone number. / Junko: _____
_____

22. Repeat phone number, say thank you, and give phone number. / Nejoom:
_____

23. Show excitement. / Junko: _____

24. Show excitement; continue the conversation or say good-bye. / Nejoom:

Reading About It

In this section, we will review pre-reading, active reading, and understanding a passage—all strategies for effective reading. In earlier chapters, you learned how to discover the meaning of new words from definition, example, and contrast context clues. Use all of these reading strategies in the following section.

Let's Read Together

As you know, when you pre-read, you first read the title of the passage; you then read the first sentence of the first paragraph; and finally you read the last sentence of the last paragraph. After you pre-read, you read actively by circling words you do not know and highlighting important ideas.

Exercise 6.29

First, pre-read the passage quickly and answer these two questions:

1. What is the topic? _____

2. What is the main idea? _____

_____

 Mabel and Her New Friend

Mabel made a new friend. Her name is Angelita. Mabel and Angelita work in the cafeteria of an office building. They both prepare food for lunch. Mabel is a new employee. She got the job a week ago. Angelita, on the other hand, has been working there for six months. Angelita helps Mabel with tasks. For example, she showed Mabel how to operate the meat cutter. Together, they are a good team. They work hard and finish their duties, or tasks, quickly. Their supervisor likes their productivity. He seems happy with their teamwork. They are happy to work together. They made a plan to go shopping together after work. Mabel is glad she made a new friend.

Now that you have pre-read the passage, go back and read it actively.

 ## Exercise 6.30

Actively read the passage about Mabel and Angelita. Follow the steps for reading actively. Review the previous chapters for more information on active reading.

 ## Exercise 6.31

Review the passage and your annotations. Then answer these questions.

1. Where did Mabel make a new friend? _____

2. What is her name? _____

3. Where do they work? _____

4. How does Angelita help Mabel? _____

5. What is their plan? _____

6. How does Mabel feel about her new friend? _____

Writing About It

Let's practice writing! In this section, you will learn the sentence structure composed of a subject, a verb, and a complement.

The SVC Sentence Structure

In Chapter 5, you learned about the subject-verb-object (SVO) sentence structure. In this chapter, we will talk about the subject-verb-complement (SVC) sentence structure. From the SVO discussion, remember these points:

- The subject usually comes at the beginning of the sentence.
- The verb, or action, follows the subject.
- The object follows the verb.

The SVC sentence structure is similar. However, there is no object. Instead, there is a complement (C). Read some examples from the earlier passage about Mabel. In each sentence, the subject is bold, the verb is underlined, and the complement is italicized:

Her **name** <u>is</u> *Angelita*.   **Mabel** <u>is</u> *a new employee*.

Together, **they** <u>are</u> *a good team*.   **He** <u>seems</u> *happy* with their teamwork.

They <u>are</u> *happy* to work together.   **Mabel** <u>is</u> *glad* she made a new friend.

What do you notice about the verbs in these sentences? Are they similar? Most of them are forms of BE. One verb is different: *seem*. Let's learn about the SVC structure.

Identifying the SVC Sentence Structure

The verb (V) in the SVC structure is a linking verb. A **linking verb** links, or connects, two things. In the SVC sentence structure, it links the subject (S) and the complement (C). Here is a list of common linking verbs:

Be	Become	Seem	Appear	Look
Feel	Taste	Smell	Sound	

Linking verbs are like an equal sign. The complement describes the subject.

Her name is Angelita. → Her name = Angelita.

Mabel is a new employee. → Mabel = a new employee.

Together, they are a good team. → They = a good team.

He seems happy with their teamwork. → He = happy.

Let's learn how to find the subject, verb, and complement in a sentence. It's similar to the strategy for the SVO structure. There are three steps:

1. Find the linking verb.

2. Find the subject. The subject is the noun that usually comes before the verb in a simple sentence.

3. Find the complement. The complement follows the linking verb and describes the subject.

Here is an example sentence:

They are happy to work together.

   S   V   C

Practice finding the subject, verb, and complement in the next exercise.

Exercise 6.32

Read the sentences, and find the SVC in each sentence. Use the steps already described to help you. For each sentence, list the verb, the subject, and the complement.

EXAMPLE   Julius appears tired.   Subject: *Julius* / Verb: *appears* / Complement: *tired*

1. Oscar sounds angry.   Subject: _____ / Verb: _____ / Complement: _____

2. Noreen and her cousin feel sad.   Subject: _____ / Verb: _____ / Complement: _____

3. My coworker is absent today.   Subject: _____ / Verb: _____ / Complement: _____

4. The doctor is very kind.   Subject: _____ / Verb: _____ / Complement: _____

5. Making friends is easy.   Subject: _____ / Verb: _____ / Complement: _____

6. Those cookies smell delicious!   Subject: _____ / Verb: _____ / Complement: _____

7. My mother seems satisfied with her meal.   Subject: _____ / Verb: _____ / Complement: _____

8. Cecilia became a high school teacher.   Subject: _____ / Verb: _____ / Complement: _____

What kinds of words are complements? They are nouns, pronouns, and adjectives. They are **not** verbs or adverbs. Let's practice identifying complements.

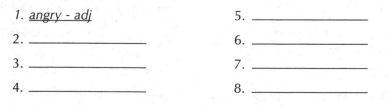

Exercise 6.33

Read the sentences in the previous exercise. Find the complement in each sentence. What part of speech is it—a noun, a pronoun, or an adjective? Note the complement on the line provided, then label it n (noun), pro (pronoun), or adj (adjective). The first one is done for you.

1. *angry - adj*

2. _____

3. _____

4. _____

5. _____

6. _____

7. _____

8. _____

Exercise 6.34

Create sentences about your life using the linking verbs provided. Form one sentence for each verb. Use the correct verb tense and form. Be sure that every complement is a noun, pronoun, or adjective and that every sentence follows the SVC sentence structure. After creating the sentence, use the three steps to check that you have a subject, verb, and complement. Label them S, V, and C, respectively.

EXAMPLE   Taste *That food tastes spicy.*

                 S   V   C

1. Be _____

2. Become _____

3. Seem _____

4. Appear _____

5. Look _____

6. Feel _____

7. Taste _____

8. Smell _____

9. Sound _____

✏ Quiz

You have finished Chapter 6. Great work! Now take the quiz to see what you remember. Choose the correct answers for each question. There may be multiple correct answers for some of the questions.

1. Choose the modals of possibility that complete the sentence correctly.

   Sanjay _____ go to the movies with Ramsay. (about 50 percent certainty)

   will   might   may   must

2. Choose the modals of obligation that complete the sentence correctly.

   Tiffany can't attend the show. She _____ to go to a doctor's appointment.

   must   has   has got   is supposed

3. Choose the modals of ability that complete the sentence correctly.

   Jessie _____ study tonight. He is working. (negative)

   must not   can't   isn't able to   can't be able to

4. What is the correct demonstrative adjective?

   I love _____ shirt. (The speaker is wearing it.)

   this   that   these   those

5. What is the correct demonstrative pronoun?

   _____ are great earrings! (The speaker's friend is wearing them.)

   This   That   These   Those

6. What is the correct possessive pronoun?

   Sheila says to her brother, "My pencil sharpener is broken. Can I use _____?"

   mine   yours   his   theirs

7. Which word replaces the underlined word correctly?

   I'm attending classes <u>at that school</u>.

   here   there

8. Which word replaces the underlined word correctly?

   He lives <u>in this apartment building</u>.

   here   there

9. What is a compliment we do *not* use in small talk?

   Your _____ is beautiful.

   dog   car   jacket   hair

10. What is a rain check? _____

    A raincoat   A postponed event   A credit card   A rain hat

Do It Out There!

Now that you have learned how to talk to people and make friends, try it out in the world. Review this chapter, and go out and use English! Put a checkmark next to each activity as you complete it.

To Do This Week

- ❑ Use two possessive pronouns in conversation.
- ❑ Use two demonstrative adjectives in conversation.
- ❑ Use two demonstrative pronouns in conversation.
- ❑ Use *here* and *there* in place of a demonstrative adjective and place.
- ❑ Make small talk by complimenting two people.
- ❑ Make small talk by asking two people questions.
- ❑ Use two different modals of obligation/necessity.
- ❑ Use two different modals of possibility.
- ❑ Use two different modals of ability.
- ❑ Make friends with someone. Follow the guidelines and conversation suggestions.

Weekly Log

Keep a weekly log of your progress. Make notes on how your practice went. What happened? Was it successful? How do you know it was successful? Was it unsuccessful? How do you know? Review all the instructions, pronunciation tips, and culture notes in Chapter 6.

_____

_____

_____

_____

_____

_____

7

Health and Medicine

In this chapter you will learn about:

Speaking
✓ How to describe symptoms and pain
✓ How to talk to a doctor
✓ How to ask for and give advice
✓ How to ask for permission

Vocabulary, Reading, and Writing
✓ Vocabulary for ailments and anatomy
✓ Time expressions with the present perfect progressive
✓ Adjectives to describe symptoms
✓ Phrasal verbs
✓ How to identify supporting evidence in a paragraph
✓ The structure of a paragraph

Grammar
✓ How to use the present perfect progressive verb tense
✓ Modals of advice
✓ Modals of permission

Body Language
✓ Thumbs-up versus thumbs-down
✓ The gesture for so-so

Talking About Illness

Sometimes we don't feel well. We feel sick. We take care of ourselves. However, sometimes we have to see a doctor for help.

Real Conversation: Describing Pain

Let's see a sample conversation between a patient and a doctor. A **patient** is someone who gets medical care.

DOCTOR: Hello, Lian. What brings you in to see me today?[1]

1. Other expressions: Why are you here to see me today? / How can I help you today? / Why are you here today?

LIAN: I don't feel well.[2] I have a fever,[3] a sore throat, and aches all over my body.[4,5]

2. Other expressions: I feel sick / so sick / very sick / really sick / terrible.

3. A **fever** is a higher-than-normal body temperature. Normal temperature is 98.6°F, or 37.0°C.

4. Lian describes her **symptoms**, meaning the feelings in her body or signs of illness.

5. Other expressions: body aches

DOCTOR: How long have you been feeling[6] this way?

6. Use the present perfect progressive verb tense to talk about events or feelings that started in the past and continue now.

LIAN: For more than a week.[7] That's a long time. I'm never sick this long.

7. To talk about a length of time, use *for* + amount of time (for three days) or *since* + day/date/time (since last Monday).

DOCTOR: Well, your vitals[8] look okay. Except your temperature, which is 100.[9] Any other aches and pains?[10]

8. *Vitals* is short for **vital signs,** which are standard clinical tests of body functions such as blood pressure and temperature.

9. 100 degrees Fahrenheit.

10. We often shorten questions. The doctor's complete question here would be *Do you have any other aches and pains?* or *Are there any other aches and pains?*

(continued)

LIAN: I also have a headache.[11] And sometimes I get a stomachache.[11]

DOCTOR: Can you describe your headache?[12] Is it dull[13] or throbbing[14]?

LIAN: It's dull. It's right here. (Points[15]) I've been taking[6] aspirin, but it doesn't help much.[16]

DOCTOR: Well, let's take a look at your throat. (Gets tongue depressor[17]) Stick out[18] your tongue and say, "Ah."

DOCTOR: Ah ha. Mm hm.[19] Well, it looks like you have strep throat.[20] There are white spots on your tongue, and your throat is raw[21] and red. That explains your symptoms.[22]

LIAN: How did I get[23] strep throat?

11. **Pronunciation note:** In English, **ch** sometimes sounds like /k/, so *ache* rhymes with *rake*. The phonetic spelling is /**eyk**/, /**eik**/, and /**eɪk**/.

12. Other expressions: What does your headache feel like? / What's your headache like? / What kind of headache is it?

13. **Dull** means steady but not too strong.

14. **Throbbing** means having a regular beat, usually strong. Synonyms include *pounding* and *pulsating*.

15. Pointing at the part of the body that hurts helps the doctor understand. It's okay to point with the index finger.

16. Other expressions: but it isn't helping much. / but it's not making a big difference. / but it's not working./ but it isn't doing anything.

17. A **tongue depressor** is a flat, wooden stick used by doctors to inspect the mouth and throat. The doctor presses it on the tongue.

18. To **stick out** means to extend.

19. These are sounds someone makes when they are inspecting and/or thinking.

20. **Strep throat** is a severe sore throat caused by a bacterium called streptococcus.

21. Here, **raw** means tender and sore.

22. In this situation, the symptoms are a headache, a sore throat, a fever, and sometimes a stomachache.

23. Another possible expression: How did I contract / What causes…?

DOCTOR: Well, it's passed[24] from person to person. It's carried by saliva.[25] You might want to[26] get a new toothbrush. And you should[26] drink out of your own glass.

LIAN: Is it serious? [27]

DOCTOR: It's not serious, because we're going to treat it.[28] If you let it go,[29] however, it would be much more serious. I'm going to take a specimen[30] and do a test just to make sure.[31] Please say, "Ah" again. I'm going to swab[32] the back of your throat to get a sample and send it to the lab. The results take about 15 minutes.

LIAN: Okay. How do we treat[28] strep throat, Doctor?[27]

DOCTOR: We treat it with antibiotics.[33] It's a common and effective treatment. I'll write you a prescription,[34] and you can get it filled in the pharmacy.

LIAN: Is there anything else I should[26] do?[35]

DOCTOR: Right now, you can sit in the waiting room. I'll call you when the results are in.[36] At home, make sure[31] you get plenty of rest and wash your hands often. Do not[37] cough into your hand; cough into a tissue or handkerchief.[38] You don't want to spread the germs.[39]

LIAN: Okay. So, can I[40] go to work?

DOCTOR: No. You had better[41] stay home and rest.

24. **Passed** means spread.

25. **Saliva** is the fluid in the mouth, or spit.

26. Modal for advice. The antonym would be *should not/shouldn't*.

27. Lian asks a question to learn about the illness.

28. To **treat an illness** means to manage it.

29. To **let something go** means to fail to manage it, to ignore it.

30. A **specimen** is a sample of a microorganism, bacteria, or virus.

31. Other expressions: to be sure / to ensure.

32. To **swab** means to wipe—in this case, to get a specimen.

33. An **antibiotic** is a medicine that stops the growth of microorganisms.

34. A **prescription** is a doctor's written order for medicine.

35. Alternative expression: What else can I do?

36. **When the results are in** means when the doctor knows the test results.

37. *Do not* is a negative imperative. See Chapter 4 for more information.

38. A **handkerchief** is a piece of fabric used for the face.

39. A **germ** is a microorganism that causes disease.

40. *Can I* and *may I* are modals of permission.

41. Modal of advice: had better = strong advice + threat of a bad result.

(continued)

Thirty minutes later

DOCTOR: It's confirmed. It's strep throat. Here's the prescription.[34] You must take *all*[42] of the antibiotics[43] until they run out.[43] You *must not*[44] stop taking them, even if you feel better. The strep will come back if you stop taking the pills. Okay? Please call my office if you have any questions.

42. The doctor stresses *all* to show the importance of the instruction.

43. To **run out** or **run out of** means to have no more; to deplete the supply.

44. *Must not* is a modal for prohibition.

LIAN: Okay. Thank you, Doctor.

DOCTOR: Take care of yourself, Lian.[45]

45. To **take care of someone/oneself** means to keep safe and healthy.

We will talk about many parts of this conversation in this chapter. Let's look first at the present perfect progressive verb tense.

Grammar: Using the Present Perfect Progressive Tense

In English, we use the **present perfect progressive** to talk about the duration of activities that began in the past and continue now. This verb tense is also called the **present perfect continuous**. The activities may be continuous or periodic. Continuous activities do not stop, whereas periodic activities start and stop.

Let's look at some example sentences. *Now* means the moment of speaking. The verb is underlined, and expressions for the duration of time are italicized. The word in parentheses is the base form of the verb.

EXAMPLE 1   (continuous activity): They <u>have been feeling</u> sick *since Wednesday*. (feel)

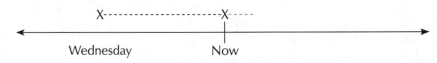

The sickness started on Wednesday, and they are still feeling sick now. This sickness is continuous, or nonstop. It will probably continue into the future.

EXAMPLE 2   (periodic activity): She <u>has been taking</u> tennis lessons *for six months*. (take)

She started tennis lessons six months ago and is still taking them now. This is *not* continuous. It is periodic; it starts and stops. She takes a tennis lesson, then later, she takes another tennis lesson. She will probably continue to take tennis lessons in the future.

EXAMPLE 3   Malcolm <u>hasn't been sleeping</u> well *lately.* (sleep)

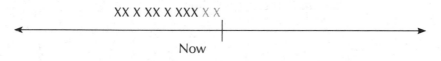

XX X XX X XXX X X

Now

Malcolm isn't sleeping well. It started at some time in the past, but we don't know when. This is *not* continuous; it is periodic. It will probably continue into the future.

Now let's study how to form the present perfect progressive verb tense.

The Present Perfect Progressive: Affirmative Form

When we form the present perfect progressive tense, we use two auxiliary verbs and the main verb: *have/has* + *been* + main verb-**ing**. As you study the following table, read the example sentences aloud.

SUBJECT OR SUBJECT PRONOUN	HAVE OR HAS*	BEEN	MAIN VERB-ING	EXAMPLE SENTENCES
I/You/We/They	have	been	studying	They have been studying English for three hours. Jack and Jill have been studying English for three hours.
He/She/It	has	been	watching	He has been watching TV since 10:00 A.M. Jack has been watching TV since 10:00 A.M.

*Be sure to use the correct form—*have* or *has*—so there is subject-verb agreement.

Note: Watch your spelling! Follow the spelling rules of the verb-**ing** form in Chapter 3.

> **Pronunciation note:** The word *been* is pronounced differently in different places. In the United States, it's often pronounced like /bɪn/ and rhymes with *in*. In parts of Canada and the United Kingdom, *been* sounds more like *bean*, or /biyn/.

Let's practice forming the present perfect progressive tense.

Exercise 7.1

Complete the following sentences with the present perfect progressive form of the verb given in parentheses.

EXAMPLE   (suffer) Venkata *has been suffering* from a headache since this morning.

*have/has + been + verb-**ing***

1. (take) I _____ _____ _____ the medicine every day for two weeks.

2. (drink) Bao _____ _____ _____ this medicinal tea all day.

3. (feel) Xiang and Feng _____ _____ _____ sick since yesterday.

4. (recover) My father _____ _____ _____ from surgery for a long time.

5. (rest) They _____ _____ _____ all afternoon.

6. (eat) His sister _____ _____ _____ organic vegetables the whole summer.

7. (read) Sam _____ _____ _____ in bed since he got the flu.

8. (feel) Carolina _____ _____ _____ better lately.

The Present Perfect Progressive: Forming Contractions

We can contract the subject pronoun and the auxiliary *have/has*. As you study these contractions, read the example sentences aloud.

SUBJECT PRONOUN	HAVE OR HAS	CONTRACTION	BEEN	MAIN VERB-ING	EXAMPLE SENTENCES
I	have	I've	been	studying	They've been studying
You		You've			English for three hours.
We		We've			
They		They've			
He	has	He's	been	watching	He's been watching TV
She		She's			since 10:00 A.M.
It		It's			

Note: We sometimes contract the third person singular subject and *has*; for example, we would write *Joe's been watching TV since 10:00 A.M.*

Note: We do *not* use stative verbs such as *be, seem, love,* and *understand* with the present perfect progressive verb tense.

Let's practice contractions with the present perfect progressive.

Exercise 7.2

Use the sentences from Exercise 7.1 to help you complete the following sentences. Use contractions. If the subject is not a pronoun, make it a pronoun. If the subject is third person singular, contract it two ways: with the subject and with the correct subject pronoun.

EXAMPLES   (I) *I've been taking* the medicine every day for two weeks.

(Bao) *He's been drinking* this medicinal tea all day. / *Bao's been drinking* this medicinal tea all day.

1. (Xiang and Feng) _____ sick since yesterday.
2. (My father) _____ from surgery for a long time.
3. (They) _____ all afternoon.
4. (His sister) _____ organic vegetables the whole summer.
5. (Sam) _____ in bed since he got the flu.
6. (Carolina) _____ better lately.

In English, we use particular time expressions with the present perfect progressive. Let's look at these.

The Present Perfect Progressive: Time Expressions

Here are some common time expressions that we use with the present perfect progressive verb tense. These expressions can come at the beginning or the end of the sentence. At the beginning, they are followed by a comma.

TIME EXPRESSION	EXAMPLE SENTENCES
Since + time/day/date	She's been sleeping since 7:00 P.M.
	Since 7:00 P.M, she's been sleeping.
For + amount of time	They've been studying for two hours.
	For two hours, they've been studying.
All + morning/day/week/month/ year	He's been complaining all morning.
	All morning, he's been complaining.
The whole + period of time (summer/day/year)	I've been skiing the whole winter.
	The whole winter, I've been skiing.
In the past + period of time (four days/few weeks/couple of years)	We haven't been feeling well in the past few days.
	In the past few days, we haven't been feeling well.
This past + period of time	He hasn't been feeling well this past week.
	This past week, he hasn't been feeling well.
Lately	She's been drinking lots of water lately.
	Lately, she's been drinking lots of water.
Recently	She's been working too much recently.
	Recently, she's been working too much.

Now that you know some time expressions for the present perfect progressive, practice identifying them.

Exercise 7.3

Go back to Exercise 7.2 and note the time expressions in each sentence.

1. _____

2. _____

3. _____

4. _____

5. _____

6. _____

Now let's practice forming sentences with the affirmative present perfect progressive and time expressions.

Exercise 7.4

Create sentences using the words given. Use the verb in the present perfect progressive verb tense and a time expression from the preceding list. Don't forget to start each sentence with a capital letter and end it with a period.

EXAMPLE 1   Virginia / walk / to school / this past week.

   Virginia has been walking to school this past week.

EXAMPLE 2   Tory and Gemma / go / to the gym / lately.

   Tory and Gemma have been going to the gym lately.

1. Kristi / study / all night / for her exam tomorrow.

   _____

2. Cathy and Ned / meditate / for 30 minutes.

   _____

3. Recently, / we / wake up / late.

   _____

4. Lately, / you / eat / a lot of fast food.

   _____

5. I / exercise / hard / the whole summer.

_____

6. He / diet / since January.

_____

Exercise 7.5

Form sentences using the present perfect progressive to talk about activities you have been doing lately. Include your friends and your family too. Use time expressions from the list. Don't forget to start each sentence with a capital letter and end it with a period.

1. _____
2. _____
3. _____
4. _____

The Present Perfect Progressive: Forming the Negative

Now let's use the negative form of the present perfect progressive. In the negative form, we use two auxiliary verbs and *not* plus the main verb: *have/has* + *not* + *been* + main verb-**ing.** As you study the following table, read the example sentences aloud.

SUBJECT OR SUBJECT PRONOUN	HAVE OR HAS	NOT	BEEN	MAIN VERB-ING	EXAMPLE SENTENCES
I/You/We/They	have	not	been	studying	They have not been studying English for three hours.
He/She/It	has	not	been	watching	He has not been watching TV since 10:00 A.M.

Let's practice using the negative form of the present perfect progressive.

Exercise 7.6

Complete the sentences with the correct negative form of the present perfect progressive verb tense. Use the preceding table to help you.

EXAMPLE   (come) Anthony *has not been coming* to basketball practice lately.

1. (feel) Solange _____ very well all day. She's been sleeping.
2. (sing) The performers _____ traditional songs all semester. They've been singing new ones.

3. (shave) Mr. Foster _____ his face. He's been growing a beard and mustache.

4. (have) Lately, we _____ fun. We've been working too hard.

5. (suffer) My daughter _____ from allergies. She's been breathing easily.

6. (go) Henrietta _____ to church this past month. She's been recovering from a broken leg.

The Present Perfect Progressive: Forming Negative Contractions

In English, we usually use contractions. It's less formal. There are two ways we can contract the negative present perfect progressive. The most common way is shown in the first table, and a less common way appears in the second table. As you look at the tables, be sure to read the example sentences aloud.

Contraction: *Have/Has + Not*

SUBJECT OR SUBJECT PRONOUN	HAVE OR HAS	NOT	CONTRACTION	BEEN	MAIN VERB-ING	EXAMPLE SENTENCES
I/You/We/They	have	not	haven't	been	studying	They haven't been studying English for three hours.
He/She/It	has	not	hasn't	been	watching	He hasn't been watching TV since 10:00 A.M.

> **Culture Note:** This type of contraction is more common in British English.

Contraction: Subject Pronoun + *Have/Has*

SUBJECT PRONOUN	HAVE OR HAS	CONTRACTION	NOT*	BEEN	MAIN VERB-ING	EXAMPLE SENTENCES
I	have	I've	not	been	studying	They've not been studying English for three hours.
You		You've				
We		We've				
They		They've				
He	has	He's	not	been	watching	He's not been watching TV since 10:00 A.M.
She		She's				
It		It's				

*When we use this form, the word *not* is stressed.

Let's practice using negative contractions of the present perfect progressive.

✏️ **Exercise 7.7**

look at the sentences you wrote in Exercise 7.6. Re-create those sentences using the most common type of contraction.

EXAMPLE   *Anthony hasn't been coming to basketball practice lately.*

1. _____

2. _____

3. _____

4. _____

5. _____

6. _____

✏️ **Exercise 7.8**

Create sentences with the words given. First, use the negative present perfect progressive verb form. Then create a sentence using the most common form of the negative contraction. Use subject pronouns and don't forget to put a period at the end of every sentence.

EXAMPLE   Brian is sick. He / NEGATIVE / go / to school / this week.

He has not been going to school this week.

He hasn't been going to school this week.

1. Charlene and Greg are in Asia for work. They / NEGATIVE / come / to the sales meetings / lately.

_____

_____

2. Kushal, Wen, and Crystal are on a safari vacation. They / NEGATIVE / check / e-mail / for two weeks.

_____

_____

3. My dog is sick. I / NEGATIVE / go / to the dog park / since Monday.

_____

_____

4. Sven is consulting with companies now. He / NEGATIVE / relax / since he retired.

_____

5. Yifei is in China now. He / NEGATIVE / play / golf / in Los Angeles / for weeks.

_____

6. Sherry just had a baby in July. She / NEGATIVE / sleep / since she had the baby.

_____

_____

The Present Perfect Progressive: Forming Yes/No Questions

In conversation, we ask yes/no questions about what people have been doing. As you know from previous chapters, we answer yes/no questions with either *yes* or *no*. See how to form these questions with the present perfect progressive in the following table.

HAVE OR HAS	SUBJECT OR SUBJECT PRONOUN	BEEN	MAIN VERB-ING	REST OF SENTENCE	EXAMPLE SENTENCES
Have	I/you/we/they	been	going	to the gym lately?	Have you been going to the gym lately?
Has	he/she/it	been	enjoying	retirement?	Has he been enjoying retirement?*

*When the duration of time is understood or unimportant, we omit the time expression.

Pronunciation Tip
Remember to use rising pitch at the end of yes/no questions because they indicate uncertainty. See the pitch chart in the Appendix for more information.

You can answer a yes/no question with a long answer, using the complete verb tense and including all parts of the sentence. Or you can give a short answer that includes only part of the verb tense. You can also give a quick answer—*yes* or *no*. All of these types of answers are acceptable. Note that long answers use the present perfect progressive tense form of the verb, and the short answer uses only the auxiliary *have/has* and sometimes *been*. Here are some examples.

YES/NO QUESTION: Have you been going to the gym lately?

Affirmative Answers

LONG ANSWER: Yes, I **have** *been going* to the gym lately.

SHORT ANSWER: Yes, I **have**. / Yes, I **have** *been*.

QUICK ANSWER: Yes. (You can also use an alternative expression for *yes*. See Chapter 1 for alternatives.)

Negative Answers

LONG ANSWER: No, I **haven't** *been going* to the gym lately.

SHORT ANSWER: No, I **haven't**. / No, I **haven't** *been*. / No, I have **not**.

QUICK ANSWER: No. (You can also use an alternative expression for *no*. See Chapter 1 for alternatives.)

> When the answer is negative, we often provide a reason or cause. For example, we might say "No, I haven't been going to the gym lately. I haven't been feeling very well." Or we might say, "No, because I haven't been feeling well." Or we say, "No, I haven't. I'm sick."

Pronunciation Tip

For long affirmative answers, stress *have/has*: *Yes, I **have** been going to the gym lately.* For short affirmative answers, stress *have/has*: *Yes, I **have**.* For long and short negative answers, stress the negative contraction or *not*: *No, I **haven't** been going to the gym lately. / No, I **haven't**. / No, I have **not**.* **Note:** Do not stress the quick answers.

The Present Perfect Progressive: Short Answers to *Yes/No* Questions

Study the rules we use to form short answers to yes/no questions.

Rules

- Omit the main verb in short answers.

- Do not contract the affirmative short answer.

YES OR NO + COMMA	SUBJECT OR SUBJECT PRONOUN	HAVE OR HAS	NEGATIVE	EXAMPLE SHORT ANSWERS
Yes,	I/you/we/they	have	—	Yes, I have. / Yes, I have been.
No,	I/you/we/they	have	not n't	No, they have not. / No, they haven't. / No, they haven't been.
Yes,	he/she/it	has	—	Yes, she has. / Yes, she has been.
No,	he/she/it	has	not n't	No, she has not. / No, she hasn't. / No, she hasn't been.

Exercise 7.9

Form yes/no questions with the present perfect progressive verb tense using the words given. Then create long, short, and quick answers to the questions. Answer the questions affirmatively (Yes) or negatively (No) as indicated.

EXAMPLE 1   Have/Has / Charlotte / jog / around the lake / lately? (Yes)

QUESTION: *Has Charlotte been jogging around the lake lately?*

LONG ANSWER: *Yes, she has been jogging around the lake lately.*

SHORT ANSWER: *Yes, she has. / Yes, she has been.*

QUICK ANSWER: *Yes.*

EXAMPLE 2   Have/Has / Charlotte / jog / around the lake / lately? (No)

QUESTION: *Has Charlotte been jogging around the lake lately?*

LONG ANSWER: *No, she hasn't been jogging around the lake lately.*

SHORT ANSWER: *No, she has not. / No, she hasn't. / No, she hasn't been.*

QUICK ANSWER: *No.*

1. Have/Has / he / recover / from his surgery? (Yes)

   QUESTION: _____

   LONG ANSWER: _____

   SHORT ANSWER: _____   QUICK ANSWER: _____

2. Have/Has / Jigar / enjoy / his vacation / so far? (Yes)

   QUESTION: _____

   LONG ANSWER: _____

   SHORT ANSWER: _____   QUICK ANSWER: _____

   > **So far** is a time expression sometimes used with the present perfect progressive. It means "up until now."

3. Have/Has / you / suffer / from allergies / in the past week? (No)

   QUESTION: _____

   LONG ANSWER: _____

   SHORT ANSWER: _____   QUICK ANSWER: _____

4. Have/Has / Joey and Carlos / play / baseball / all spring? (Yes)

QUESTION: _____

LONG ANSWER: _____

SHORT ANSWER: _____   QUICK ANSWER: _____

5. Have/Has / Marion / take / her medicine / since the doctor's visit? (No)

QUESTION: _____

LONG ANSWER: _____

SHORT ANSWER: _____   QUICK ANSWER: _____

6. Have/Has / she / prepare dinner / for an hour? (Yes)

QUESTION: _____

LONG ANSWER: _____

SHORT ANSWER: _____   QUICK ANSWER: _____

The Present Perfect Progressive: Forming WH Questions

In conversation, we ask people about activities that began in the past and continue now. As you know from previous chapters, we use WH questions, or information questions, to ask about the time of, location of, manner of, and reason for an action. WH questions begin with WH question words or phrases such as *who, what, when, where, why, how, how long, how many,* and *how much.* For a list of WH question words, refer to the Appendix. The following table shows how to form these questions with the present perfect progressive.

WH QUESTION WORD	HAVE OR HAS	SUBJECT OR SUBJECT PRONOUN	BEEN	MAIN VERB-ING	EXAMPLE SENTENCES
Where	have	I/you/we/they	been	studying	Where have you been studying for the test?
How long	has	he/she/it	been	living	How long has she been living in Singapore?
What	have	I/you/we/they	been	doing	What have they been doing for the past hour?
Why	has	he/she/it	been	drinking	Why has he been drinking so much coffee lately?

For the WH question *who*, we use only *has*—never *have*. Do not add another subject. *Who* is the subject of the sentence. See the example in the following table.

WHO (SUBJECT OF SENTENCE)	HAS	BEEN	MAIN VERB-ING	EXAMPLE SENTENCE
Who	has	been	eating	Who has been eating all of my cereal?

Pronunciation Tip

We usually use falling pitch at the end of WH questions. However, if you need the speaker to repeat information, use rising pitch. See the pitch chart in the Appendix for more information.

Just like with yes/no answers, we can answer WH questions in different ways. We can give long answers using complete sentences. We can also give short answers with only the essential information.

Exercise 7.10

Form WH questions with the present perfect progressive verb tense using the statements given. The appropriate question words and information for answering them are given in parentheses. Form both long and short answers; use subject pronouns in the long answers.

EXAMPLE   Jeremy has been taking his medicine. (How often / every day)

     QUESTION: *How often has Jeremy been taking his medicine?*

     LONG ANSWER: *He's been taking his medicine every day.* (complete sentence)

     SHORT ANSWER: *Every day.* (essential information only)

1. Prisca has been working with international professionals. (Where / in Switzerland)

     QUESTION: _____

     LONG ANSWER: _____

     SHORT ANSWER: _____

2. Danielle and Mike have been planning a round-the-world trip. (How long / for a month)

     QUESTION: _____

     LONG ANSWER: _____

     SHORT ANSWER: _____

3. Hailey has been seeing her doctor every week. (Why / for back pain)

QUESTION: _____

LONG ANSWER: _____

SHORT ANSWER: _____

4. Eveline and Paul have been saving for a new house. (How much / half of their paychecks every month)

QUESTION: _____

LONG ANSWER: _____

SHORT ANSWER: _____

5. Michelle has been teaching yoga in her new studio. (How long / since January)

QUESTION: _____

LONG ANSWER: _____

SHORT ANSWER: _____

6. Gerard has been visiting his mother. (Where / in Florida)

QUESTION: _____

LONG ANSWER: _____

SHORT ANSWER: _____

Communication Strategy: Describing Symptoms

When we see a doctor, we describe our symptoms, meaning we explain how we feel and explain signs of the problem. We use two verbs to describe symptoms: *have* and *feel*. Let's look at examples of these verbs in sentences.

HAVE/HAS	FEEL
I have a rash on my arm.	I feel tired all the time.
My son has a toothache.	My daughter feels sick.
I have a stomachache.	I don't feel well.

Vocabulary: Symptoms and Ailments

Now, let's look at some vocabulary for symptoms and ailments. An **ailment** is a sickness. Most of the vocabulary uses the verb *have*. The only vocabulary that uses *feel* is the adjective *dizzy*.

Exercise 7.11

Match the illustration and the vocabulary with the definition.

ILLUSTRATION	VOCABULARY	DEFINITION / SYMPTOMS
	1. A cough _____	a. A sudden forceful release of air through the nose and mouth; protects the lungs from germs
	2. A toothache _____	b. Nausea, pain, and discomfort in the stomach
	3. A sore throat _____	c. Red spots on the skin
	4. Sinus pressure _____	d. Pain in the head area
	5. (Feel) dizzy _____	e. Above-normal body temperature
	6. A stomachache/bellyache/ tummyache _____	f. A feeling of extreme cold; shivering and shaking
	7. A rash _____	g. A pain in the tooth
	8. A sneeze _____	h. A pain in the ear
	9. A fever _____	i. To spew food from the stomach
	10. A headache _____	j. A push of air from the lungs; releases fluid from the lungs through the mouth

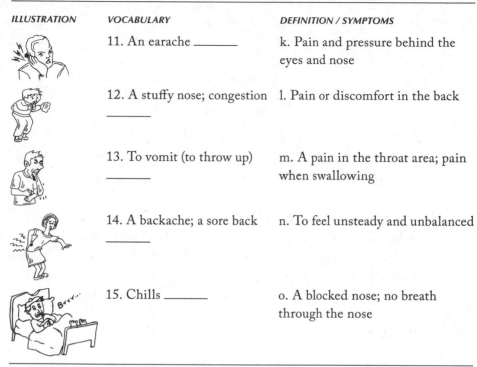

ILLUSTRATION	VOCABULARY	DEFINITION / SYMPTOMS
	11. An earache _____	k. Pain and pressure behind the eyes and nose
	12. A stuffy nose; congestion _____	l. Pain or discomfort in the back
	13. To vomit (to throw up) _____	m. A pain in the throat area; pain when swallowing
	14. A backache; a sore back _____	n. To feel unsteady and unbalanced
	15. Chills _____	o. A blocked nose; no breath through the nose

Now that we have discussed symptoms and ailments, let's practice vocabulary for different parts of the body, or **anatomy**. When you see a doctor, you need to describe the problem in your body. Here is some vocabulary to help you

Exercise 7.12

Look at the illustration of the human body, with numbers pointing to the different parts. Match the names of the body parts from the following list to the numbers on the illustration. Number 1 is done for you (see following page).

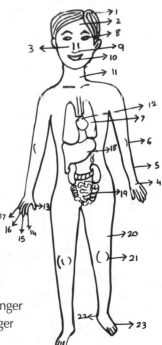

Intestines	Thumb	Pinkie	Lungs	Heart	Forehead
Stomach	Wrist	Ankle	Knee	Elbow	Middle finger
Ring finger	Eyes	Hand	Sinus	Thigh	Index finger
Throat	Nose	Mouth	Foot	Hair	

1. _Hair_	9. _____	17. _____
2. _____	10. _____	18. _____
3. _____	11. _____	19. _____
4. _____	12. _____	20. _____
5. _____	13. _____	21. _____
6. _____	14. _____	22. _____
7. _____	15. _____	23. _____
8. _____	16. _____	

Adjectives and Adverbs to Describe Pain

Sometimes, you need to describe the intensity of the pain you are experiencing. How do you describe how much pain you feel? We use adjectives and adverbs to describe how we feel.

Exercise 7.13

Look at some common expressions we use to describe pain. Note where these expressions belong on the scale of pain.

No pain   A lot of pain

←————————————————————————————————→

Really hurts   A little pain
Severe pain   Kind of hurts

1. _____   2. _____   3. _____   4. _____

Here are some example sentences using adjectives and adverbs. The adjectives and adverbs are in bold. The verb in each sentence is underlined.

1. I <u>feel</u> **a little** pain.

2. It **kind of** <u>hurts</u> here. (point to pain)

3. It **really** <u>hurts</u>, Doctor.

4. I <u>am</u> in **severe** pain. / I <u>feel</u> **severe** pain here.

Culture Note
In the United States, we sometimes use gestures to describe how we feel. Here are different ways we do this.

Thumbs-Up
Meaning: I feel good. / Things are fine.
You learned how to give a thumbs-up in Chapter 5.

Thumbs-Down
Meaning: I don't feel well. / I feel bad. / Things are *not* fine.
A thumbs-down is the opposite of a thumbs-up.

So-So
Meaning: I feel okay—not good and not bad. / I feel so-so.
To make this gesture, we use one hand with the palm down and pivot it left and right quickly a couple of times.

Consulting a Doctor

When you are sick, you **consult**—or ask advice from—a doctor. The doctor gives you advice on health, illness, and medicines. It's important to understand what your doctor tells you. Let's talk about some of the expressions and communication skills you will need when you go to the doctor.

Communication Strategy: Giving Advice

Many people give **advice**, which is guidance or help. Doctors give advice to their patients; parents give advice to their children; teachers give advice to their students; friends give advice to each other; and supervisors give advice to their employees. Do you give advice—maybe to your children, friends, or spouse? Make a list of people to whom you give advice.

_____   _____   _____

Make a list of people who give advice to you.

_____   _____   _____

What are different ways to give advice? List some expressions you've used or heard.

_____   _____   _____

When you give advice, be polite. We are less direct with new friends or people who are superior to us personally or professionally. We are more direct with family and friends. Let's look at some ways to give advice.

Modals of Advice

For advice, we use modal auxiliary verbs. Here are some examples:

> You **should** get plenty of rest.

> She **ought to** take vitamins.

> Tony **had better** take his medicine, or he'll get worse.

> He **might want to** eat more vegetables.

As you learned in Chapter 6, modal auxiliary verbs, or modals, are used with main verbs. We always use the base form of the main verb. Here's how to form modals of advice.

SUBJECT OR SUBJECT PRONOUN	MODAL OF ADVICE	BASE FORM OF MAIN VERB	EXAMPLE SENTENCES	MEANING/USE
I	should	exercise	I should exercise more.	Advice
We	had better	pass	We had better pass the final exam. (Or we'll fail the class.)	Strong advice with the threat of a bad result; more direct
She	ought to*	relax	She ought to relax.	Advice
You	might want to*	eat	You might want to eat healthier foods.	Polite advice; less direct; more of a suggestion

*These modals require *to*.

 Caution

Had better is strong and direct. If the subject is *you*, the speaker is usually a superior or a good friend. For example, in the advice *You had better do your homework on time*, the speaker is probably a teacher; a teacher is superior to a student. The advice *You had better eat all your vegetables or you won't get dessert* is probably spoken by a parent; a parent is superior to a child. A good friend might give this advice: *You had better let me come with you to the party.* Superiors, good friends, and family can be more direct with each other. Use this modal of advice only when appropriate.

Use the base form of the main verb, which is the same for all subjects—*I*, *you*, *we*, *they*, *he*, *she*, and *it*. Let's practice forming sentences with modals of advice.

Exercise 7.14

Create sentences using the words provided. Form four sentences for each question. Review how to form modals of advice, and remember to include to *with* ought *and* might want.

EXAMPLE   We / MODAL OF ADVICE / study / more / for the test.

Answer 1: *We should study more for the test.*

Answer 2: *We had better study more for the test.*

Answer 3: *We ought to study more for the test.*

Answer 4: *We might want to study more for the test.*

1. You / MODAL OF ADVICE / drink / more water / every day.

   _____

   _____

   _____

2. Melody / MODAL OF ADVICE / get / eight hours of sleep / every night.

   _____

   _____

   _____

3. They / MODAL OF ADVICE / pay / the rent / on time.

   _____

   _____

   _____

4. Fawn / MODAL OF ADVICE / do / her homework / every night.

   _____

   _____

   _____

5. He / MODAL OF ADVICE / take / his antibiotics / every day until they're gone.

   _____

   _____

   _____

6. You / MODAL OF ADVICE / go / to the dentist / soon.

_____

_____

_____

7. I / MODAL OF ADVICE / talk / to my supervisor / about the problem.

_____

_____

_____

8. She / MODAL OF ADVICE / make / an appointment / with the doctor.

_____

_____

_____

 Exercise 7.15

When you give advice to people, be polite. Complete each sentence with the modal of advice that is appropriate to the situation.

1. Jenny and Tasha are best friends. Tasha is giving Jenny advice about homework.

   Jenny, you _____ finish the project fast so we can go shopping!

2. Jordan is Derek's older brother. He is babysitting Derek and giving his little brother advice about behaving.

   Jordan: Derek, you _____ behave, or I'll tell Mom and Dad.

3. Miss Tango is Stephanie's fifth-grade teacher. She is giving Stephanie advice about her science project.

   Miss Tango: Stephanie, you _____ research three topics first. Then you can choose your favorite.

4. Jody is a new neighbor meeting Aida for the first time. They are talking about flower gardens. Jody is giving Aida advice about flowers.

   Jody: You _____ plant roses here. Do you like roses?

Exercise 7.16

Create four sentences in which you give advice to someone you know. Review how to form modals of advice.

1. should _____

2. had better _____

3. ought to _____

4. might want to _____

Now that you have practiced giving advice, let's learn how to ask for advice.

Communication Strategy: Asking for Advice

Sometimes, we need to ask people for guidance. Students ask teachers for advice; patients ask doctors; friends ask friends; employees ask supervisors; and children ask parents. To ask for advice, we use *should*. Read the following situations to see how people ask for help.

Situation 1: Simone wants advice on her hair. She asks her friend Deb.

Simone: My hair is getting too long. Should I get it cut?

Situation 2: Paul wants advice about which college to attend. He asks his guidance counselor at school.

Paul: I like Paley College, but I also like Shubert Community College. Where should I go?

Situation 3: Fiona is in sixth grade. Another student cheated on the recent math test by copying Fiona's answers. Fiona asks her mother for advice.

Fiona: Should I tell the teacher? I don't want to get anyone in trouble. But she cheated off *my* test! I studied hard. What should I do?

Grammar: Yes/No Questions with *Should*

We ask yes/no and WH questions with *should*. Here's how to form yes/no questions.

MODAL OF ADVICE	SUBJECT OR PRONOUN	BASE FORM OF MAIN VERB	EXAMPLE SENTENCES
Should	I/you/we/they/ he/she/it	go study be	Should I go to the party? Should she study all night for the test? Should the party be on Friday night?

Pronunciation Tip
Remember to use rising pitch at the end of yes/no questions, which indicate uncertainty. See the pitch chart in the Appendix for more information.

You can answer yes/no questions with long answers that use all parts of the sentence. You can also give a short answer using only *should*. Or you can give a quick answer—*yes* or *no*. All of these answers are acceptable.

Exercise 7.17

Ask for advice by forming yes/no questions with should *using the words given. Then create long, short, and quick answers to each question. Answer the questions affirmatively (Yes) or negatively (No) as indicated. Follow the examples. Stressed words or syllables are in bold.*

EXAMPLE 1   Should / I / work / late today? (Yes)

QUESTION: *Should I work **late** today?*

LONG ANSWER: *Yes, you **should** work late today.*

SHORT ANSWER: *Yes, you **should**.*

QUICK ANSWER: *Yes.*

EXAMPLE 2   Should / I / work / late today? (No)

QUESTION: *Should I work **late** today?*

LONG ANSWER: *No, you **should**n't work late today.*

SHORT ANSWER: *No, you **should**n't. / No, you should **not**.*

QUICK ANSWER: *No.*

1. Should / she / clean / the house / today? (Yes)

    QUESTION: _____

    LONG ANSWER: _____

    SHORT ANSWER: _____   QUICK ANSWER: _____

2. Should / Trevor / take / this job? (Yes)

    QUESTION: _____

    LONG ANSWER: _____

    SHORT ANSWER: _____   QUICK ANSWER: _____

3. Should / Marlene and Joyce / eat / at the new restaurant? (No)

QUESTION: _____

LONG ANSWER: _____

SHORT ANSWER: _____ QUICK ANSWER: _____

4. Should / Cheryl / join / the gym? (Yes)

QUESTION: _____

LONG ANSWER: _____

SHORT ANSWER: _____ QUICK ANSWER: _____

5. Should / Bobby / fix / his car? (No)

QUESTION: _____

LONG ANSWER: _____

SHORT ANSWER: _____ QUICK ANSWER: _____

6. Should / Jeanine / color / her hair? (Yes)

QUESTION: _____

LONG ANSWER: _____

SHORT ANSWER: _____ QUICK ANSWER: _____

Exercise 7.18

Ask for advice by creating four yes/no questions using should. Review and use the example sentences in the previous exercise to guide you.

1. _____

2. _____

3. _____

4. _____

Grammar: WH Questions with *Should*

Now that you have practiced yes/no questions, let's study WH questions. Look at the following table, and read the example sentences aloud.

WH QUESTION WORD	MODAL OF ADVICE	SUBJECT OR SUBJECT PRONOUN	BASE FORM OF MAIN VERB	EXAMPLE SENTENCES
Where	should	I/you/we/they/	buy	Where should I buy a new dress?
When		he/she/it	talk	When should she talk to the boss?
How			tell	How should I tell her?
Which one/			choose	Which one should I choose?
Which + noun				Which college should I choose?
Who/Whom (object of verb)			ask	Who/Whom should we ask for directions?

When *who* is the subject of the sentence, we do not add another sub-ject. We do not add *I*, *you*, *we*, *they*, *he*, *she*, or *it*. The following table gives examples.

WHO (SUBJECT OF SENTENCE)	MODAL OF ADVICE	BASE FORM OF MAIN VERB	EXAMPLE SENTENCES
Who	should	buy	Who should buy dinner?
		stay	Who should stay late?

Pronunciation Tip

We usually use falling pitch at the end of WH questions. However, if you need the speaker to repeat something, use rising pitch. See the pitch chart in the Appendix for more information.

Like yes/no answers, we answer WH questions in different ways. A long answer is a complete sentence; a short answer gives only the essential infor-mation that answers the question.

Exercise 7.19

Ask for advice concerning others by forming WH questions with should *using the information given. The question word is in parentheses, and the answer to the ques-tion is underlined. Use subject pronouns in the long answer.*

EXAMPLE   Jonathan and his wife should go <u>to Bali</u> on vacation. (Where)

    QUESTION: *<u>Where should Jonathan and his wife go on vacation?</u>*

    LONG ANSWER: *<u>They should go to Bali.</u>* (complete sentence)

    SHORT ANSWER: *<u>Bali.</u>* (essential information only)

1. Myron should take his medication <u>every morning</u>. (When)

   QUESTION: _____

   LONG ANSWER: _____

   SHORT ANSWER: _____

2. Nick and Sara should buy a house <u>in Peabody</u>. (Where)

   QUESTION: _____

   LONG ANSWER: _____

   SHORT ANSWER: _____

3. Peter and Jeanine should buy <u>the red car</u>. (Which car)

   QUESTION: _____

   LONG ANSWER: _____

   SHORT ANSWER: _____

4. David should go to bed <u>now</u>. (When)

   QUESTION: _____

   LONG ANSWER: _____

   SHORT ANSWER: _____

5. Jackson should study <u>economics</u>. (What)

   QUESTION: _____

   LONG ANSWER: _____

   SHORT ANSWER: _____

6. Stacey should move <u>to California</u>. (Where)

   QUESTION: _____

   LONG ANSWER: _____

   SHORT ANSWER: _____

Exercise 7.20

Ask for advice concerning others by creating four WH questions using should. *Review the example sentences from the previous exercise to guide you.*

1. _____

2. _____

3. _____

4. _____

Communication Strategy: Asking for Permission

Sometimes, we ask for permission to do things, as illustrated in the following examples.

Situation 1: Frankie is five years old. He wants an ice cream cone. He asks his father for permission.

FRANKIE: Daddy, *can I* have an ice cream cone?

Situation 2: Vicky is at work. She is meeting with her supervisor and would like to open the window because it's warm. She asks her boss for permission.

VICKY: *May I* open the window?

Modals of Permission

In English, there are two common ways to ask for permission: *can I* and *may I*. *Can I* is informal, and *may I* is more formal. These are yes/no questions. To make any sentence more polite, add *please*. We usually say *please* after *can I* or *may I*, but you can also put *please* at the end of the sentence. If you do put it at the end, use rising intonation. Let's see how to form modals of permission.

MODAL OF PERMISSION	SUBJECT OR SUBJECT PRONOUN	BASE FORM OF MAIN VERB	EXAMPLE SENTENCES
Can	I/you/they/we/ he/she/it	take	Can I take the medicine in the morning?
May	I*	borrow	May I please borrow the car?

*Notice that we only use the subject pronoun *I* for *may*.

Pronunciation Tip
Remember to use rising pitch at the end of yes/no questions, which indicate uncertainty. See the pitch chart in the Appendix for more information.

Let's practice forming questions that ask for permission.

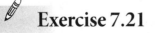

Exercise 7.21

Create questions using the information provided. Review how to form modals of permission, and be sure to put a question mark after each question.

EXAMPLE   MODAL OF PERMISSION / I / go / back to work, Doctor?

Can I go back to work, Doctor?

May I go back to work, Doctor?

1. MODAL OF PERMISSION / I / watch / TV / now?

_____

_____

2. MODAL OF PERMISSION / I / wear / your necklace / to the party?

_____

_____

3. MODAL OF PERMISSION / I / get / a new pair of shoes, Mom?

_____

_____

4. MODAL OF PERMISSION / I / take / vacation in July?

_____

_____

Exercise 7.22

Create four questions that ask for permission. Review how to form modals of permission, and be sure to use the appropriate language. If the situation is formal, use may I. _To be polite, use_ please.

1. Can I _____

2. Can I _____

3. May I _____

4. May I _____

Vocabulary: Phrasal Verbs for Health

We use some common phrasal verbs when we talk about health, sickness, hospitals, and medicine. Let's look at these verbs.

Exercise 7.23

*Read the phrasal verbs on the left, then read the definitions on the right. You may know some of these terms. Match the verbs with their appropriate definitions. For the phrasal verbs you do not know, take a guess. Some can be separated with a noun or pronoun; these are shown in **bold**.*

1. _____ To look over **something**/ to look **something** over
2. _____ To fill out **something**/to fill **something** out (American); to fill in **something**/to fill **something** in (British)
3. _____ To call around
4. _____ To come down with **something**
5. _____ To run out of **something**
6. _____ To cross out **something**/to cross **something** out
7. _____ To pass out
8. _____ To pass away
9. _____ To get over **something**
10. _____ To take care of **someone**
11. _____ To take care of **something**
12. _____ To make sure
13. _____ To throw up **something**/to throw **something** up

a. To faint
b. To have no more supply
c. To keep **someone** safe and healthy
d. To check/examine
e. To die
f. To complete (such as a form or an application)
g. To become sick
h. To vomit
i. To call different places on the phone
j. To manage **something**
k. To be sure; to ensure
l. To draw a line through **something**
m. To recover from **something**

Exercise 7.24

Complete the following sentences with the appropriate phrasal verb from the preceding chart. Be sure to use the correct verb tense and form. Review previous chapters for verb tenses if you need help.

EXAMPLE   Lowell *has been filling out* that application for over an hour. (present perfect progressive)

1. Paulette _____ (simple past) the flu a week ago, but she's starting to feel better. She's _____ (present progressive) it.

2. Marie and John _____ their son's homework. They _____ that he did it. (present progressive)

3. Annette's mother is old, so Annette brings her meals and helps her. Annette _____ her mother. (present progressive)

4. I made a mistake on the test. I didn't have an eraser, so I _____ it _____. (simple past)

5. On Sunday, Mr. Wilson _____ his medicine. He needed more, so he _____ to find an open pharmacy. (simple past)

6. Mr. Wilson's neighbor went to the pharmacy and picked up the medicine. He _____ it. (simple past)

Conversation: Putting It All Together

In this chapter, you have learned the following:

1. How to use the present perfect progressive verb tense to talk about activities that started in the past and continue now
2. How to talk to a doctor
3. Some vocabulary for symptoms and ailments
4. Phrasal verbs
5. How to give and ask for advice
6. How to ask for permission

Now let's try to put it all together.

Exercise 7.25

Complete the conversation. Use the present perfect progressive verb tense, time expressions for this tense, communication strategies, and the vocabulary and expressions you learned in this chapter. Review the example conversation at the beginning of the chapter to help you. In this situation, Denise has the flu and she goes to see her doctor. This is their conversation. The doctor begins the conversation.

1. Greet patient. / Doctor: _What brings you in to see me today, Denise?_

2. Describe symptoms. / Denise: _____

3. Ask more about the symptoms. / Doctor: _____

4. Answer question. / Denise: _____

5. Ask duration of symptoms using present perfect progressive. / Doctor:

_____

6. Answer question. / Denise: _____

7. Examine patient; give name of illness (flu). / Doctor: _____

8. Ask question about illness (flu). / Denise: _____

9. Answer question. / Doctor: _____

10. Tell patient about treatment (rest and lots of liquids). / Doctor: _____
    _____

11. Thank doctor. / Denise: _____

12. Say good-bye. / Doctor: _____

Reading About It

In this section, you will learn to identify supporting sentences in a paragraph. We will also review how to pre-read and read actively.

Let's Read Together

Let's read a story about Rohit and his ailment. First, pre-read the passage. Then read it actively. Finally, answer questions about the passage to see if you understand what you read.

Pre-Read

How do you pre-read? To pre-read, you first read the title of the passage; then you read the first sentence of the first paragraph; and finally you read the last sentence of the last paragraph.

Exercise 7.26

First, pre-read the passage quickly and answer these two questions:

1. What is the topic? _____

2. What is the main idea? _____

_____

 **Rohit's Illness**

Rohit Malisetty was very sick. One Saturday, he woke up feeling awful. He had a sore throat, a headache, and a fever of 101°F. His body ached, and he couldn't stand up or walk around easily. He had to move very slowly because his body and head hurt so much. Sometimes, Rohit felt very hot. Other times, he got the chills and shivered. He took some aspirin and stayed in bed all day. However, the next day he felt worse. To make sure he was all right, Rohit called his doctor. The doctor asked Rohit some questions, and Rohit described his symptoms. The doctor confirmed that Rohit had the flu. He had never had the flu before. The doctor prescribed bed rest, lots of liquids, and a fever-reducing painkiller. Rohit followed the doctor's orders. Seven days later, he got over the flu. He was very sick, but he finally recovered.

Read Actively

After you pre-read, you should read actively by circling words you do not know and highlighting important ideas.

To Read Actively
- Underline the topic.
- Note new vocabulary.
- Put a question mark (?) next to unclear parts.
- Take notes.
- Highlight the main idea and key words.
- Mark examples with "Ex."
- Number main points, lists, or ideas.
- List comments or questions.

Identifying Supporting Ideas in a Paragraph

Each paragraph has one main idea, which is usually stated in the first sentence or two of the paragraph. This is the topic sentence. The main idea of a paragraph is always supported with evidence such as reasons, details, examples, or data. **Data** are numbers that prove a fact. Supporting sentences give evidence for the topic sentence. In the paragraph about Rohit, the main idea is his illness. He was very sick. How do you know this? Is there evidence to prove it? What reasons, details, examples, or data support this main idea? His symptoms are details that describe his illness. Therefore, his symptoms are supporting evidence.

Exercise 7.27

Actively read the passage about Rohit. Follow the steps for reading actively.

Exercise 7.28

Explain the main idea of the paragraph. Then list Rohit's symptoms as supporting evidence.

1. Main idea: _____

2. Supporting evidence (symptoms): _____

Exercise 7.29

Read the paragraph again. Find more details, examples, and data that show that Rohit was ill. Note the details, examples, and data here.

1. Details and examples: _____

2. Data: _____

    In the next chapter, you will practice identifying the supporting evidence in a paragraph.

Understand What You Read

Active reading helps you understand the information in the passage. Check your understanding of the passage details by answering the following questions.

Exercise 7.30

Review the passage and your annotations. Then answer these questions about the passage.

1. What illness did Rohit have? _____
2. Had he had this illness before? _____
3. What were his symptoms? _____
4. How did he recover? _____
5. How long did it take for him to recover? _____

Writing About It

Now let's practice writing! The foundation of writing is the sentence. You have been learning how to form sentences—statements and questions—throughout this book. You have also learned two types of sentence structure: the subject-verb-object (SVO) and the subject-verb-complement (SVC). Now we will study the structure of a paragraph.

Structure of a Paragraph

There are three main parts of a paragraph:

1. The topic sentence
2. The supporting sentences
3. The concluding sentence

    Let's take a look at each of these parts.

The Topic Sentence

The topic sentence states the topic and the main idea of the paragraph. It is usually the first sentence. Let's practice identifying the topic sentence. Look back at the paragraph about Rohit. You already know the topic and the main idea of the paragraph. Make a note of them.

TOPIC: _____

MAIN IDEA: _____

Exercise 7.31

Now find the sentence that states this topic and main idea. Where is it? Make a note of the first sentence.

TOPIC SENTENCE: _____

Supporting Sentences

As you learned in the reading section, supporting sentences give evidence that supports the main idea in the topic sentence. There are usually 3 to 20 supporting sentences in a paragraph. They give reasons, details, explanations, descriptions, examples, and data to prove or reinforce the main idea. In the passage about Rohit, most of the sentences are supporting sentences. They show evidence that Rohit was very sick. Some sentences give details such as symptoms, while others describe his actions, such as calling the doctor. One symptom includes data—his 101°F temperature.

Exercise 7.32

Go back to the paragraph about Rohit's illness. Count the supporting sentences in the paragraph.

How many supporting sentences are there? _____

Concluding Sentence

The last part of a paragraph is the concluding sentence, which ends the paragraph. It is the last sentence in the paragraph and usually restates the main idea. Sometimes, the concluding sentence also gives a resolution to a problem.

Exercise 7.33

What is the last sentence in Rohit's story?

Concluding sentence. _____

The last sentence of the paragraph states the main idea again: Rohit was very sick. It also concludes by stating that he recovered. This gives a resolution (recovery) to a problem (sickness).

Quiz

You have finished Chapter 7. Great work! Now take the quiz to see what you remember. Choose the correct answers for each question. There may be multiple correct answers for some of the questions.

1. Select the choices that complete the sentence correctly.

   Samsara _____ to make an appointment with the doctor.

   should   ought

   had better   might want

2. Select the choices that complete the sentence correctly.

   Robby has been feeling sick since _____.

   yesterday   one week

   two days   Friday

3. Select the choices that complete the sentence correctly.

   Sandra has been feeling better for _____.

   yesterday   one week

   two days   Friday

4. Which phrase describes the largest amount of pain? _____

   Really hurts   Severe pain

   A little pain   Kind of hurts

5. You form the present perfect progressive like this: *have/has* + *been* + verb-**ing**. True or False?

6. Mary and Joan are good friends. Mary wants permission to borrow Joan's pen. Which question is appropriate for this situation?

   May I borrow your pen, Joan?   Can I borrow your pen, Joan?

7. Which phrasal verb completes this sentence best?

   Jerry _____ the flu last weekend.

   called around   threw up

   passed out   came down with

8. Which ailment matches the symptoms of feeling unsteady and unbalanced?

   _____

   Cold   Flu

   Dizziness   Indigestion

9. Where is the topic sentence in a paragraph? _____

   First sentence   Middle of the paragraph   Last sentence

10. Where are the supporting sentences in a paragraph? _____

    First sentence   Middle of the paragraph   Last sentence

Do It Out There!

Now that you have learned how to talk about symptoms and ailments, ask for and give advice, and ask for permission, try these skills out in the world. Review this chapter, and go out and use English! Put a checkmark next to each activity as you complete it.

To Do This Week

- ☐ Use the affirmative and negative present perfect progressive verb tense to talk about activities that began in the past and continue now.
- ☐ Use time expressions for the present perfect progressive.
- ☐ Ask for advice using *should*.
- ☐ Give advice using *should*, *ought to*, *might want to*, and *had better*.
- ☐ Describe your symptoms, or physical sensations, to a friend, family member, or doctor.
- ☐ Practice using the vocabulary for human anatomy.
- ☐ Practice using vocabulary for symptoms and ailments.
- ☐ Practice using new phrasal verbs.

Weekly Log

Keep a weekly log of your progress. Make notes on how your practice went. What happened? Was it successful? How do you know it was successful? Was it unsuccessful? How do you know? Review all the instructions, pronunciation tips, and culture notes in Chapter 7.

_____

_____

_____

_____

_____

_____

_____

8

Shopping and Clothing

In this chapter you will learn about:

Speaking
✓ How to ask for help
✓ How to offer help
✓ How to ask for and give opinions
✓ How to describe clothes

Vocabulary, Reading, and Writing
✓ Vocabulary for clothing
✓ Time expressions with the future tense
✓ Adjectives and adverbs to describe clothing
✓ Prepositions used with time
✓ Phrasal verbs
✓ How to write a paragraph

Grammar
✓ How to use the future tense
✓ Object pronouns
✓ Expressions for opinions
✓ How to use comparatives and superlatives

Talking About Shopping

Sometimes we go shopping for clothes. There are many reasons we buy clothes—for a special occasion or to give as gifts. We may need to buy clothes for ourselves, our children, or our spouses. Let's talk about shopping for clothes.

301

Conversation: At a Clothing Store

Read the example conversation that follows between Genevieve, a shopper, and various employees at a department store.

DEPARTMENT STORE CUSTOMER SERVICE SPECIALIST: How may I help you today?[1]

1. A common expression used to offer help.

GENEVIEVE: Hello. I'm looking for[2] the shoe department. Where is it, please[3]?

2. An expression used to ask for help finding something.

3. *Please* makes every question more polite.

DEPARTMENT STORE CUSTOMER SERVICE SPECIALIST: It's on the fourth floor. When you get off the escalator, turn right. It's right there.[4]

4. See Chapter 4 to review giving and receiving directions.

GENEVIEVE: So, I take a right off the escalator on the fourth floor?[4] Thank you so much!

In the shoe department

GENEVIEVE: Excuse me. Can you help me[5] find a pair of boots, please?

5. An expression used to ask for help.

SHOE SALESPERSON: Sure! What are you looking for?

GENEVIEVE: I'm looking for[2] tall, black boots that have a flat heel.

SHOE SALESPERSON: What is your size?

GENEVIEVE: I'm a 7.[6]

6. Alternative expressions: I take a size 7. / My shoe size is 7.

SHOE SALESPERSON: Okay. Well, we have some new boots that just came in over here. (Points) There are three pairs that are tall, black, and flat. What do you think of these?[7]

7. A question used to ask for an opinion.

GENEVIEVE: Well, I don't like[8] these because they are too[9a] fancy.[10] Can I try on[11] the other two pairs, please?

8. Both *like* and *don't like* are expressions to show opinions.

9. *Too* has two meanings:

a. An intensifier that means "more than very" (see Chapter 1); it has a negative connotation.

b. Also.

10. **Fancy** means not plain or simple.

SHOE SALESPERSON: Yes, let me go in the back and check for your size.

Five minutes later

SHOE SALESPERSON: We have both styles in size 7. Try these on.[11]

After Genevieve tries on the first pair

SHOE SALESPERSON: What do you think?[7]

GENEVIEVE: Hm. Well, I like[8] the fit. They're very comfortable. But they're too[9a] wide at the top. I'll try the other pair on.[11]

Five minutes later

GENEVIEVE: I like these boots too.[9b] They are narrower[12] than the others. What do you think?[7] Which ones do you like[8] better?

SHOE SALESPERSON: They're both nice. Which pair makes you happier[12]?

GENEVIEVE: I think the second pair. They fit tighter[12] in the leg, and I like that. Yes, I really like these. Thank you!

SHOE SALESPERSON: My pleasure! Let me box these for you and ring them up.[13]

11. To **try on** means to wear briefly to check the fit.

12. This is a comparative, which is used to identify similarities between things.

13. To **ring something up** is to complete the transaction on a cash register.

Now that you have read a conversation between a customer and a salesperson, let's look at the individual parts of this conversation. We'll start with the future verb tense.

Grammar: Using the Future Verb Tense

In English, we use the *future* verb tense to talk about actions in the future. There are four ways to show future time. We use different ways for different reasons. Study the table that follows.

FUTURE VERB TENSE	USES
Will + base form of the verb	1. To make predictions
	2. To make promises
	3. To make offers
	Note: We do not use *will* to talk about certain plans.

(continued)

FUTURE VERB TENSE	USES
BE going to + base form of the verb	1. To talk about plans or intentions 2. To make predictions for immediate future from evidence **Note:** For plans, this future verb form and the next one are sometimes used interchangeably.
The present progressive verb tense	To talk about plans already arranged **Note:** For plans, this future verb form and the preceding one are sometimes used interchangeably. **Note:** We often use this verb tense with phrases such as *go shopping* and *go swimming*. See Chapter 5 for a list of some of these actions with *go*. Example: He's going shopping this afternoon.
The simple present verb tense	For set schedules such as train and bus schedules

Let's look at some example sentences about the future. The verb is in bold, and time expressions for the future are italicized. The word in parentheses is the base form of the verb.

EXAMPLE 1   John: We **will have** fun at the party *tonight*. (have)

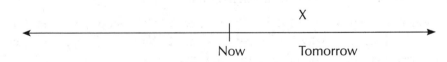

The moment of speaking is 11:00 A.M. The party is in the future—tonight. John predicts that he and his friend are going to have fun at the party. In this example, *will* + base form of the verb is used.

EXAMPLE 2   Jack and Jill **are going to buy** new clothes *tomorrow*. (buy)

The moment of speaking is now. Jack and Jill have a plan to buy new clothes in the future—tomorrow. In this example, *BE going to* + base form of the verb is used.

EXAMPLE 3   He **is flying** to Europe *on Saturday.* (fly)

The moment of speaking is now. He has a plan to travel to Europe in the future—Saturday. He already has his plane ticket. In this example, the present progressive is used because arrangements are already made. You learned about the present progressive in Chapter 3.

EXAMPLE 4   The train **leaves** for Halifax *in an hour.* (leave)

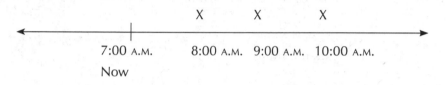

The moment of speaking is now—7:00 A.M. The train runs every hour (8:00 A.M., 9:00 A.M., and 10:00 A.M.). The next train leaves the station at its scheduled departure time an hour from now, which is 8:00 A.M. In this example, we use the simple present because it is a transportation schedule. You learned about the simple present verb tense for schedules in Chapter 4.

Forming the Future Tense

Now, let's learn how to form the future verb tense using *will* and *BE going to.* As you study the tables that follow, be sure to read the example sentences aloud.

The Future: Affirmative Form with *Will*

SUBJECT OR SUBJECT PRONOUN	WILL	BASE FORM OF MAIN VERB	EXAMPLE SENTENCES
I/You/We/ They/He/She/It	will	look	You will look great in your new dress tonight! (prediction)
		give	I will give you the money tomorrow. (promise)
		carry	Do you need help? I will carry the boxes. (offer)

The Future: Affirmative Form with *BE Going To*

SUBJECT OR SUBJECT PRONOUN	BE GOING TO*	BASE FORM OF MAIN VERB	EXAMPLE SENTENCES
I	am going to	buy	I am going to buy a new coat. (plan/intention)
You/We/ They	are going to	leave	We are going to leave at 5:00. (plan/intention)
He/She/It	is going to	rain	Look at those dark clouds. It is going to rain. (prediction from evidence)

*Be sure to use the correct form of BE so there is subject-verb agreement.

> **Pronunciation Note:** Native speakers sometimes say *going to* very quickly, and it sounds like *gonna*.

Let's practice the future verb tenses using *will*, *BE going to*, the present progressive and the simple present.

Exercise 8.1

Complete the following sentences with the future form of the verb given in parentheses. Decide which form is correct for the situation. Use the clue to guide you. Review the different uses for each future verb tense in the previous table.

EXAMPLES   Prediction from evidence: (step) Watch out! You *are going to step* on dog poo!

Promise: (call) I *will call* you next week.

Arranged plan: (play) He *is playing* tennis with his father this weekend.

Schedule: (arrive) The bus *arrives* in 30 minutes.

1. Plan/intention: (do) Jack _____ the homework before class.

2. Prediction: (have) Psychic: You _____ many children!

3. Prediction from evidence: (hit) Be careful, Serafina! You _____ that parked car!

4. Arranged plan: (see) Fred _____ Ben this Tuesday morning.

5. Offer: (hold) I _____ the door open for you.

6. Prediction from evidence: (be) What a clear sky! It _____ a sunny day today.

7. Promise: (finish) I _____ the project by noon tomorrow.

8. Prediction: (win) Fortune cookie: You _____ a lot of money this year.

9. Plan/intention: (clean) Jessie and I _____ the house this weekend.

10. Schedule: (depart) The 56 bus _____ in a few minutes.

11. Arranged plan: (meet) My boss _____ with me later.

12. Promise: (pick up) I _____ the kids at school this afternoon.

Forming Contractions with the Future Tense

We often use contractions when we talk about the future. Let's look at how to contract the future verb tense with *will* and *BE going to*.

The Future: Forming Contractions with *Will*

SUBJECT OR SUBJECT PRONOUN	WILL	CONTRACTION	BASE FORM OF MAIN VERB	EXAMPLE SENTENCES
I	will	I'll	give	I'll give you the money tomorrow.
You		You'll	look	You'll look great in your new dress!
We		We'll	help	We'll help you study for the test.
They		They'll	drive	They'll drive you to the concert.
He		He'll	pass	He'll pass the test easily.
She		She'll	be	She'll be the first one to the mountain.
It		It'll	take	It'll take an hour to drive there.

Pronunciation Note: Some of these contractions sound like other words.

Contraction	Sounds Like	Contraction	Sounds Like
I'll	Aisle, isle	You'll	Yule
We'll	Wheel	He'll	Heel, heal
It'll	Little (rhymes)		

The Future: Forming Contractions with *BE Going To*

SUBJECT OR SUBJECT PRONOUN	BE	CONTRACTION	GOING TO	BASE FORM OF MAIN VERB	EXAMPLE SENTENCES
I	am	I'm	going to	buy	I'm going to buy a new coat.
You	are	You're	going to	leave	We're going to leave at 5:00.
We		We're			
They		They're			
He	is	He's	going to	rain	Look at those dark clouds.
She		She's			It's going to rain.
It		It's			

Pronunciation Note: Some of these contractions sound like other words. For example, *you're* sounds like *your*, and *they're* sounds like *there* and *their*.

Let's practice contractions with the future.

Exercise 8.2

Use the sentences from the previous exercise to complete the following sentences. Use contractions. If the subject is not already a pronoun, make it one. For example, in the first sentence, Jack *becomes* he.

EXAMPLES   Watch out! You*'re going to step* on dog poo!

I*'ll call* you next week.

He*'s playing* tennis with his father this weekend.

It *arrives* in one hour.

Note: We do not use contractions for the simple present tense.

1. (do) Jack _____ the homework before class.

2. (have) You _____ many children!

3. (hit) Be careful, Serafina! You _____ the parked car!

4. (see) Fred _____ Ben this Tuesday morning.

5. (hold) I _____ the door open for you.

6. (be) What a clear sky! It _____ a sunny day today.

7. (finish) I _____ the project by noon tomorrow.

8. (win) Fortune cookie: You _____ a lot of money this year.

9. (clean) Jessie and I _____ the house this weekend.

10. (depart) The 56 bus _____ in a few minutes.

11. (meet) My boss _____ with me later.

12. (pick up) I _____ the kids at school this afternoon.

The Future: Time Expressions

Here are some common time expressions that we use with the future verb tense. The expressions can come at the beginning or the end of the sentence. If at the beginning, follow with a comma as shown in the examples.

TIME EXPRESSIONS	EXAMPLES
In + amount of time (one week, two minutes, three years)	The bus arrives in five minutes. In five minutes, the bus arrives.
This + morning/afternoon/evening/day/ week/month/year	She's going to travel this summer. This summer, she's going to travel.
Next + week/year/name of day or month	He'll pay you next week. Next week, he'll pay you.
Tonight	We're going to see a movie tonight. Tonight, we're going to see a movie.
Tomorrow	He's seeing the dentist tomorrow. Tomorrow, he's seeing the dentist.
Later	I'll do the homework later. Later, I'll do the homework.
Soon	He'll visit soon. Soon, he'll visit.
By + date/time/day*	We'll finish the job by dinnertime. By dinnertime, we'll finish the job.
Before + event/time	I'm going to call her before Friday. Before Friday, I'm going to call her.
After + event/time	I'm going to do it after class. After class, I'm going to do it.

*This phrase is usually used with promises.

Now that you know some time expressions used for the future, practice identifying them.

Exercise 8.3

Go back to Exercise 8.2 and find the time expression in each sentence. Some sentences may not have one.

1. _____   7. _____
2. _____   8. _____
3. _____   9. _____
4. _____   10. _____
5. _____   11. _____
6. _____   12. _____

Now let's practice forming sentences with the affirmative future and time expressions.

Exercise 8.4

Construct sentences using the words given. Put the verb in the future tense, and use time expressions from the previous list. Don't forget to start each sentence with a capital letter and end it with a period.

EXAMPLES   Promise: Ivy / walk / you / to school / this week.

<u>Ivy will walk you to school this week.</u>

Arranged plan: Allen and Leon / start / a guitar lessons/ next Wednesday.

<u>Allen and Leon are starting guitar lessons next Wednesday.</u>

1. Promise: I / complete / the report / by Monday night.

_____

2. Schedule: The train / arrive / in an hour.

_____

3. Offer: I / help/ you / with homework / after class.

_____

4. Plan/intention: Tomorrow night, / we / eat / dinner at the new restaurant.

_____

5. Prediction: You / be / famous / someday soon.

_____

6. Arranged plan: Ella / meet / with her tutor / tomorrow afternoon.

_____

Exercise 8.5

Now form your own sentences using future verb tenses. Talk about activities you will be doing in the future. Include your friends and family, and use time expressions from the list. Don't forget to start each sentence with a capital letter and end it with a period.

1. Promise: _____

2. Plan/intention: _____

3. Prediction: _____

4. Arranged plan: _____

5. Offer: _____

6. Schedule: _____

7. Prediction from evidence: _____

Forming the Negative in the Future Tense

Now let's use the negative form of the future verb tense. As you study the following tables, read the example sentences aloud.

The Future: Negative Form with _Will_*

SUBJECT OR SUBJECT PRONOUN	WILL	NOT	BASE FORM OF MAIN VERB	EXAMPLE SENTENCES
I/You/We/They/ He/She/It	will	not	worry fail	You will not worry about money in your life. (prediction) I will not fail the test tomorrow. (promise/refusal)

*_Will_ + _not_ can mean refusal. For example, _I will not fail the test_ can mean _I refuse to fail the test_.

The Future: Negative Form with *BE Going To**

SUBJECT OR SUBJECT PRONOUN	BE	NOT	GOING TO	BASE FORM OF MAIN VERB	EXAMPLE SENTENCES
I	am	not	going to	buy	I am not going to buy a new coat.
You/We/They	are	not	going to	leave	We are not going to leave at 3:00.
He/She/It	is	not	going to	rain	Look at that clear sky! It is not going to rain today!

*BE + *not going to* can also mean refusal. For example, *I am not going to fail the test* can mean *I refuse to fail the test.*

Let's practice the negative form of the future verb tenses.

 ## Exercise 8.6

Complete the following sentences with the correct negative form of the future verb tense. Use the preceding table to help you, and follow the examples.

EXAMPLES   (play / BE going to) Nguyen *is not going to play* in the tournament this weekend.

(shop / will) Mary *will not shop* in that store. It's too expensive.

1. (go / will) Arielle _____ to the mall this afternoon.

2. (buy / BE going to) My mother _____ any more clothes online.

3. (write / will) Professor Jackson _____ on a chalkboard. He prefers a whiteboard.

4. (work / BE going to) Josie _____ next week. It's a vacation week.

5. (read / will) Carl _____ the newspaper on his tablet. He likes to read a real newspaper.

6. (subscribe / BE going to) We _____ to any more fashion magazines. We already get too many magazines every month.

The Future: Forming Negative Contractions

In English, we usually use contractions when speaking because it's less formal. There is only one way to contract the negative future with *will*. However, there are two ways to contract the negative future with *BE going to*. Look at all of these types of contractions in the following tables.

Negative Contractions with *Will*

SUBJECT OR SUBJECT PRONOUN	WILL	NOT	CONTRACTION	BASE FORM OF MAIN VERB	EXAMPLE SENTENCES
I/You/We/They/	will	not	won't	worry	You won't worry about money in your life. (prediction)
He/She/It				fail	I won't fail the test tomorrow. (promise/refusal)

You already learned about the following type of contraction in Chapter 1, but here is a brief review.

Negative Contraction 1: *BE Going To* (Subject Pronoun + BE)

SUBJECT OR SUBJECT PRONOUN	BE	CONTRACTION*	NOT	GOING TO	BASE FORM OF MAIN VERB	EXAMPLE SENTENCES
I	am	I'm	not	going to	buy	I'm not going to buy a new coat.
You We They	are	You're We're They're	not	going to	leave	We're not going to leave at 5:00.
He She It	is	He's She's It's	not	going to	rain	Look at that clear sky! It's not going to rain today!

*When we use this type of contraction, the word *not* is stressed.

You are also familiar with the next type of contraction from Chapter 1. Here is a quick review.

Negative Contraction 2: *BE Going To* (BE + *Not*)

SUBJECT OR SUBJECT PRONOUN	BE	NOT	CONTRACTION	GOING TO	BASE FORM OF MAIN VERB	EXAMPLE SENTENCES
I	am	not	—	going to	buy	I'm not* going to buy a new coat.
You/We/They	are	not	aren't	going to	leave	We aren't going to leave at 5:00.
He/She/It	is	not	isn't	going to	rain	Look at that clear sky! It isn't going to rain today!

*We never contract *am* + *not*.

Let's practice negative contractions of the future verb tenses.

Exercise 8.7

Look at the sentences you wrote in Exercise 8.6. Re-create those sentences so they are negative contractions. Use all the types of contractions for that future verb tense. Change the subjects to subject pronouns.

EXAMPLES   Nguyen (play / BE going to) in the tournament this weekend.

He's not going to play in the tournament this weekend.

He isn't going to play in the tournament this weekend.

Mary (shop / will) in that store. It's too expensive.

She won't shop in that store. It's too expensive.

1. _____

2. _____

3. _____

4. _____

5. _____

6. _____

Exercise 8.8

Create sentences using the words that follow. First, use the negative future verb form. Then create sentences that use all forms of the negative contraction. Don't forget to put a period at the end of every sentence.

EXAMPLE 1   Toni has no money. She / BE going to/ NEGATIVE / buy / new shoes / this month.

She's not going to buy new shoes this month. / She isn't going to buy new shoes this month.

EXAMPLE 2:   Bill and Tessa have to work late. They / will / NEGATIVE / join / us / for happy hour / this evening.

> **Happy hour** is a period of time when restaurants and bars offer special prices for drinks and food.

They won't join us for happy hour this evening.

1. Charlotta is sick right now. She / BE going to / NEGATIVE / come / to my party / today.

_____

_____

2. Abdul, Chen, and Joe are cooking dinner at home tonight. They / will / NEGATIVE / spend / money on food / tonight.

_____

3. I am home in China. I / BE going to / NEGATIVE / practice / English / every day / here.

_____

4. You are studying for the test tonight. You / will / NEGATIVE / attend / the play / at the theater / tonight.

_____

The Future: Forming Yes/No Questions

In conversation, we ask yes/no questions about what people will do in the future. As you know from previous chapters, we answer yes/no questions with either *yes* or *no*. See how to form these questions in the following tables.

Yes/No Questions with *Will*

WILL	SUBJECT OR SUBJECT PRONOUN	BASE FORM OF MAIN VERB	REST OF SENTENCE	EXAMPLE SENTENCES
Will	I/you/we/they/ he/she/it	come	to the concert tonight?	Will you come to the concert tonight?
Will	I/you/we/they/ he/she/it	hold	these books, please?	Will you hold these books, please? (request)

Yes/No Questions with *BE Going To*

BE VERB	SUBJECT OR SUBJECT PRONOUN	GOING TO	BASE FORM OF MAIN VERB	REST OF SENTENCE	EXAMPLE SENTENCES
Am	I	going to	study	this weekend?	Am I going to study this weekend?
Are	you/we/they	going to	move	into the new apartment Saturday?	Are they going to move into the new apartment Saturday?
Is	he/she/it	going to	graduate	high school this year?	Is she going to graduate high school this year?

Pronunciation Tip

Remember to use rising pitch at the end of yes/no questions, which indicate uncertainty. See the pitch chart in the Appendix for more information.

You can answer yes/no questions with long answers, using the complete verb tense and including all parts of the sentence. You can also give a short answer that includes only part of the verb tense. Finally, you can give a very quick answer—*yes* or *no*. All of these types of answers are acceptable. Note that long answers use the future verb tense and that the short answer uses only part of the verb tense, as in the examples.

EXAMPLE 1　*Will*

YES/NO QUESTION: Will she want any pizza?

Affirmative Answers

LONG ANSWER: Yes, she *will* want some pizza.

SHORT ANSWER: Yes, she *will*.

QUICK ANSWER: Yes. (See Chapter 1 for alternative expressions for *yes*.)

Negative Answers

LONG ANSWER: No, she *won't* want any pizza.

SHORT ANSWER: No, she *won't*. / No, she will *not*.

QUICK ANSWER: No. (See Chapter 1 for alternative expressions for *no*.)

Pronunciation Tip: For both long and short affirmative answers, stress *will*. For both long and short negative answers, stress the negative contraction *won't* or *not*. **Note:** Do not stress quick answers.

EXAMPLE 2   *BE going to*

YES/NO QUESTION: Is she going to graduate high school this year?

Affirmative Answers

LONG ANSWER: Yes, she *is* going to graduate high school this year.

SHORT ANSWER: Yes, she *is*. / Yes, she *is* going to.

QUICK ANSWER: Yes.

Negative Answers

LONG ANSWER: No, she *is*n't going to graduate high school this year.

SHORT ANSWER: No, she *is*n't. / No, she isn't *going* to. / No, she's *not*. / No, she's *not* going to.   QUICK ANSWER: No.

> **Tip**
> When the answer is negative, we often provide a reason or cause. For example, we might say, "No, she isn't going to graduate high school this year. She missed too many classes." Or we might say, "No, because she missed too many classes." For both long and short affirmative answers, stress BE. For long and short negative answers, stress the negative contraction or *not*. **Note:** Do not stress the quick answers.

Let's look at rules for short answers.

Rules

We omit the main verb in short answers.

We never contract the affirmative short answer.

The Future: Short Answers to Yes/No Questions with *Will*

YES *OR* NO + COMMA	SUBJECT OR SUBJECT PRONOUN	WILL	*NEGATIVE*	*NEGATIVE CONTRACTION**
Yes,	I/you/we/they/he/she/it	will	—	Yes, I will.
				~~Yes, I'll.~~
No,	I/you/we/they/he/she/it	will	not n't	No, it will not. / No, it won't.

*We do not use contractions in affirmative answers.

The Future: Short Answers to Yes/No Questions with *BE Going To*

YES OR NO + COMMA	SUBJECT OR SUBJECT PRONOUN	BE	NEGATIVE	NEGATIVE CONTRACTION*
Yes,	I	am	—	Yes, I am. / ~~Yes, I'm.~~
No,	I	am	not	No, I'm not.
Yes,	you/we/they	are	—	Yes, we are. / ~~Yes, we're.~~
No,	you/we/they	are	not n't	No, we're not. / No, we aren't.
Yes,	he/she/it	is	—	Yes, it is. / ~~Yes, it's.~~
No,	he/she/it	is	not n't	No, it's not. / No, it isn't.

*We do not use contractions in affirmative answers.

Exercise 8.9

Form yes/no questions with the future verb tense using the words given. Then create long, short, and quick answers for each question. Answer the questions affirmatively (Yes) or negatively (No) as indicated. Add a reason when the answer is negative.

EXAMPLE 1   Will / Carmella / take / classes / this summer? (Yes)

QUESTION: *Will Carmella take classes this summer?*

LONG ANSWER: *Yes, she will take classes this summer.*

SHORT ANSWER: *Yes, she will.*

QUICK ANSWER: *Yes.*

EXAMPLE 2   Will / Carmella / take / classes / this summer? (No, she's working.)

QUESTION: *Will Carmella take classes this summer?*

LONG ANSWER: *No, she will not/won't take classes this summer. She's working.*

SHORT ANSWER: *No, she will not. / No, she won't. She's working this summer.*

QUICK ANSWER: *No. She's working this summer.*

EXAMPLE 3:   BE going to / Carmella / take / classes / this summer? (Yes)

QUESTION: _Is Carmella going to take classes this summer?_

LONG ANSWER: _Yes, she is going to take classes this summer._

SHORT ANSWER: _Yes, she is._

QUICK ANSWER: _Yes._

EXAMPLE 4:   BE going to / Carmella / take / classes / this summer? (No, she's working.)

QUESTION: _Is Carmella going to take classes this summer?_

LONG ANSWER: _No, she's not/ she isn't going to take classes this summer. She's working._

SHORT ANSWER: _No, she's not. / No, she isn't. She's working this summer._

QUICK ANSWER: _No. She's working this summer._

1. Will / they / have / a yard sale / this Sunday? (No, on Saturday.)

   QUESTION: _____

   LONG ANSWER: _____

   SHORT ANSWER: _____

   QUICK ANSWER: _____

> A **yard sale** (also **garage sale**) is the sale of one's possessions, such as clothes, furniture, and books, in a yard, garage, or driveway.

2. BE going to / Lee / lease / a new car / next year? (No, he'll buy.)

   QUESTION: _____

   LONG ANSWER: _____

   SHORT ANSWER: _____

   QUICK ANSWER: _____

3. Will / you / please / show / me / some evening dresses? (Yes.)

   QUESTION: _____

   LONG ANSWER: _____

   SHORT ANSWER: _____

   QUICK ANSWER: _____

4. BE going to / Liam and Shelby / rent / a boat / this summer? (Yes.)

QUESTION: _____

LONG ANSWER: _____

SHORT ANSWER: _____

QUICK ANSWER: _____

The Future: Forming WH Questions

When we ask people about activities in the future, we use WH questions, or information questions, to ask about the time of, location of, manner of, and reason for an action. As you know from previous chapters, WH questions begin with WH question words or phrases such as *who, what, when, where, why, how, how long, how many,* and *how much.* For a list of WH question words, refer to the Appendix. The following table shows how to form these questions.

WH Questions with *Will*

WH QUESTION WORD	WILL	SUBJECT OR SUBJECT PRONOUN	BASE FORM OF MAIN VERB	EXAMPLE SENTENCES
Where	will	I/you/we/they/ he/she/it	go	Where will you go for vacation?
How long	will	I/you/we/they/ he/she/it	be	How long will she be in Spain?
What	will	I/you/we/they/ he/she/it	do	What will they do for the next hour?
Why	will	I/you/we/they/ he/she/it	work	Why will he work late?

For the WH question *who,* do not add another subject. *Who* is the subject of the sentence, as illustrated in the following table.

WHO (SUBJECT OF SENTENCE)	WILL	BASE FORM OF MAIN VERB	EXAMPLE SENTENCE
Who	will	go	Who will go to the grocery store for me?

Pronunciation Tip
We usually use falling pitch at the end of WH questions. However, if you need the speaker to repeat something, use rising pitch. See the pitch chart in the Appendix for more information.

WH Questions with *BE Going To*

WH QUESTION WORD	BE VERB	SUBJECT OR SUBJECT PRONOUN	GOING TO	BASE FORM OF MAIN VERB	EXAMPLE SENTENCES
Where	am	I	going to	study	Where am I going to study this weekend?
How long	are	you /we/they	going to	do	How long are you going to do that?
What	is	he/she/it	going to	buy	What is he going to buy online?
Why	are	you /we/they	going to	sell	Why are they going to sell their house?

Just like with yes/no answers, we can answer WH questions in different ways: with long answers that are complete sentences or short answers with only the essential information to respond to the question. Let's practice using WH questions with *will* and *be going to*.

Exercise 8.10

Form WH questions with the future verb tense using the statements given. The question word and the information you will need to answer the question are given in parentheses. Use subject pronouns and contractions.

EXAMPLE 1   Henry will research computer prices. (When / after school)

QUESTION: *When will Henry research computer prices?*

LONG ANSWER: *He'll research computer prices after school.* (complete sentence)

SHORT ANSWER: *After school.* (essential information only)

EXAMPLE 2   I am going to go shopping tonight. (Where / at the mall)

QUESTION: *Where are you going to go shopping tonight?*

LONG ANSWER: *I'm going shopping at the mall.*

SHORT ANSWER: *At the mall.*

> We usually use the present progressive verb tense with phrases such as *go shopping*. See Chapter 5 for more information.

1. My brother will fix her bicycle. (Where / in the garage)

   QUESTION: _____

   LONG ANSWER: _____

   SHORT ANSWER: _____

2. She will do her homework. (When / after dinner)

   QUESTION: _____

   LONG ANSWER: _____

   SHORT ANSWER: _____

3. Christian is going to take classes this summer. (Which / art and history)

   QUESTION: _____

   LONG ANSWER: _____

   SHORT ANSWER: _____

4. Evie and Lorraine are going to buy a new stove. (Why / stove is broken)

   QUESTION: _____

   LONG ANSWER: _____

   SHORT ANSWER: _____

Now let's practice offering and asking for help.

Communication Strategy: Offering and Asking for Help

In the conversation at the beginning of the chapter, the customer service specialist offered Genevieve help. Many jobs such as customer service specialists, salespeople, and salesclerks are **service jobs**. These jobs serve, or help, people. Hotel receptionists, restaurant servers, and hostesses also serve customers. But anyone can offer help to someone else.

Offering Help

We use a few different expressions to offer help. In the following examples, the offers of help are italicized.

SITUATION	OFFERING HELP	RESPONSE
1. A man approaches the front desk at a hotel. The receptionist offers him help.	Hotel receptionist: Hello there! Welcome to Hotel California! *How may I help you*, sir?	Man: Thank you. I have a reservation. My name is Reynaldo Hernandez.

SITUATION	OFFERING HELP	RESPONSE
2. A customer at a mall is reading a map. She looks confused.	Mall security guard: *Can I help you* find something?	Alice: Yes, please. I'm lost. Where is Plum Bookstore? I can't find it.
3. A shopper is carrying many bags. She's trying to open the store door.	Another customer in store: *Can I help you* with the door?	Shopper: Oh, yes. Thank you so much!

In the first situation, a customer approaches a service desk. In this case, we usually say, "How may I help you?" In the second situation, a service employee approaches a customer to offer assistance: "Can I help you find something?" In the third situation, one customer offers help to another: "Can I help you with the door?" In these cases, we usually say, "Can I help you . . . ?" Study the following table.

QUESTIONS TO OFFER HELP	WHO USES THIS EXPRESSION	SITUATION
How may I help you?	Employees in the service sector: Hotel employees Restaurant employees Tourism employees Salesclerks	A customer approaches a service desk, the front desk of a hotel, the hostess station at a restaurant, the cash register counter at a grocery store, or the customer service desk at a department store.
Can I help you . . . ?	Employees in the service sector Anyone	A service employee approaches a customer. Anyone offers assistance to someone else.

There are many ways to offer help. In this section, we look at two ways:

1. How may I help you? (formal)
2. Can I help you . . . ? (informal)

Let's examine these expressions.

QUESTIONS TO OFFER HELP	WAYS TO ASK	EXAMPLES
How may I help you?	Sometimes, we add *sir* or *ma'am* to the end of the question.	How may I help you? How may I help you, sir? How may I help you, ma'am?
	Sometimes we add *today*, *this morning*, etc. Use falling pitch.	How may I help you today? How may I help you this morning?

(continued)

QUESTIONS TO OFFER HELP	WAYS TO ASK	EXAMPLES
Can I help you . . . ?	1. *Can I help you* + do something. Use base form of verb and rising pitch.	Can I help you look for something? Can I help you choose a restaurant?
	2. *Can I help you* + *with* something. Use rising pitch.	Can I help you with that? Can I help you with your bags?

Let's practice offering help.

 ## Exercise 8.11

Look at the following situations, and complete each offer using the clues given.

EXAMPLE   A person approaches the customer service desk at a clothing store.

Customer service specialist: *How may I help you today?*

1. A salesclerk approaches a shopper in a store.

   (look for something) Salesclerk: _____

2. A hotel clerk approaches a guest in a hotel lobby.

   (with that luggage) Hotel clerk: _____

3. Someone approaches a salesclerk at a shop.

   Salesclerk: _____

4. A person is looking around on the street. He seems confused.

   (find something) Another person: _____

Exercise 8.12

Create an offer of help for each of the following situations.

1. A customer approaches a cash register counter at a store.

   Salesclerk: _____

2. A store clerk approaches a customer.

   Store clerk: _____

3. A woman is looking at a train schedule. She seems confused.

Someone at the train station: _____

Asking for Help

Sometimes, we need help, so we must ask for it. Let's look at some example situations. The requests for help are italicized.

SITUATION	ASKING FOR HELP	RESPONSE
1. A woman approaches a salesclerk at a department store.	WOMAN: Excuse me. *Could you help me* find the men's shoe department?	SALESCLERK: Yes. It's on the third floor. Take a right off the escalator. WOMAN: Thank you.
2. A man at a mall can't find the jewelry store. He approaches a shopkeeper.	MAN: Pardon me. *Can you help me?* I can't find the jewelry store.	SHOPKEEPER: Sure. It's right down here on the left. It's next to the shoe store. MAN: Thank you very much!

There are many ways to ask for help. In this section, we will look at two:

1. Could you help me . . . ?

2. Can you help me . . . ?

Let's examine these expressions in more detail.

QUESTIONS TO ASK FOR HELP	WAYS TO ASK	EXAMPLES
Could you help me? Can you help me?	Ask these questions, then say the problem. Use *I can't* + do something Use rising pitch.	Could you help me? I can't carry these. They're too heavy. Can you help me, please? I can't find the children's clothing department.
Could you help me . . . ? Can you help me . . . ?	1. *Can/Could you help me* + do something. Use base form of verb and rising pitch.	Could you help me find the bookstore? Can you help me open this door, please?
Could you help me . . . ? Can you help me . . . ?	2. *Can/Could you help me* + *with* something. Use rising pitch.	Could you help me with these packages? Can you help me with this, please?

Note: Saying *please* makes every question more polite. Begin each question for help with *Excuse me* or *Pardon me*.

Now let's practice asking for help.

Exercise 8.13

Look at the following situations, and complete the question for help using the clues given.

EXAMPLE   A person doesn't understand the bus schedule. He asks a bus driver for help.

Traveler: *Excuse me. Could you help me, please? I can't find the weekend bus schedule.*

1. A customer must find a bathroom quickly. She asks a security guard for help.

   Customer: _____

2. A guest at a hotel has lost his room key. He asks the hotel clerk for a new key.

   Guest: _____

3. A customer at a restaurant can't decide what to order for dinner. She asks the server for help.

   Customer: _____

4. An office worker is trying to make a copy. The copy machine isn't working. He asks the receptionist for help.

   Office worker: _____

Exercise 8.14

Form a question asking for help in each of the following situations.

1. A customer can't find the price of a shirt. She asks a salesclerk for help.

   Customer: _____

2. An elderly man can't read the train schedule. He asks a person at the train station for help.

   Elderly man: _____

3. A student can't find the library on the college campus. She asks another student for help.

   Student: _____

Now that we learned ways to offer help and ways to ask for help, let's learn some vocabulary.

Vocabulary: Clothing

Let's learn some vocabulary for clothes.

Exercise 8.15

For each of the following illustrations, match the words from the list with letters corresponding to the correct pieces of clothing. There is sometimes more than one word for the same piece of clothing.

Athletic shoes Baseball cap Boots Belt Coat Dress
Flip-flops Galoshes Gloves Hat Hood Hoodie
Jeans Mittens Skirt Pants Rain boots Raincoat
Scarf Shorts Socks Sneakers Sweatshirt T-shirt
Tennis shoes Trench coat Trousers Umbrella
Wellies Winter jacket Tank top Jumper Sweater
Shirt Blouse Top Sandals High-heeled sandals
High-heeled shoes

Culture Note:
Wellies is a British term. A *jumper* in American usage is a type of dress for young girls, while in British usage, it is a sweater.

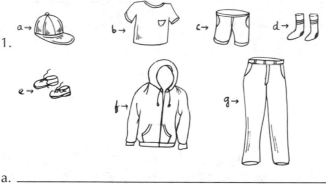

1.

a. _____

b. _____

c. _____

d. _____

e. _____

f. _____

g. _____

2.

a. _____

b. _____

c. _____

d. _____

e. _____

f. _____

g. _____

h. _____

i. _____

j. _____

3.

a. _____

b. _____

c. _____

d. _____

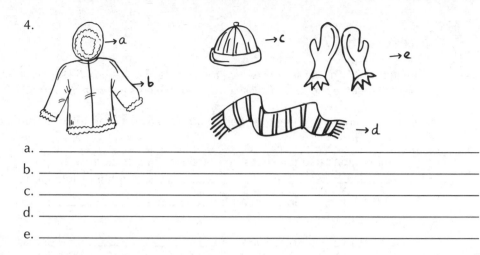

4.

a. _____

b. _____

c. _____

d. _____

e. _____

Vocabulary: Phrasal Verbs for Shopping

We use some common phrasal verbs when we talk about shopping and clothes. Let's look at some of them.

Exercise 8.16

Read the phrasal verbs on the left, then read the definitions on the right. You may know some of these terms. Match the verbs with their appropriate definitions. For the phrasal verbs you do not know, take a guess. Some can be separated with a noun or pronoun; these are shown in **bold**.

1. To pick out **something**/to pick **something** out
2. To break in **something**/to break **something** in
3. To shop around
4. To grow out of **something**
5. To put on **something**/to put **something** on
6. To try on **something**/to try **something** on
7. To grow into **something**
8. To come apart
9. To send back **something**/to send **something** back
10. To ring up **something** + **someone**/to ring **something** + **someone** up

a. To wear something
b. To return a product through the mail
c. To select or choose
d. To grow big enough to fit into something
e. To compare prices at different stores
f. To separate into pieces
g. To grow too big for something
h. To wear clothing briefly to check fit
i. To wear footwear enough to make it comfortable
j. To complete a transaction of buying something at the cash register

Culture Note: In British usage, *to ring someone up* means to call someone on the phone.

Exercise 8.17

Complete the following sentences with the correct phrasal verb. Be sure to use the correct verb tense and form. Review previous chapters for verb tense forms.

EXAMPLE   Herman *is going to shop around* for a sports car. (plan or intention / future)

1. Stanley didn't like the shoes he bought online. Tomorrow, he _____ them _____. (plan or intention / future)

2. The threads on Dolores's scarf are separating. It _____. (present progressive)

3. Daisy is five years old. Soon, she _____ her older sister's clothes. (prediction)

4. Stella is in the department store. She wants to buy a new raincoat. She _____ some raincoats _____. (present progressive)

5. It's snowing out there! You had better _____ your winter jacket. (base form of the verb)

6. Sally, we've been in this store for an hour. Hurry up and _____ a pair of shoes! (imperative)

Prepositions of Time

In Chapter 4, you learned some prepositions of place. In this section, we will talk about prepositions of time, as shown in the following table.

PREPOSITION OF TIME	EXAMPLES	PREPOSITION OF TIME	EXAMPLES
In + amount of time	In five minutes In two days	*On* + day	On Tuesday On Saturday
For + amount of time (duration)	For three hours For nine months	*In* + month/year/decade/century	In January In 2025 In the 1980s In the 1700s
At + specific time	At 10:35 P.M. At noon	*In the morning/afternoon/evening*	In the morning In the evening
At night	At night	*On the weekend/a weekday*	On the weekend On a weekday

Now, let's practice using prepositions of time.

Exercise 8.18

Complete the sentences with the correct preposition of time. Review the preceding table if you need help.

EXAMPLE   Mary and Joseph ate dinner *at* 6:30 p.m.

1. Do you like to exercise _____ the morning or _____ the afternoon?
2. I take night classes. I go to school _____ night.
3. The dresses _____ the 1960s were short.
4. The skirts _____ the 1970s were long.
5. When do you shop for clothes: _____ a weekday or _____ the weekend?
6. His uncle shopped _____ eight hours _____ Sunday!
7. I'll be ready _____ 15 minutes.
8. I go school shopping _____ August.

Grammar: Object Pronouns

You learned in Chapter 1 that we sometimes use a pronoun in place of a noun. A **pronoun** replaces a noun. An **object pronoun** replaces a noun in any object position of the sentence. Here are two types of object pronouns:

- The object of a verb
- The object of a preposition

The object of a verb usually follows the verb. The object of a preposition follows the preposition. Do you know any object pronouns? Make a list of the ones you know.

> Remember: A **noun** is a person, place, or thing

Study the object pronouns listed in the chart and the example sentences that follow.

Object Pronouns

	SINGULAR	PLURAL
First person	Me	Us
Second person	You	You
Third person	Him (male)	Them
	Her (female)	
	It	

*John knows **me**.*   *Dr. Nguyen recommended **you**.*
*Jessica asked about **him**.*   *My friend met **her**.*
*She walked along **it**.*   *My mother invited **us** to dinner.*
*I like **them**.*

As you learned in the subject-verb-object (SVO) sentence structure section in Chapter 4, to find the object of the verb in a sentence, ask the question "What?" for things or "Whom?" for people after the verb. Do this to find the object pronoun too. Let's look at some examples.

SENTENCE WITH OBJECT PRONOUN	VERB + WHAT OR WHOM	OBJECT PRONOUN
John knows me.	Knows whom?	Me
Dr. Nguyen recommended you.	Recommended whom?	You
My friend met her.	Met whom?	Her
My mother invited us to dinner.	Invited whom?	Us
I like them a lot.	Like what?	Them

You can also find the object of a preposition this way. **Prepositions** are little words that show position or direction such as *in, on, for, with,* and *to.* See the Appendix for a list of prepositions.

SENTENCE WITH OBJECT PRONOUN	PREPOSITION + WHAT OR WHOM	OBJECT PRONOUN
Jessica asked about him.	About who?	Him
She walked along it.	Along what?	It

Let's practice identifying object pronouns in a sentence.

Exercise 8.19

Note the object pronoun for each sentence. Refer to the preceding tables if you need help.

EXAMPLE   Jonathan noticed it.   *it*

1. Alice bought it. _____

2. Jeff got along with him. _____

3. My parents spent money on her. _____

4. We took them to the store. _____

5. They heard you. _____

6. My sister wore it. _____

7. Call me! _____

8. The store owner showed us. _____

Now let's practice using object pronouns.

Exercise 8.20

Read the following sentences. In each sentence, there is an object of the verb or an object of the preposition. Restate the sentence, replacing the underlined object noun with an object pronoun.

EXAMPLE   She walked to <u>the shoe store</u>.   *She walked to it.*

1. Jenny and Lori shopped for <u>shoes</u>. _____

2. She likes <u>secondhand stores</u>. _____

3. My aunt got a good deal on <u>that car</u>. _____

4. I like shopping with <u>Anna</u>. _____

5. I found a T-shirt for <u>Mike</u>. _____

6. How much money does <u>the dress</u> cost? _____

> **Secondhand stores** sell pre-owned clothing, furniture, and other home goods such as kitchenware. They are also called **thrift stores** and **consignment shops**.

Exercise 8.21

Create sentences about clothes and shopping using object pronouns as indicated.

1. me _____

2. you _____

3. him _____

4. her _____

5. it _____

6. us _____

7. them _____

Talking About Clothes

Sometimes we talk with our friends about clothes. We want their opinions, and they provide them. In this section, you will learn how to do the following:

- Ask for opinions
- Give positive opinions
- Give negative opinions politely
- Make suggestions
- Describe how clothes fit and look

Vocabulary: Adverbs and Adjectives

When we talk about how clothes fit and look, we use adverbs and adjectives. Let's look first at some intensifier adverbs. The scale shows intensifiers from *a lot* to *a little*. You learned some of these in Chapter 1. Remember: we use *too* to give negative opinions, not positive ones.

A lot
↑ Too (negative; more than desired)
   Very + so*
   Really
   Quite (North America)
   Kind of
   A bit / a little / a little bit / a tad / slightly / quite (British)
↓ Not very (negative)
A little
So is used for emphasis.

The following pairs of adjectives describe clothes; each pair shows opposites.

Loose / tight	Big / small
Long / short	Fancy / plain *or* simple
Trendy / classic	Dark / light
Wide / narrow	Formal *or* dressy / informal *or* casual
Beautiful / ugly	Professional / sporty
Appropriate / inappropriate	

Here are some other adjectives used for clothing:

Colorful   Perfect   Nice   Fabulous   Pretty   Fashionable

Sometimes we ask our friends for their opinion on our clothes. We say "What do you think of this?" They can answer with a positive or negative opinion. Let's look at some example sentences using these adverbs and adjectives.

POSITIVE OPINIONS	NEGATIVE OPINIONS
That shirt is really nice on you. I think that shirt is really nice on you.	That T-shirt is too sporty. Maybe you could wear a blouse for our business meeting.
Those shoes are so fashionable. I think those shoes are so fashionable.	Those shoes aren't very comfortable. Maybe you could wear athletic shoes for the hike.
This outfit is very professional. I think this outfit is very professional.	That outfit isn't appropriate. Maybe you could wear something more casual for lunch.

Now, let's practice using adverbs and adjectives to describe clothes and give positive and negative opinions.

Exercise 8.22

Your friend asks you for your opinion. Form sentences using the clues given. Start positive and negative opinions with I think. *Use the preceding table for guidance.*

EXAMPLE   What do you think of this hat?

(too big) *I think that hat is too big for you.*

1. What do you think of this dress?

   (very pretty) _____

2. What do you think of this outfit for the party?

   (too casual) _____

3. What do you think of these shoes?

   (so lovely) _____

4. What do you think of this coat?

   (quite trendy) _____

Vocabulary: Comparatives

We often compare things such as clothes or prices. To do this, we use **comparatives**. Comparative words and phrases identify the differences between things. There are two ways to form comparatives, as shown in the following table.

1. ADJECTIVE + -ER + THAN		**2. MORE + ADJECTIVE + THAN**	
This hat is nicer than that hat.		That outfit is more appropriate than this one.	
That dress is cheaper than the other dress.		This dress is more expensive than the other dress.	

When do we use these two different comparatives? Here are some rules.

ADJECTIVE	EXAMPLE ADJECTIVES	RULE	EXAMPLE COMPARATIVES
One-syllable adjectives	Small	Add **-er**	Smaller
	Big	If the word is spelled with a consonant-vowel-consonant, double the final consonant and then add **-er**.	Bigger
Two-syllable adjectives (usually ending in *y*)	Dressy	Change *y* to *i* and add **-er**	Dressier
	Ugly		Uglier
Two- or three-syllable adjectives	Expensive	Add *more* + adjective	More expensive
	Formal	Add *less* + adjective	Less formal

Let's practice using comparatives in sentences.

✏ Exercise 8.23

Complete the sentences with the correct form of the comparative of the adjective given.

EXAMPLES   (short) This belt is <u>shorter than</u> that belt.

(appropriate) The blue dress is <u>more appropriate than</u> the red one.

1. (trendy) The black shoes are _____ the tan boots.

2. (casual) His outfit is _____ hers.

3. (wide) These shoes are _____ the other ones.

4. (professional) This coat is _____ that coat.

5. (beautiful) This shirt is _____ the sweater.

6. (expensive) This store is _____ the other store.

Vocabulary: Superlatives

To talk about the most or the least, we use superlatives. There are two ways to form superlatives, as shown in the following table.

1. THE + ADJECTIVE + -EST	2. THE MOST/THE LEAST + ADJECTIVE
These shoes are the nicest.	Those shoes are the least expensive.
That dress is the longest.	That outfit is the most professional.

When do we use these two different superlatives? Here are some rules.

ADJECTIVE	EXAMPLE ADJECTIVES	RULE	EXAMPLE SUPERLATIVES
One-syllable adjectives	Small	Add *the* before adjective	The smallest
	Big	Add **-est** to the adjective	The biggest
		If the word is spelled with a consonant-vowel-consonant, double the final consonant and then add **-est**.	
Two-syllable adjectives (usually ending in *y*)	Dressy	Add *the* before adjective	The dressiest
	Ugly	Change *y* to *i*	The ugliest
		Add **-est**	
Two- or three-syllable adjectives	Expensive	Add *the*	The most expensive
	Formal	Add *most/least* before adjective	The least formal

Now let's practice using superlatives in sentences.

Exercise 8.24

Complete the sentences with the correct form of the superlative of the adjective given.

EXAMPLES   (short) This belt is *the shortest*.

(most / appropriate) The blue dress is *the most appropriate*.

1. (trendy) The black shoes are _____.

2. (most / casual) His outfit is _____.

3. (wide) These shoes are _____.

4. (least / professional) This coat is _____.

5. (most / beautiful) This shirt is _____.

6. (least / expensive) This store is _____.

Communication Strategy: Asking for and Giving Opinions

Sometimes, we want to ask people for their opinions. For example, customers ask retail clerks for their opinions on products and friends ask friends for opinions on many things. To do this, we use a few different expressions. Read the following situations and the examples of people asking for opinions.

SITUATION	ASKING FOR SOMEONE'S OPINION	GIVING AN OPINION
1. Shoshana wants her friend's opinion on a dress.	SHOSHANA: I bought this new dress today. What do you think?	PENELOPE: I think it's perfect for you!
2. Vladimir is shopping for a new suit. He asks his friend for his opinion.	VLADIMIR: Check out this black suit. What do you think?	SASHA: Hm. It's too big. Maybe you could try a smaller size.

In the first situation, Penelope is giving a positive opinion. In the second situation, Sasha is giving a negative opinion. However, Sasha offers a suggestion (*Maybe you could try a smaller size.*) When giving a negative opinion, it's polite to offer an alternative suggestion. Let's look more closely at how to give opinions.

QUESTIONS TO ASK FOR OPINIONS	GIVING POSITIVE OPINIONS	GIVING NEGATIVE OPINIONS POLITELY + OFFERING A SUGGESTION
What do you think? *What do you think of* + noun	*I think* + (subject + verb)	*It's too* + adjective *Maybe you could* + base form of verb
Examples	I think the dress (S) is (V) perfect.	It's too big (Adj). Maybe you could try (base form of verb) a smaller size.

Now, let's practice giving positive and negative opinions.

Exercise 8.25

Create answers to the following questions using the clues given. You will provide both positive and negative opinions. Review the meaning and use of each modal of advice.

EXAMPLES   (positive / pretty) What do you think of this scarf?

I think it's pretty.

(negative / dressy / SUGGESTION / wear boots) What do you think of these shoes?

They're too dressy. Maybe you could wear boots.

1. (positive / perfect) What do you think of this sweater?

   _____

2. (negative / small / SUGGESTION / try a bigger size) What do you think of this sweater?

   _____

3. (positive / professional) What do you think of this suit?

   _____

4. (negative / loose / SUGGESTION / try a smaller size) What do you think of this suit?

   _____

Conversation: Putting It All Together

In this chapter, you have learned the following:

1. How to use the future verb tense to talk about activities in the future

2. How to offer and ask for help

3. Some vocabulary for describing clothes

4. Phrasal verbs

5. How to ask for and give opinions politely

Now let's try to put it all together.

Exercise 8.26

To complete the following conversation, use the future verb tense, time expressions for the future, communication strategies, and the vocabulary and expressions you learned in this chapter. Use the example conversation at the beginning of the chapter as an example. In this situation, Ben is in a department store. He wants to buy a dress for his wife. The conversation is between Ben and a salesclerk in the dress department. Ben begins the conversation.

1. Greet salesclerk and ask for help finding a dress. / Ben:

   _____

2. Greet Ben and ask about the type of dress. / Salesclerk:

   _____

3. Describe dress as long, formal, and black. / Ben:

   _____

4. Ask about size. / Salesclerk:

   _____

5. Give size as 6. / Ben:

   _____

6. Offer Ben three different dresses in size 6 and ask for his opinion. / Salesclerk: _____

7. Give positive opinion of dress 1 as very pretty. / Ben:

   _____

8. Ask Ben's opinion of dress 2. / Salesclerk:

   _____

9. Give negative opinion on dress 2 as too simple. / Ben:

   _____

10. Ask Ben's opinion of dress 3. / Salesclerk:

    _____

11. Give positive opinion on dress 3 as really trendy. / Ben:

    _____

12. Ask salesclerk for opinion. / Ben:

    _____

13. Compare dresses 1 and 3. Describe dress 1 as beautiful. / Salesclerk:

    _____

14. Agree using superlative to describe dress 1 as beautiful. / Ben:

_____

15. Suggest ringing up the dress. / Salesclerk:

_____

16. Thank salesclerk. / Ben:

_____

Reading About It

In this section, we will review the elements of a paragraph, as well as how to pre-read and read actively.

Let's Read Together

Let's read a story about Julia's new outfit. First, pre-read the passage. Then read it actively. Finally, check to see whether you understand what you read by answering questions about the passage.

Pre-Read

As you know from previous chapters, there are three steps to pre-reading: (1) read the title of the passage; (2) read the first sentence of the first paragraph; and (3) read the last sentence of the last paragraph.

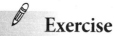

Exercise 8.27

First, pre-read the passage quickly and answer these two questions:

1. What is the topic? _____

2. What is the main idea? _____

Julia's New Outfit

Julie went shopping and bought a new outfit. She just got a job as a secretary, so she needs new clothes. She's very excited about this outfit. It is her first pantsuit. She shopped around for a week. Finally, she found a store that carried pantsuits and was not expensive. Julia tried on many pantsuits. She picked out a navy blue one. It is the most professional-looking and the most comfortable. She bought a few blouses to wear with the suit—a white one, a tan one, and a green one. Julia also got a new pair of black shoes with flat heels. They were the most comfortable shoes she tried on. Julia is very happy with her purchase. She looks really good in her new pantsuit. She's glad she bought a new outfit.

Read Actively

After you pre-read, what do you do? You should read *actively* by circling words you do not know and highlighting important ideas.

To Read Actively
- Underline the topic.
- Note new vocabulary.
- Put a question mark (?) next to unclear parts.
- Take notes.
- Highlight the main idea and key words.
- Mark examples with "Ex."
- Number main points, lists, or ideas.
- List comments or questions.

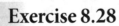
Exercise 8.28

Actively read the passage about Julia's new outfit. Follow the steps for reading actively.

Understand What You Read

Active reading helps you understand the information in a passage. Check your understanding of the passage details by answering the following questions.

Exercise 8.29

Review the passage and your notes. Then answer these questions.

1. What three things did Julia buy? _____

2. How does she feel about her new outfit? _____

3. Why did she buy a new pantsuit? _____

4. Was it expensive? _____

5. How long did it take her to find the new outfit? _____

Reviewing Elements of a Paragraph

As you know, a paragraph has one main idea, which is usually stated in the first sentence or two. This is the topic sentence. The main idea of the paragraph is always supported with evidence such as reasons, details, examples, or data. The sentences that support the main idea are supporting sentences. Finally, a paragraph ends with a concluding sentence that restates the topic sentence.

Exercise 8.30

Explain the main idea of the paragraph about Julia.

Main idea: _____

All of the sentences between the first and the last should support the main idea. Every sentence should relate to the topic sentence.

Exercise 8.31

Read the paragraph again, and answer these questions.

1. Do all the sentences between the topic sentence and the concluding sentence support the main idea? _____

2. How many supporting sentences are there? _____

Exercise 8.32

Find the elements of the paragraph.

1. What is the topic sentence? _____

2. What is the concluding sentence? _____

Writing About It

Let's practice writing! As you know, the foundation of writing is the sentence, and sentences create a paragraph. You have been studying how to create sentences using the SVO and SVC structures. You have also been studying the structure of a paragraph. Now it's time to create a paragraph.

Review: Structure of a Paragraph

Remember that a paragraph has three parts:

1. The topic sentence

2. The supporting sentences

3. The concluding sentence

Exercise 8.33

Create a paragraph about clothes you have purchased. Use the paragraph about Julia and her outfit as a guide. Start with a topic sentence, then use sentences with details, examples, and explanations to support the main idea. Finally, create a concluding sentence. Check your verb tenses, subject-verb agreement, and SVO/SVC sentence structure. Use everything you have learned about English in this book. Good luck!

Quiz

You have finished Chapter 8. Great work! Now take the quiz to see what you remember. Choose the correct answers for each question. There may be multiple correct answers for some of the questions.

1. Select the choices that complete the sentence correctly.

   (plan / intention) Samantha and Julian _____ to the park tomorrow.

   will go   go

   are going to go   went

2. Select the choices that complete the sentence correctly.

   (offer) I _____ you move this weekend.

   am going to help   help

   will help   am helping

3. Select the choices that complete the sentence correctly.

(promise / refusal) Georgette: I _____ the test tomorrow!

am not going to fail   will not fail

don't fail   fail

4. Select the choice that completes the sentence correctly.

(schedule) The bus _____ at 9:00 every morning.

is going to leave   is leaving

leaves   will leave

5. Select the choices that complete the sentence correctly.

(arranged plan) Max and Mary _____ next summer.

are going to get married   marry

married   are getting married

6. Complete the sentence with the superlative.

Ann and Francis have _____ cat. (fluffy)

the fluffy   the fluffier

the fluffiest   a fluffiest

7. Complete the sentence with the superlative.

Joseph is _____ baseball player on his team. (talented)

a most talented   the talentedest

the most talented   talented

8. Complete the sentence with the comparative.

Audrey is _____ all the kids in her class. (smart)

more smart than   smartest

smarter than   the smartest

9. How many parts are there to a paragraph?

5   2   18   3

10. How do you ask for opinions?

What do you think?   How do you think?

What do you think of . . . ?   How do you think of . . . ?

Do It Out There!

Now that you have learned how to talk about shopping and clothes, ask for and give opinions, and offer and ask for help, try these skills out in the world. Review this chapter, and go out and use English! Put a checkmark next to each activity as you complete it.

To Do This Week

- ❑ Use the future verb tense to talk about activities and plans for the future.
- ❑ Use time expressions for the future.
- ❑ Ask for opinions using *What do you think?*
- ❑ Give positive opinions using *I think*.
- ❑ Give negative opinions politely and make a suggestion using *Maybe you could*.
- ❑ Describe clothes using the vocabulary, phrasal verbs, adverbs, and adjectives in this chapter.
- ❑ Practice pre-reading and reading actively.
- ❑ Practice writing a paragraph.

Weekly Log

Keep a weekly log of your progress. Make notes on how your practice went. What happened? Was it successful? How do you know it was successful? Was it unsuccessful? How do you know? Review all the instructions, pronunciation tips, and culture notes in Chapter 8.

_____

_____

_____

_____

_____

_____

_____

Appendix

Useful Resources for ESL Students

Capitals (Uppercase alphabet)

A B C D E F G H I J K L M N O P Q R S T U V W X Y Z

Small Letters (Lowercase alphabet)

a b c d e f g h i j k l m n o p q r s t u v w x y z

Consonants and Vowels

Vowels: a, e, i, o, u (Note: Sometimes *y* is called a *semi-vowel* because it acts like a vowel.)

Consonants: b, c, d, f, g, h, j, k, l, m, n, p, q, r, s, t, v, w, x, y, z

Punctuation Marks

Comma ,	**Ellipsis** ...	**Quotation marks** "To be or not to be."
Period .	**Hyphen** good-bye	**Ampersand** &
Question mark ?	**Em dash** —	**Asterisk** *
Exclamation point !	**En dash** –	**Angle brackets** < >
Apostrophe John's	**Parentheses** ( )	**Square brackets** [ ]
Semicolon ;		**Braces** { }
Colon :		

Phonetic Symbols for Vowel Sounds

The following symbols are used in this book.

PHONETIC SYMBOLS	EXAMPLES OF THIS VOWEL SOUND
/ɪy/	sleep, piece, eat
/ɪ/	slip, it
/ey/	say, eight, fail
/ɛ/	bed, head
/æ/	cat, bad, malice
/ɑ/	father, calm
/ə/ (unstressed)	about, pronunciation
/ʌ/ (stressed)	productive, money
/a/	talk, bought, audience
/oʊ/	know, no, show, note
/ʊ/	good, would, put, book
/u/	new, food
/ay/	hi, night, site
/aʊ/	now, how, about, shout
/oy/	boy, toil

Vowels Followed by /r/

/ɚ/	first, research, turn, journal
/or/	four, or, short
/ɛr/	where, air, pair, fare
/ir/	near, here, fear
/ɑr/	far, partial, heart
/yʊɚ/	pure
/ayɚ/	fire, hire, mire, higher
/aʊɚ/	flour, flower, hour

British English

/ɔ/	talk, bought, sauce

Phonetic Symbols for Consonant Sounds

PHONETIC SYMBOLS	EXAMPLES OF THIS SOUND
/b/	boy, robber
/p/	pay, zipper
/d/	do, red
/t/*	time, better
/g/	go, bigger

* /t/ has many different sounds in North American English
depending on where it is positioned in a word or sentence.

PHONETIC SYMBOLS	EXAMPLES OF THIS SOUND
/k/	cat, kite, pickle
/v/	vest, moving
/f/	fun, roof
/ð/	the, breathe
/θ/	think, breath
/z/	zip, phrase, is
/s/	sit, miss
/ʃ/	show, washer
/ʒ/	beige, television
/ʧ/	catch, church
/dʒ/	judge
/h/	hello
/m/	make, summer
/n/	none
/ŋ/	sing, ringer
/l/	love, feel, feeling
/r/	risk, hear
/w/	will, which
/hw/** (regional)	which, when
/y/	you, joy

** The /hw/ sound is most commonly heard in the southern region of the United States.

Pitch Chart

English has four major pitches. We use different patterns for different reasons, as shown in the chart

PITCH	PITCH PATTERN	USED FOR
Falling Pitch		
4 Highest pitch		Statements; WH questions to show certainty and to offer a choice (the most commonly used pitch pattern)
3		
2		
1 Lowest pitch		

(continued)

PITCH	PITCH PATTERN	USED FOR

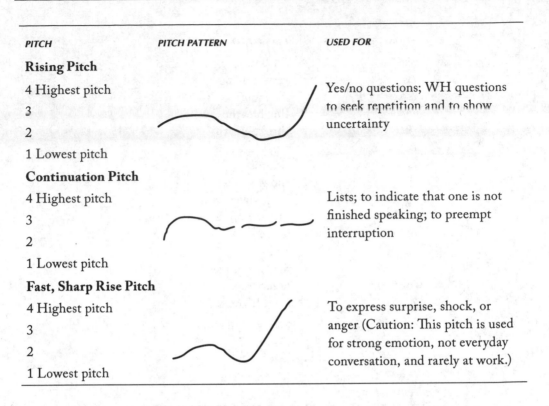

Rising Pitch

4 Highest pitch

3

2

1 Lowest pitch

Yes/no questions; WH questions to seek repetition and to show uncertainty

Continuation Pitch

4 Highest pitch

3

2

1 Lowest pitch

Lists; to indicate that one is not finished speaking; to preempt interruption

Fast, Sharp Rise Pitch

4 Highest pitch

3

2

1 Lowest pitch

To express surprise, shock, or anger (Caution: This pitch is used for strong emotion, not everyday conversation, and rarely at work.)

Parts of Speech (Glossary of Grammar Terms)

Subject (subj): A subject is the main noun of a sentence. It usually comes before the verb. The subjects in these two example sentences are in italics: The *children* are playing in the park. *Jason* and *Marcy* love movies.

Verb (v): A verb is an action word. Examples of verbs are *call, be, learn, write, go, do, have,* and *win.*

Object (obj): The object of the verb (also known as a *direct object*) takes the action of the verb. For example, in the sentence *I eat breakfast every day*, the verb is *eat* and the object that takes the action is *breakfast*. It answers the question *Eat what?* The object of a preposition is similar: *We walked along the beach.* Ask the question *Along what?* The answer is *the beach*, so *beach* is the object. See Chapter 8 for information on object pronouns.

Subject-verb-object (SVO): This is one type of English sentence structure. An example is *She studies English. She* is the subject, *studies* is the verb, and *English* is the object.

Subject-verb-complement (SVC): This is one type of English sentence structure. An example is *She is a teacher*. *She* is the subject, *is* is the verb, and *a teacher* is the complement.

Noun (n): A noun is a person, place, or thing. Examples are *George Washington, Brazil, pencil*, and *love*.

Adjective (adj): Adjectives describe or modify nouns as in *The **white** car is mine*.

Adverbs (adv): These words describe or modify verbs (**Example:** He ran *quickly*) and adjectives (**Example:** He is *very* tired).

Article (art): English has two types of articles: definite (*the*) and indefinite (*a, an*).

Preposition (prep): Prepositions are small words that show position or direction such as *in, on, for, with*, and *to*.

Conjunction (conj): A conjunction joins two clauses to make a sentence. Examples are *and, or, but*, and *because*.

***Who* vs. *whom*:** *Who* is used to replace a subject, and *whom* is used to replace an object. They are used as WH question words and relative pronouns.

Common Stative Verbs

appreciate	approve	believe	belong	consist	cost
desire	dislike	doubt	equal	forget	hate
know	like	match	matter	need	owe
own	possess	prefer	recognize	remember	resemble
seem	understand	want			

The following can be stative (nonaction) or regular (action) verbs, depending on how they are used: appear, be, feel, fit, guess, have, hear, imagine, look, love, mean, mind, see, smell, sound, taste, think, and weigh.

Common Irregular Verbs

BASE FORM OF WORD	SIMPLE PAST	PAST PARTICIPLE	BASE FORM OF WORD	SIMPLE PAST	PAST PARTICIPLE
be	was/were	been	have	had	had
begin	began	begun	leave	left	left
bring	brought	brought	make	made	made
buy	bought	bought	meet	met	met
catch	caught	caught	pay	paid	paid
come	came	come	put	put	put

(continued)

BASE FORM OF WORD	SIMPLE PAST	PAST PARTICIPLE	BASE FORM OF WORD	SIMPLE PAST	PAST PARTICIPLE
do	did	done	say	said	said
drink	drank	drunk	see	saw	seen
drive	drove	driven	sleep	slept	slept
eat	ate	eaten	speak	spoke	spoken
feel	felt	felt	take	took	taken
forget	forgot	forgotten	tell	told	told
get	got	gotten	understand	understood	understood
give	gave	given	wake up	woke up	woken up
go	went	gone	write	wrote	written
hear	heard	heard			

Common WH Question Words

who	what	when	where	why
how	what kind	which one	how long	how many
how much	how old	whose	whom	how far
what time	how often			

Spelling Rules for Simple Present Third Person Singular

1. Add **-s** to most verbs (**Example:** put → puts).

2. If a word ends in a *y*, change the *y* to an *i* and add **-es** (**Example:** study → studies).

3. Add **-es** if the verb ends in *ch, sh, tch, ss, x,* or *z* (**Example:** match → matches).

4. Irregular verbs have different spellings (**Example:** do → does; go → goes; have → has).

Common Prepositions

about	above	across (from)	against	around
at	behind	beneath	beside(s)	between
by	down	during	for	from
in	in back of	in front of	inside (of)	into
near	of	off (of)	on	onto
out (of)	outside (of)	over	past	through
throughout	to	toward(s)	under	up
with	within	without		

Answer Key

Chapter 1   Meeting People
Exercise 1.1

Formal	Informal	Neutral
Hello.	Hello.	Hello.
How are you?	Hello there.	How are you?
Good morning.	Howdy.	Good morning.
Good afternoon.	Hi.	
Good evening.	Hi there.	
	Hey.	
	Hey there.	
	How are you?	
	Hey, how are you doing?	
	How are you doing?	
	What's up?	
	What's happening?	
	Long time no see!	

Exercise 1.2

1. Inappropriate. "Hey, what's up?" is too informal for Brenda's supervisor. She should speak more formally to show respect for her boss.   2. Appropriate. "What's happening?" is appropriate because Jason and José are good friends.   3. Inappropriate. "Good night" is inappropriate because it means "Good-bye," or "I'm going to bed." Harry just arrived at his job, so he should say, "Good evening," meaning "Hello," instead.

Exercise 1.3

1. Brenda is greeting her supervisor, so she should be formal or neutral. Possible answers are: Hello. / How are you? / Good afternoon.   2. Dan and Sunil are friends, so informal greetings are fine. Possible answers are: Hello. / Hello there. / Howdy. / Hi. / Hi there. / Hey. / Hey there. / How are you? / Hey, how are you doing? / How are you doing? / What's up?   3. Klara is greeting her teacher, so she should be formal or neutral. Possible answers are: Hello. / How are you? / Good evening.   4. Possible answers are: Hello. / Hello there. / Howdy. / Hi. / Hey. / How are you? / Hey, how are you doing?   5. Possible answers are: Hello. / How are you? / Good morning.

Exercise 1.4

Answers will vary.

Exercise 1.5

1. Make eye contact.   2. Make small talk.   3. Introduce yourself.   4. Look for a connection.   5. Learn about each other.   6. End the conversation.

Exercise 1.6

1. Make eye contact.   2. Begin with small talk. Be positive   3. Food   4. Have you tried the . . . ?   5. I'm . . .   6. Yes   7. Look in the person's eyes.   8. How people know each other, such as through friends, family, or coworkers   9. Information (WH) questions and yes/no questions   10. To find someone, use the restroom, get food or a drink, leave an event

Exercise 1.7

1. c   2. b   3. b

Exercise 1.8

Answers will vary.

Exercise 1.9

1. They   2. We   3. He   4. She   5. It   6. They

Exercise 1.10

1. They   2. He   3. He   4. You   5. You   6. We   7. He   8. I

Exercise 1.11

1. He is a mechanic.   2. We are students.   3. We are married.   4. She is a dog walker.
5. I am a dog walker.   6. I am a police officer.   7. You are an author.   8. He is an engineer.
9. He is a mechanic. *or* He is my husband.   10. You are married.

Exercise 1.12

1. is   2. is   3. am   4. are   5. is   6. are   7. is   8. is   9. are   10. is

Exercise 1.13

1. am   2. is   3. are   4. are   5. is   6. are   7. is   8. is   9. are   10. am

Exercise 1.14

1. Tomas is my supervisor. / He's my supervisor.   2. Gerald and I are great today. / We're great today.   3. My sisters are here. / They're here.   4. Mary and Will are my friends. / They're my friends.   5. Today is a great day! / It's a great day!

Exercise 1.15

1. isn't   2. aren't   3. isn't   4. aren't   5. aren't   6. 're not   7. 'm not   8. 's not   9. 're not   10. 's not

Exercise 1.16

1. Marty and Joe aren't cousins. / They're not cousins.   2. You aren't a mechanic. / You're not a mechanic.   3. Cheryl and I aren't siblings. / We're not siblings.   4. Mr. Jones isn't happy. / He's not happy.   5. My computer isn't not old. / It's not old.   6. Mrs. Weatherby isn't strict. / She's not strict.   7. The road isn't straight. / It's not straight.   8. I'm not a teacher. / I'm not a teacher.   9. Francisco isn't a student. / He's not a student.   10. Rose isn't sleepy. / She's not sleepy.

Exercise 1.17

Answers will vary.

Exercise 1.18

Answers will vary. But sentences should begin like this:
1. / 7. She is… / She's…   2. / 8. He is… / He's…   3. / 9. It is… / It's …   4. / 10. You are… / You're…   5. / 11. We are… / We're…   6. / 12. They are… / They're…

Exercise 1.19

Answers will vary. But sentences should begin like this:
1. / 7. She is not… / She's not… / She isn't…   2. / 8. He is not… / He's not… / He isn't…   3. / 9. It is not… / It's not… / It isn't…   4. / 10. You are not… / You're not… / You aren't…   5. / 11. We are not… / We're not… / We aren't…   6. / 12. They are not… / They're not… / They aren't…

Exercise 1.20

1. QUESTION: *Is Alejandrina an employee?*
   LONG ANSWER: *Yes, she is an employee. / Yes, she's an employee.*
   SHORT ANSWER: *Yes, she is.*   QUICK ANSWER: *Yes.*

2. QUESTION: *Is Dean late?*
   LONG ANSWER: *No, he is not late. / No, he isn't late. / No, he's not late.*
   SHORT ANSWER: *No, he is not. / No, he isn't. / No, he's not.*   QUICK ANSWER: *No.*

3. QUESTION: *Is Jenna your sister?*
   LONG ANSWER: *Yes, she is my sister. / Yes, she's my sister.*
   SHORT ANSWER: *Yes, she is.*   QUICK ANSWER: *Yes.*

4. QUESTION: *Are you a student at the community college?*
   LONG ANSWER: *No, I am not a student at the community college. / No, I'm not a student at the community college.*
   SHORT ANSWER: *No, I'm not.*   QUICK ANSWER: *No.*

5. QUESTION: *Are you a student at the nursing school?*
   LONG ANSWER: *Yes, I am a student at the nursing school. / Yes, I'm a student at the nursing school.*
   SHORT ANSWER: *Yes, I am.*   QUICK ANSWER: *Yes.*

Exercise 1.21

1. QUESTION: *When is Xin home?*
   LONG ANSWER: *She is home at 3:00 P.M. / She's home at 3:00 P.M.*
   SHORT ANSWER: *At 3:00 P.M.*

2. QUESTION: *Why is Michael unhappy?*
   LONG ANSWER: *He is unhappy because he failed the test. / He's unhappy because he failed the test.*
   SHORT ANSWER: *Because he failed the test.*

3. QUESTION: *How often are Harry and William at baseball practice?*
   LONG ANSWER: *They are /They're at baseball practice every day after school.*
   SHORT ANSWER: *Every day after school.*

4. QUESTION: *Where is he now?*
   LONG ANSWER: *He is at home. / He's at home.*
   SHORT ANSWER: *At home.*

5. QUESTION: *How is she?*
   LONG ANSWER: *She is fine. / She's fine.*
   SHORT ANSWER: *Fine.*

6. Who / BE verb / he? (the boss)
   QUESTION: *Who is he?*
   LONG ANSWER: *He is the boss. / He's the boss.*
   SHORT ANSWER: *The boss.*

Exercise 1.22

1. Benjamin is great.   2. Evelyn and Rocco are okay.   3. Diana is all right.   4. Sonja and I are excellent.   5. They are good.   6. I am very good.

Exercise 1.23

1. It's sunny today.   2. It's cloudy today.   3. It's stormy today.   4. It's partly sunny today.   5. It's windy today.

Exercise 1.24

1. It is not rainy. / It's not rainy. / It isn't rainy.   2. It is not sunny. / It's not sunny. / It isn't sunny.   3. It is not hot. / It's not hot. / It isn't hot.   4. It is not warm. / It's not warm. / It isn't warm.   5. It is not dry. / It's not dry. / It isn't dry.

Exercise 1.25

1. a bit   2. pretty   3. quite

Exercise 1.26

1. fed up with   2. cut down on   3. look up   4. break into   5. Check out   6. drop in on

Exercise 1.27

1. Rita Learns English   2. Rita   3. At night   4. a, c, d   5. Rita is learning English.

Exercise 1.28

1. N   2. h   3. p   4. B   5. Q   6. e   7. K   8. W   9. y   10. D

Exercise 1.29

1. R   2. I   3. S   4. H   5. W   6. Y

Exercise 1.30

Answers will vary. Be sure that every sentence begins with a capital letter. Use the uppercase alphabet in the Appendix to guide you.

Exercise 1.31

1. Correct   2. Incorrect / My friend is from Morocco.   3. Incorrect / What time does the restaurant open?   4. Correct   5. Incorrect / Are you happy today?   6. Correct   7. Correct   8. Incorrect / This is my brother.   9. Incorrect / Maura is a student, isn't she?   10. Incorrect / Where is Vivek?

Exercise 1.32

1. ,   2. ?   3. ,   4. ?   5. ?   6. ?   7. ?   8. ,   9. ,   10. ?

Exercise 1.33

1. Where do you live?   2. I live in Lakeview.   3. Is that your dog?   4. Yes, it is.   5. When do you study?   6. I study every night.   7. How much does it cost?   8. It costs a lot.   9. Is he a good student?   10. Ali is a good student.

Exercise 1.34

Answers will vary. Be sure that every sentence begins with a capital letter. Every statement must end with a period, and every question must end with a question mark.

Quiz

1. Good morning.   2. A pleasure meeting you.   3. Make eye contact.   4. Firmly   5. They   6. is   7. aren't   8. Circling new vocabulary   9. Reading the first and last paragraphs of long passages   10. ,

Chapter 2   Habits, Customs, and Routines

Exercise 2.1

The following are a few possible answers:
Every day: Take a shower; Go to work/school; Eat lunch; Exercise
Every week: Play in the park; Exercise
Every six months: Go to the dentist; Take a vacation
Every year: Go to the dentist; Celebrate your birthday; Take a vacation

Exercise 2.2

1. parents   2. siblings   3. wife   4. children (also *kids* in North America)   5. brother
6. sister   7. Jack / Aidan / Madeleine / Mason   8. niece   9. nephew   10. brother-in-law
11. sister-in-law   12. cousins

Exercise 2.3

Answers will vary.

Exercise 2.4

Answers will vary.

Exercise 2.5

1. gets up   2. makes   3. walk   4. arrives   5. finishes   6. picks up   7. eats   8. watches
9. puts   10. relax   11. goes

Exercise 2.6

1. plays   2. plays   3. eat   4. do   5. celebrate   6. go   7. works   8. walk
9. has   10. is

Exercise 2.7

1. /z/   2. /s/   3. /ɪz/   4. /z/   5. /z/   6. /z/   7. /z/   8. /s/

Exercise 2.8

Various answers are possible.

Exercise 2.9

Various answers are possible. Be sure that two of the answers use the third person singular.

Exercise 2.10

1. does not   2. do not   3. does not   4. does not   5. do not   6. do not

Exercise 2.11

1. Charlie does not play hockey. / Charlie doesn't play hockey.   2. Cindy does not drive to work. / Cindy doesn't drive to work.   3. Jack does not play a musical instrument. / Jack doesn't play a musical instrument.   4. Joshua and Sybil do not go to college. / Joshua and Sybil don't go to college.   5. Sharon and her sister do not work at night. / Sharon and her sister don't work at night.   6. I do not exercise in the morning. / I don't exercise in the morning.   7. We do not finish work at the same time every day. / We don't finish work at the same time every day.

Exercise 2.12

1. Takako and Jun always eat breakfast.   2. Solomon often takes a shower in the morning.   3. They usually drive to work Monday through Friday.   4. I am hardly ever late for work.   5. She seldom walks to work.   6. Hildegard sometimes exercises before work.   7. Julius and his brother frequently take the bus to school.   8. You are occasionally late for school.   9. We hardly ever miss class.   10. Oscar is always tired by 9:00 P.M.

Exercise 2.13

Answers will vary.

Exercise 2.14

1. How often does Etta watch TV?   2. How often do Jay and Marcy go to the mall?   3. How often does Mom shop for groceries?   4. How often do you do your homework?   5. How often do they eat dinner at restaurants?   6. How often does your sister make your breakfast?   7. How often do we miss the bus?   8. How often does Adele visit her grandparents?

Exercise 2.15

1. QUESTION: How often does Cindy drive to work?
   SHORT ANSWER: Never.

2. QUESTION: How often does Jim have lunch at a restaurant?
   SHORT ANSWER: Often.

3. QUESTION: How often does Madeleine do her homework after dinner?
   SHORT ANSWER: Always.

4. QUESTION: How often do Cindy and Jim relax before going to bed?
   SHORT ANSWER: Always.

5. QUESTION: How often does Cindy take a walk in the park?
   SHORT ANSWER: Sometimes.

Exercise 2.16

1. When does your mother-in-law arrive?   2. What time do your children get home from school?   3. What do Peter, Paul, and Mary do on the weekends?   4. Where does Donna play hockey?   5. Which day do you sleep late?   6. How many employees does the company have?   7. How much time do we get for each break?   8. How long does summer vacation last?

Exercise 2.17

Answers will vary.

Exercise 2.18

1. Who wants vanilla ice cream for dessert?   2. Who needs the car tomorrow?   3. Who needs to sleep more than six hours a night?   4. Who takes a vacation every year?   5. Who gets paid on Fridays?   6. Who visits the zoo every year?

Exercise 2.19

Answers will vary.

Exercise 2.20

1. Do Marjorie and Tomas sing in the choir?   2. Do your parents go on vacation to Europe every year?   3. Does Davida have the same work schedule?   4. Does Michel play football?

Exercise 2.21

1. QUESTION: Do Felicity and her boyfriend go to an art museum every month?
   LONG ANSWER: Yes, they do go to an art museum every month.
   SHORT ANSWER: Yes, they do.   QUICK ANSWER: Yes.

2. QUESTION: Do Alexandra and Petrov vacation in Thailand every winter?
   LONG ANSWER: No, they don't vacation in Thailand every winter.
   SHORT ANSWER: No, they don't.   QUICK ANSWER: No.

3. QUESTION: Does Minzhi play on a tennis team?
   LONG ANSWER: Yes, she does play on a tennis team.
   SHORT ANSWER: Yes, she does.   QUICK ANSWER: Yes.

4. QUESTION: Does Chun-Chieh attend music school?
   LONG ANSWER: No, he doesn't attend music school.
   SHORT ANSWER: No, he doesn't.   QUICK ANSWER: No.

Exercise 2.22

1. d   2. e   3. f   4. a   5. g   6. c   7. b

Exercise 2.23

1. wakes up   2. hangs out   3. takes / out   4. gets up   5. dresses up   6. work out

Exercise 2.24

Answers will vary. Be sure to use the guide in the sample conversation.

Exercise 2.25

1. Ravi   2. He misses his family.   3. Peng.   4. He is getting a new education. / He is learning a new way of learning. / He is learning a new education system.

Exercise 2.26

The following are a few possible answers:

School: How to study, different topics studied in school, school teachers and administrators, private versus public schools, school uniforms

Work: Different jobs, getting a job, interviewing for a job, working at a large versus a small company, working for yourself, benefits at work, freelancing, how to work effectively, time management, being an effective boss

Hobbies: Different types of hobbies, hobby groups, time management for hobbies, outdoor hobbies, gaming

Exercise 2.27

Peng Gets an Education

Peng is learning a new education system. He moved to the United States six months ago. He is studying Business and Finance at a university. In China, he didn't go to his undergraduate classes. Instead, he read and studied the textbook. Peng passed all of the exams easily. He has great memorization skills. In the U.S, however, it is a different way of learning. In the university, you must attend classes. The professors talk about new ideas and discuss them with the students. They expect the students to have opinions about the topic. The exams are usually essay exams. Peng doesn't prepare for the exams by memorizing. Peng has a new way of studying. He studies the textbook and all of his class notes. He also discusses the topics with classmates. Peng practices writing for the essays, too. Peng works hard to pass the exams. For Peng, this new way of learning is difficult but also fun.

1. a. He must attend classes.   b. He discusses new ideas in class with his professor and classmates.   c. He must have opinions about the ideas discussed.   d. The exams are essays.

2. a. He studies his notes from class.   b. He discusses topics with classmates.   c. He practices writing for essay exams.

Exercise 2.28

1. China   2. The United States   3. Business and finance   4. No   5. He memorized the textbooks.   6. No   7. Yes   8. A new education system: (1) a different way to learn and (2) a different way to study   9. Yes   10. Yes

Exercise 2.29

Subjects are underlined, and simple present tense verbs are bold.

Ravi and his Family

Ravi **lives** far from his family in India. He **misses** his parents, siblings, and relatives. He moved to a new country for a job as a programmer at a computer company that **makes** software. Right now, the company is creating a new product. Ravi **works** on this product, so he **is** very busy. He **works** from 7:00 A.M. to 8:00 P.M. Monday through Friday. He usually **works** on Saturdays too. Sometimes, he even **goes** to work on Sundays. Ravi **wants** to call his parents, but the time difference **is** big. They are usually sleeping when he calls. Ravi **likes** his new job, but he **misses** his family very much.

Exercise 2.30

1. Incorrect / She wants ice cream for dessert.   2. Correct   3. Incorrect / The grocery store takes cash only.   4. Correct   5. Correct   6. Incorrect / We drive 10 miles to work every day.   7. Incorrect / They celebrate every holiday with a big festival.   8. Correct

Exercise 2.31

Answers will vary.

Exercise 2.32

Jennifer, Mr. Blumenthal, the White House, Whiting High School, Flint Bank, Queen Elizabeth, Nordstrom, Manhattan

Exercise 2.33

Answers will vary.

Exercise 2.34

Answers will vary.

Quiz

1. Habits / Weekly activities / Customs   2. Aunt   3. He / She / It   4. do not take / don't take   5. Hardly ever   6. This is / I want you to meet / I'd like you to meet   7. False; one arm is best.   8. How often   9. False; it's the *subject* of the passage. The primary point of the topic is the main idea.   10. True

Chapter 3   Food: Shopping and Restaurants

Exercise 3.1

1. d   2. c   3. a   4. b

Exercise 3.2

1. is   2. are   3. is   4. are   5. am

Exercise 3.3

1. taking   2. buying   3. choosing   4. drinking   5. stopping   6. showing

Exercise 3.4

1. are driving   2. is calling   3. is attending   4. is buying   5. is cooking   6. are saving   7. is selling   8. am making

Exercise 3.5

Answers will vary.

Exercise 3.6

1. is not   2. are not   3. is not   4. am not   5. are not   6. are not

Exercise 3.7

Answers will vary.

Exercise 3.8

1. Hiro is playing soccer for the summer.
   Hiro isn't playing soccer for the summer.
   Hiro's not playing soccer for the summer.

2. I am studying English these days.
   I am not studying English these days.
   I'm not studying English these days.

3. Ian and Catherine are arguing at this moment.
   Ian and Catherine aren't arguing at this moment.
   They're not arguing at this moment. (Note: Use the subject pronoun *they* to contract the plural subject *Ian* and *Catherine*.)

4. My dog is chewing on a bone.
   My dog isn't chewing on a bone.
   My dog's not chewing on a bone.

5. Sara and I are talking on the phone.
   Sara and I aren't talking on the phone.
   We're not talking on the phone. (Note: Use the subject pronoun *we* to contract the plural subject *Sara and I*.)

Exercise 3.9

Answers will vary.

Exercise 3.10

1. QUESTION: Is Miguel going to adult school for English?
   LONG ANSWER: Yes, Miguel is going to adult school for English.
   SHORT ANSWER: Yes, he is.   QUICK ANSWER: Yes.

2. QUESTION: Is Sheila reading a book right now?
   LONG ANSWER: No, she isn't reading a book right now. / No, she's not reading a book right now.
   SHORT ANSWER: No, she isn't. / No, she's not.   QUICK ANSWER: No.

3. QUESTION: Are Jeff and Henry working at the ice cream shop?
   LONG ANSWER: No, they aren't working at the ice cream shop. / No, they're not working at the ice cream shop.
   SHORT ANSWER: No, they aren't. / No, they're not.   QUICK ANSWER: No.

4. QUESTION: Are you studying at the community college?
   LONG ANSWER: Yes, I am studying at the community college. / Yes, I'm studying at the community college.
   SHORT ANSWER: Yes, I am.   QUICK ANSWER: Yes.

5. QUESTION: Is Bethany learning computer programming at school this year?
   LONG ANSWER: Yes, she is learning computer programming at school this year. / Yes, she's learning computer programming at school this year.
   SHORT ANSWER: Yes, she is.   QUICK ANSWER: Yes.

Exercise 3.11

1. QUESTION: When is Miguel going to school?
   LONG ANSWER: He's going to school at night.
   SHORT ANSWER: At night.

2. QUESTION: How many books is Sheila reading right now?
   LONG ANSWER: She's reading three books.
   SHORT ANSWER: Three.

3. QUESTION: How often are Jeff and Henry working at the ice cream shop?
   LONG ANSWER: They're working at the ice cream shop every weekday.
   SHORT ANSWER: Every weekday.

4. QUESTION: Why are you studying at the community college?
   LONG ANSWER: I'm studying at the community college because it's affordable.
   SHORT ANSWER: Because it's affordable.

5. QUESTION: How is Bethany doing in the computer programming class?
   LONG ANSWER: She's doing very well.
   SHORT ANSWER: Very well.

Exercise 3.12

1. QUESTION: Who is going to dinner with Rex? / Who is going to dinner? / Who is?
   LONG ANSWER: Lara is going to dinner with Rex.
   SHORT ANSWER: Lara is.
   QUICK ANSWER: Lara.

2. QUESTION: Who is eating dinner at her sister's house? / Who is eating dinner? / Who is?
   LONG ANSWER: Margarita and her son are eating dinner at her sister's house.
   SHORT ANSWER: Margarita and her son are.
   QUICK ANSWER: Margarita and her son.

3. QUESTION: Who is cooking Sunday dinner? / Who is cooking? / Who is?
   LONG ANSWER: Roshana's mother is cooking Sunday dinner.
   SHORT ANSWER: Roshana's mother is.
   QUICK ANSWER: Roshana's mother.

4. QUESTION: Who is getting sandwiches at a deli? / Who is getting sandwiches? / Who is?
   LONG ANSWER: Lorraine and her friends are getting sandwiches at a deli.
   SHORT ANSWER: Lorraine and her friends are.
   QUICK ANSWER: Lorraine and her friends.

5. QUESTION: Who is bringing food to the park? / Who is bringing food? / Who is?
   LONG ANSWER: Ludwig and Cy are bringing food to the park.
   SHORT ANSWER: Ludwig and Cy are.
   QUICK ANSWER: Ludwig and Cy.

Exercise 3.13

1. **Count nouns:** pizzas / **Noncount nouns:** soda, potato chips (Note: Pizza can be either count or noncount, depending on how it's used. In this sentence, we are talking about whole pizzas, so it is a count noun. If you have a slice of the pizza, it is noncount but you can count the slices.)

2. **Noncount nouns:** coffee, tea, water, juice

3. **Count nouns:** airport, friends, store / **Noncount nouns:** luggage, clothes

4. **Noncount nouns:** tennis, news

5. **Count nouns:** apples, banana / **Noncount nouns:** chocolate, ice cream

Exercise 3.14

1. spoons   2. forks   3. knives   4. eggs   5. children   6. teeth   7. batches   8. recipes
9. potatoes   10. boysenberries   11. hens   12. loaves

Exercise 3.15

1. g, h   2. g, h   3. a, c, d   4. b, c   5. a, c, d   6. e   7. f   8. b

Exercise 3.16

1. Several / my   2. Five / the   3. Three / her   4. Every / this / two   5. My / five / the
6. That / many

Exercise 3.17

Answers will vary.

Exercise 3.18

1. How much   2. How many   3. How much   4. How much   5. How many
6. How many   7. How many   8. How much

Exercise 3.19

Answers will vary.

Exercise 3.20

1. an / the   2. a / The   3. a / the   4. a / The   5. an / the

Exercise 3.21

1. the   2. the   3. any   4. the   5. a

Exercise 3.22

Answers will vary. The following answers are guidelines:
1. Either *a* or *an;* must have an article   2. *The;* must have an article   3. *Some* for affirmative sentences; *any* for questions or negatives; omit the article   4. *The* or omit the article   5. *Some* for affirmative sentences; *any* for questions or negatives; omit the article   6. *The* or omit the article

Exercise 3.23

1. f   2. c   3. a   4. d   5. b   6. e

Exercise 3.24

1. is tidying up/ is cleaning up   2. is filling / up   3. is adding up   4. are eating out   5. are chipping in

Exercise 3.25

Answers will vary. Be sure to use polite expressions for ordering food. Use phrasal verbs related to eating at restaurants. Use the sample conversation as a guide.

Exercise 3.26

TOPIC: Sally
MAIN IDEA: She grows her food. / She grows the food she eats in her garden. / She eats food from her garden. (Or something similar)

Exercise 3.27

1. an outdoor market where farmers sell directly to consumers   2. vegetables that grow on a vine and climb   3. dino kale and Tuscan kale   4. foods with many nutrients   5. natural chemicals in plants

Exercise 3.28

Answers will vary.

Quiz

1. BE + verb-**ing**   2. Drop the e and add -**ing**.   3. Every day   4. does not eating   5. At the café.   6. Yes, she is.   7. Mixes   8. Salt   9. A teaspoon of   10. A orange

Chapter 4   Getting Around Town

Exercise 4.1

1. A stop sign and a traffic light   2. A streetlight   3. A pedestrian   4. A parking lot
5. A pharmacy   6. The doughnut shop, the grocery store, the café, the bakery, the Chinese restaurant, and the Italian restaurant   7. A street and a road   8. A sidewalk
9. An intersection   10. Four blocks

Exercise 4.2

Exercise 4.3

1. b   2. d   3. e   4. a   5. c

Exercise 4.4

1. Cross the street. / Don't cross the street.   2. Go straight for two blocks. / Don't go straight for two blocks.   3. When you get to the hospital, go right. / When you get to the hospital, don't go right.   4. At the intersection, make a left. / At the intersection, don't make a left.   5. After you pass the movie theater, turn right. / After you pass the movie theater, don't turn right.

Exercise 4.5

1. Cross the street. / Don't cross the street.   2. Go straight / Don't go straight   3. go right / don't go right   4. make a left / don't make a left   5. turn right / don't turn right

Exercise 4.6

1. café or Chinese restaurant   2. office building   3. police station / doughnut shop   4. park or parking lot   5. The hospital or The bank or The hardware store or City Hall   6. parking lot   7. post office   8. Chinese restaurant

Exercise 4.7

1. on the corner of / and   2. next to or next door to   3. next to or next door to   4. between or in between / and   5. across from or across the street from   6. next to or next door to   7. across from or across the street from   8. across from or across the street from

Exercise 4.8

1. The parking lot   2. The doughnut shop   3. The pharmacy

Exercise 4.9

Answers will vary. Here are some suggestions.
1. Take a right out of the Chinese restaurant and walk to the Intersection. Cross River Road. It's on your right after City Hall.   2. Take a left out of the Chinese restaurant. Go past the movie theater and make another left. It's just past the movie theater on the left.   3. Cross the street. Walk between the office building and the bank. It's behind the office building on the left.

Exercise 4.10

1. parking lot   2. fire station   3. Italian restaurant   4. office building   5. parking lots
6. trees   7. six/several/many/some   8. hardware store

Exercise 4.11

1. There are   2. there are   3. There is   4. there is   5. There are   6. there is   7. there is
8. There are

Exercise 4.12

1. There aren't   2. there isn't   3. There isn't   4. there aren't   5. There isn't   6. There aren't
7. there aren't   8. There isn't

Exercise 4.13

1. There is a bakery next to the post office.   2. There are two/a couple of parking lots in downtown Porter City.   3. There isn't a café on the corner of Main Street and River Road.
4. There is a library across from/across the street from a/the park.   5. There aren't two Indian restaurants in downtown Porter City.   6. There is a hospital across from/across the street from a/the bank.   7. There isn't a library on Main Street.   8. There are many/some/a few trees in the park.

Exercise 4.14

Here are some suggested answers. You can also provide other helpful information when giving a short answer.

1. No, there isn't. There is one on River Road.   2. Yes, there is. There's a grocery store on Broad Street.   3. Yes, there are. There is a parking lot on Main Street next to the hospital, and there is one behind the Chinese restaurant on Main.   4. No, there isn't. There is only one bank downtown. It's on the corner of Main and River.   5. Yes, there is. There's a department store next to the fire station.

Exercise 4.15

1. Are there / No, there aren't.   2. is there / No, there isn't.   3. Are there / Yes, there are.
4. Is there / Yes, there is.   5. Is there / Yes, there is.

Exercise 4.16

1. Where is there a police station downtown?   2. Where is there a place to get breakfast?   3. Where is there a café with Wi-Fi?   4. Where is there a place to donate clothes?

Exercise 4.17

Maps will differ.

Exercise 4.18

Answers will vary.

Exercise 4.19

Answers will vary.

Exercise 4.20

Answers will vary. Here are some suggestions:
1. Could you repeat that, please?   2. Sorry, I didn't catch that. Could you please repeat that?

Exercise 4.21

Answers will vary. Here are some suggestions:
1. So, I should go to the intersection, cross River Road, and the hotel is on the right?
2. You mean I take a right at the intersection, and it's on my right after the café?

Exercise 4.22

1 Pardon me. Do you know where the movie theater is?
7 Ok great! Thank you very much!
3 So, I should take a right and it will be on my right?
2 Yes. Walk down this street and take a left at the traffic light. You'll see it on the right.
4 No. Actually, you take a LEFT and it's on the right.
6 Just ½ a block.
5 Ah, ok. I take a left and it's on the right. How far down is it on the right?
8 Sure.

Exercise 4.23

Answers will vary.

Exercise 4.24

1. A bus station   2. A bus driver   3. A bus stop   4. A customer service agent   5. A ticket counter   6. A train station   7. A terminal   8. A ticket   9. A kiosk   10. A conductor   11. A schedule

Exercise 4.25

1. Oakland 11   2. Alameda 8   3. Berkeley 5   4. Alameda 31   5. Oakland 27   6. Oakland 11

Exercise 4.26

Answers will vary. Here are some possibilities.
1. The Oakland 11 runs/comes every half hour until/till 9:30 A.M.   2. The Emeryville 3 runs/comes every hour/on the hour/every hour on the hour until/till 9:00 A.M.   3. The Berkeley 29 runs/comes every 10 minutes until /till 7:00 A.M.   4. The Alameda 31 runs/comes every half hour until/till 8:30 A.M.

Exercise 4.27

Answers will vary.

Exercise 4.28

1. b   2. d   3. e   4. c   5. f   6. g   7. a

Exercise 4.29

1. figure out *or* look up   2. pick / up   3. top off   4. figure out *or* look up   5. get around
6. ask around

Exercise 4.30

1. Josie   2. She likes Porter City because it's easy to get around.

Exercise 4.31

Here is an example of what active reading looks like.

Josie Gets Around Porter City

Josie enjoys living and working in Porter City. She lives on the (outskirts) or the outer area, of the city. She works downtown in the financial district. The public transportation system is very (convenient.) Every week day, she takes the bus to work because it is too far to walk. She catches the bus at 8:00 A.M. At 6:15 P.M, she takes the bus back home, where she arrives at 7:00 P.M. Every Saturday, Josie walks to the grocery store to buy food for the week. On Sundays, she rides her bicycle to the park. Her neighborhood park is five blocks from her house. There are many activities to do in the park such as exercising, barbecuing, and relaxing. Right now, Josie is playing tennis in the park with her friend. Porter City is a nice place to live, and Josie likes Porter City because it is easy to get around.

Exercise 4.32

1. 8:00 A.M.   2. 7:00 P.M.   3. In the park   4. Yes   5. It's easy to get around.

Exercise 4.33

1. tax benefits and discounted tolls   2. drive to work with a family member, a friend, or a coworker   3. saves gas and decreases air pollution   4. the vanpool and company shuttles   5. space for bicyclists to ride alongside cars

Exercise 4.34

1. Subject: Jacob / Verb: gets / Object: a paycheck   2. Subject: Sandra / Verb: is walking / Object: her dog   3. Subject: Geraldo / Verb: likes / Object: movies   4. Subject: the bus / Verb: takes / Object: Audrey   5. Subject: Joseph / Verb: plays / Object: baseball   6. Subject: Mike / Verb: is taking / Object: a taxi   7. Subject: Tanaka / Verb: is studying / Object: economics   8. Subject: The Williams family / Verb: plans / Object: a vacation

Exercise 4.35

Answers will vary.

Exercise 4.36

Answers will vary.

Quiz

1. Imperative   2. There are   3. Behind   4. Near to   5. True   6. Simple present   7. Such as / For example / Like / Including   8. SVO   9. Make a right. / Turn right. / Go right.   10. Paraphrase

Chapter 5   Recreation and Hobbies

Exercise 5.1

1. cooked   2. exercised   3. raked   4. walked   5. biked   6. worked   7. grilled   8. carried

Exercise 5.2

1. /ɪd/   2. /t/   3. /t/   4. /d/   5. /ɪd/   6. /t/   7. /d/   8. /d/

Exercise 5.3

Answers will vary.

Exercise 5.4

1. swam   2. ran   3. drank   4. bought   5. slept   6. sang   7. forgot   8. made

Exercise 5.5

1. Denise and Kerry danced all night at the party.   2. Jeremy and his friends rode their motorcycles last weekend.   3. On Friday, she drove to the country.   4. Earlier this week, Matt moved in to a new apartment.   5. I hiked the mountain yesterday afternoon.   6. They enjoyed the weather this past weekend.

Exercise 5.6

1. did not cook   2. did not run   3. did not come   4. did not have   5. did not win
6. did not hike

Exercise 5.7

1. Vera did not like the movie. / Vera didn't like the movie.   2. Hilal and her mother did not go to the store. / Hilal and her mother didn't go to the store.   3. He did not understand the math class. / He didn't understand the math class.   4. I did not forget the concert tickets. / I didn't forget the concert tickets.

Exercise 5.8

1. c   2. e   3. a   4. d   5. b

Exercise 5.9

Answers may vary. Here are possible answers.
1. Raman went sailing over the weekend.   2. Tamara didn't go waterskiing last week.   3. This morning, my mom went shopping.   4. Last weekend, he didn't go hunting.   5. Gretel didn't go boating on Saturday.   6. Ulya went skiing all winter.

Exercise 5.10

1. QUESTION: Did Felicia go to the museum on Saturday?
   LONG ANSWER: Yes, she did go to the museum on Saturday. / Yes, she went to the museum on Saturday.
   SHORT ANSWER: Yes, she did.   QUICK ANSWER: Yes.

2. QUESTION: Did Manny catch his flight to Hong Kong this morning?
   LONG ANSWER: Yes, he did catch his flight to Hong Kong this morning. / Yes, he caught his flight to Hong Kong this morning.
   SHORT ANSWER: Yes, he did.   QUICK ANSWER: Yes.

3. QUESTION: Did Dr. Lane run the marathon last week?
   LONG ANSWER: No, Dr. Lane didn't run the marathon last week.
   SHORT ANSWER: No, she didn't.   QUICK ANSWER: No.

4. QUESTION: Did you get the tickets for the musical?
   LONG ANSWER: Yes, I did get the tickets for the musical. / Yes, I got the tickets for the musical.
   SHORT ANSWER: Yes, I did.   QUICK ANSWER: Yes.

5. QUESTION: Did Salvatore register for ballroom dancing lessons?
   LONG ANSWER: No, Salvatore didn't register for ballroom dancing lessons.
   SHORT ANSWER: No, he didn't.   QUICK ANSWER: No.

Exercise 5.11

1. QUESTION: When did Eveline and Jack go to the symphony? / When did they go to the symphony? / When did they go?
   LONG ANSWER: Eveline and Jack went to the symphony on Sunday evening. / They went to the symphony on Sunday evening.
   SHORT ANSWER: Sunday evening.

2. QUESTION: Who quilted a beautiful blanket for the raffle? / Who did?
   LONG ANSWER: Ingrid and her mother quilted a beautiful blanket for the raffle.
   SHORT ANSWER: Ingrid and her mother.

3. QUESTION: What did her aunt bake for the picnic? / What did her aunt bake?
   LONG ANSWER: Her aunt baked three delicious berry pies for the picnic. / Her aunt baked three delicious berry pies.
   SHORT ANSWER: Three delicious berry pies.

4. QUESTION: Where did Paul and Martin walk last spring? / Where did they walk last spring? / Where did they walk?
   LONG ANSWER: Paul and Martin walked in Spain. / They walked in Spain.
   SHORT ANSWER: In Spain.

5. QUESTION: How long did the meditation group live in the Himalayas? / How long did the group live in the Himalayans? / How long did they live in the Himalayas? **Note:** Although *it* is the correct pronoun for *group,* most people will refer to the group as *they* because it is a group of people.
   LONG ANSWER: The meditation group lived in the Himalayas for one month. / They lived in the Himalayas for one month.
   SHORT ANSWER: One month.

Exercise 5.12

1. was   2. was   3. was   4. were   5. was   6. were   7. was   8. was   9. were   10. was

Exercise 5.13

1. was   2. was   3. were   4. were   5. was   6. were   7. was   8. was   9. were   10. was

Exercise 5.14

1. wasn't   2. weren't   3. wasn't   4. weren't   5. weren't   6. weren't   7. wasn't   8. wasn't
9. weren't   10. wasn't

Exercise 5.15

1. Marion and Trudy weren't at the café this morning.   2. They weren't happy yesterday.
3. Cheyenne and I weren't bad students last year.   4. Lucy wasn't worried.   5. My computer wasn't broken.   6. We weren't hungry at lunch.

Exercise 5.16

Answers will vary.

Exercise 5.17

Answers will vary.

Exercise 5.18

Answers will vary.

Exercise 5.19

1. QUESTION: Were they the owners of the store?
   LONG ANSWER: Yes, they were the owners of the store.
   SHORT ANSWER: Yes, they were.   QUICK ANSWER: Yes.

2. QUESTION: Was is a good movie?
   LONG ANSWER: No, it was not a good movie. / No, it wasn't a good movie.
   SHORT ANSWER: No, it was not. / No, it wasn't.   QUICK ANSWER: No.

3. QUESTION: Were we at school at that time?
   LONG ANSWER: Yes, we were at school at that time.
   SHORT ANSWER: Yes, we were.   QUICK ANSWER: Yes.

4. QUESTION: Was she a student at the art school last semester?
   LONG ANSWER: Yes, she was a student at the art school last semester.
   SHORT ANSWER: Yes, she was.   QUICK ANSWER: Yes.

5. QUESTION: Were you happy yesterday afternoon?
   LONG ANSWER: Yes, I was happy yesterday afternoon.
   SHORT ANSWER: Yes, I was.   QUICK ANSWER: Yes.

Exercise 5.20

1. QUESTION: When were Vivian and Marcelle there?
   LONG ANSWER: They were there in the afternoon.
   SHORT ANSWER: In the afternoon.

2. QUESTION: Why was the car dead?
   LONG ANSWER: It was dead because it ran out of gas.
   SHORT ANSWER: Because it ran out of gas.

3. QUESTION: How often were you at the beach?
   LONG ANSWER: I was at the beach every weekend.
   SHORT ANSWER: Every weekend.

4. QUESTION: Where was he last week?
   LONG ANSWER: He was on vacation.
   SHORT ANSWER: On vacation.

5. QUESTION: How was she?
   LONG ANSWER: She was okay.
   SHORT ANSWER: Okay.

6. QUESTION: What was the problem?
   LONG ANSWER: The problem was the printer ran out of paper.
   SHORT ANSWER: The printer ran out of paper.

Exercise 5.21

1. Verb: prefers / to go: Infinitive   2. Verb: hates / going to: Gerund   3. Verb: like / listening: Gerund   4. Verb: love / bungee jumping: Gerund   5. Verb: prefers / to take: Infinitive   6. Verb: hate / to wait: Infinitive

Exercise 5.22

1. a. to fish / b. fishing   2. a. scuba diving / b. to scuba dive   3. a. to snorkel / b. snorkeling   4. a. waterskiing / b. to waterski

Exercise 5.23

Answers will vary.

Exercise 5.24

1. Their   2. My   3. His   4. My / your   5. Her   6. Her / my   7. They / my   8. Our / our

Exercise 5.25

1. They took their daughter to the park last Saturday.   2. She swam for one hour yesterday afternoon in her pool.   3. They brought their guitars to the beach.   4. He painted a mural on his front yard fence.

Exercise 5.26

Answers will vary. Be sure that the verb is in the simple past tense. Confirm that the subject pronouns are correct (male/female), and check that the possessive adjectives are appropriate.

Exercise 5.27

Answers will vary.

Exercise 5.28

1. d   2. c   3. a   4. g   5. f   6. e   7. b

Exercise 5.29

1. warms up   2. showed up   3. cools down   4. let / down   5. looks forward to
6. come down

Exercise 5.30

1. damaging / b   2. very tired / e   3. doesn't release negative feelings / c   4. not exciting to look at / a   5. not funny / d

Exercise 5.31

1. Khaled's adventures   2. His first adventure was skydiving.

Exercise 5.32

Khaled's First Adventure

On his first adventure, Khaled jumped out of an airplane. He graduated from college a month ago, and he is celebrating by doing new recreational activities. He works full time, so he planned exciting weekends for the summer. Last weekend, he went sky diving. He jumped out of an airplane and free-fell until he opened the parachute. His parachute worked perfectly, and Khaled landed safely. After he landed, he yelled, "Woooohoooooooo!" He loved it. It was scary but also exhilarating. He is very excited about his adventure next weekend – parasailing. But he won't forget his first skydiving adventure – free-falling from an airplane.

Exercise 5.33

1. To celebrate his graduation   2. One month ago   3. Skydiving   4. Yes   5. Parasailing

Exercise 5.34

Exclamation Point Interjections (!)

No way!
Get out!
Wow!
Nice!
Woohoo!
Yes!
Rock on!
That's amazing!
Yay!
Good for you!
Right on!

Question Mark Interjections (?)

Really?
You did?
Are you kidding me?
What?

Exercise 5.35

Answers will vary.

Quiz

1. went camping   2. yesterday / last summer / all summer / on Friday   3. bought   4. saw
5. False   6. Did Anne-Marie have a good weekend? / Who had a good weekend? / Where did Anne-Marie go last weekend? / What did Anne-Marie do last weekend?   7. Like / Love / Hate / Prefer   8. Its   9. Exciting   10. True

Chapter 6   Making Friends

Exercise 6.1

In every example, the people have something in common.

Exercise 6.2

1. Look at all the sweaters the knitting club made! <u>His</u> is the green one.   2. My brother has a beautiful flower garden. It's much prettier than <u>mine</u>.   3. See that shiny new car over there? It's <u>hers</u>.   4. Their nature photographs are in this gallery. <u>Theirs</u> are the pictures of mountains and lakes.   5. Is this pencil <u>yours</u>?   6. Here are two coats. Are the coats <u>theirs</u>?

Exercise 6.3

1. Ours was the red house on the right. It's not ours any longer. We sold it.   2. Those shoes are hers.   3. The kids in the pool are mine.   4. The children eating popcorn are theirs.

Exercise 6.4

Answers will vary.

Exercise 6.5

1. hat, bicycle   2. this, that   3. pants, chocolate chip cookies   4. these, those

Exercise 6.6

1. These flowers smell nice.   2. Those bikes cost a lot of money.   3. This money is mine.
4. That house is Maddy's.

Exercise 6.7

Answers will vary.

Exercise 6.8

1. We live here.   2. Penelope studies there.   3. Gwen sings there.   4. He works here.   5. They often eat dinner there.   6. My parents live here.

Exercise 6.9

Answers will vary.

Exercise 6.10

1. Those   2. that   3. this   4. This   5. these   6. That   7. These   8. that

Exercise 6.11

1. We love these!   2. Those are Sherry's.   3. These are my kids.   4. Those are Jim's kids.

Exercise 6.12

Answers will vary.

Exercise 6.13

Do you wanna go together sometime? I'd be happy to show you around and give you some tips on the best yarns.

Exercise 6.14

Answers can vary. Here are some possible answers.
1. Shradha: Hey, would you like to study for the test together this Friday afternoon? / Do you want to study for the test together this Friday afternoon? / Are you free Friday afternoon? Wanna study for the test together? 2. Christine: Do you want to hike a new trail Sunday morning? / Are you free Sunday morning? / Can you hike a new trail Sunday morning? 3. Margie: Would you and your son like to join us at the park Wednesday after school? 4. Seth: Are you busy after the conference today? Would you like to join me for dinner? / Are you interested in joining me for dinner after the conference today? 5. Henry: Are you free Saturday night? Can you come to a party at my house? / Are you free Saturday night? Do you want to come to a party at my house?

Exercise 6.15

Answers will vary. Check level of formality.
1. Suggestion: This situation is informal, so use informal language. (*I won't be able to* and *must* are too formal.) Example answers: Sorry, but I can't. I'm babysitting my brother. / Bummer! I have to babysit my brother. / Oh, I can't go. I've got to babysit my brother. / I'd love to, but I'm supposed to babysit my brother.

2. This situation is more formal, so use more formal language. **Note:** *BE supposed to* is not the best answer. Example answers: I wish I could, but I won't be able to. I've got to attend a business meeting during lunch. / I'm sorry, but I have to attend a business meeting during lunch. / I'd love to, but I must attend a business meeting during lunch. / I'm afraid I can't. I have to attend a business meeting during lunch. / I can't make it. I've got to attend a business meeting during lunch.

Exercise 6.16

1. We have to have dinner with my parents Thursday evening.
   We have/We've got to have dinner with my parents Thursday evening.
   We must have dinner with my parents Thursday evening.
   We are/We're supposed to have dinner with my parents Thursday evening.

2. I have to walk my dogs after dinner.
   I have/I've got to walk my dogs after dinner.
   I must walk my dogs after dinner.
   I'm supposed to walk my dogs after dinner.

3. He has to finish his research paper this weekend.
   He has/He's got to finish his research paper this weekend.
   He must finish his research paper this weekend.
   He's supposed to finish his research paper this weekend.

4. They have to visit their sister that day.
   They have/They've got to visit their sister that day.
   They must visit their sister that day.
   They are/They're supposed to visit their sister that day.

5. She has to clean her house this afternoon.
   She has/She's got to clean her house this afternoon.
   She must clean her house this afternoon.
   She is/She's supposed to clean her house this afternoon.

6. I have to work on my résumé Wednesday evening.
   I have/I've got to work on my résumé Wednesday evening.
   I must work on my résumé Wednesday evening.
   I am/I'm supposed to work on my résumé Wednesday evening.

7. We have to do our homework tonight.
   We have/We've got to do our homework tonight.
   We must do our homework tonight.
   We are/We're supposed to do our homework tonight.

8. I have to meet with my supervisor that morning.
   I have/I've got to meet with my supervisor that morning.
   I must meet with my supervisor that morning.
   I am/I'm supposed to meet with my supervisor that morning.

Exercise 6.17

Answers will vary.

Exercise 6.18

Answers can vary. See following examples.
1. Christine: Do you want to hike a new trail Sunday morning?
   Julia: Oh, I'd love to, but I have plans on Sunday morning. Can we take a raincheck?

2. Margie: Would you and your son like to join us at the park Wednesday after school?
   Lynette: That would be great! We would love to join you.

3. Seth: Are you busy after the conference today? Would you like to join me for dinner?
   Howard: I can't. I have to finish a work project after the conference. But thank you for asking.

4. Henry: Are you free Saturday night? Can you come to a party at my house?
   Rishi: That sounds like fun. Can I bring my wife?

Exercise 6.19

Possible answers:
1. Let's work on the art project Thursday evening. / Why don't we work on the art project Thursday evening? / Should we work on the art project Thursday evening? / Shall we work on the art project Thursday evening?   2. Let's play the game today. / Why don't we play the game today? / Should we play the game today? / Shall we play the game today?   3. Let's get together soon. / Why don't we get together soon? / Should we get together soon? / Shall we get together soon?   4. Let's eat lunch today. / Why don't we eat lunch today? / Should we eat lunch today? / Shall we eat lunch today?

Exercise 6.20

1. We will cook brunch for Leyla's birthday on Sunday.   2. Seamus might/may not do his presentation on Monday.   3. I might/may pass the test in math class.   4. My boss will give me a raise next year.   4. Professor Dunn might/may give a test in computer class next week.

Exercise 6.21

Answers will vary.

Exercise 6.22

1. He can't understand the math problem.   2. Janice is able to understand the math problem.   3. Paul isn't able to understand the math problem.   4. The Greggs family might/may be able to go camping.   5. Sheena and her daughter might/may not be able to go camping.
6. Preston and his son aren't able to go camping.

Exercise 6.23

Answers will vary, but these rules must be followed:
1. Must use *can*   2. Must use *can't* or *cannot*   3. Must use *BE able to*; use correct form of BE (*am*, *is*, or *are*)   4. Must use *BE able to + not*; use correct form of BE (*am*, *is*, or *are*)   5. Must use *might* or *may + BE able to*; use correct form of BE (*be*)   6. Must use *might* or *may + not + BE able to*; use correct form of BE (*be*)

Exercise 6.24

1. eight-eight-eight / six-two-five /oh-oh-four-eight   2. five-oh-eight / seven-two-two / nine-five-four-six   3. nine-seven-eight / four-four-five / one-one-oh-five *or* eleven-oh-five   4. nine-one-nine / two-three-six / nine-eight-one-five

Exercise 6.25

Verbal exercise; no answers.

Exercise 6.26

1. c   2. d   3. a   4. n   5. b   6. m   7. e   8. l   9. k   10. f   11. j   12. h   13 g   14. i

Exercise 6.27

1. made up   2. passed up   3. are cheering up   4. call / back   5. backs up   6. called off
7. ended up   8. do / over

Exercise 6.28

Answers will vary.

Exercise 6.29

1. Mabel   2. She made a new friend, Angelita.

Exercise 6.30

Mabel and Her New Friend

Mabel made a new friend. Her name is Angelita. Mabel and Angelita work in the cafeteria of an office building. They both prepare food for lunch. Mabel is a new employee. She got the job a week ago. Angelita, on the other hand, has been working there for six months. Angelita helps Mabel with tasks. For example, she showed Mabel how to operate the meat cutter. Together, they are a good team. They work hard and finish their duties, or tasks, quickly. Their supervisor likes their productivity. He seems happy with their teamwork. They are happy to work together. They made a plan to go shopping together after work. Mabel is glad she made a new friend.

Exercise 6.31

1. At work. / Mabel made her new friend at work. / Mabel made her new friend at her new job. 2. Angelita. / Her name is Angelita. 3. In a cafeteria. / They work in a cafeteria. / They work in the cafeteria of an office building. 4. Angelita shows Mabel how to do tasks. / She shows Mabel how to do things. / She shows Mabel how to slice the meat. 5. They are going shopping after work. / Their plan is to go shopping after work. 6. Glad. / Mabel is glad about her new friend.

Exercise 6.32

1. **Subject:** Oscar / **Verb:** sounds / **Complement:** angry 2. **Subject:** Noreen and her cousin / **Verb:** feel / **Complement:** sad 3. **Subject:** My coworker / **Verb:** is / **Complement:** absent 4. **Subject:** The doctor / **Verb:** is / **Complement:** very kind 5. **Subject:** Making friends / **Verb:** is / **Complement:** easy 6. **Subject:** Those cookies / **Verb:** smell / **Complement:** delicious 7. **Subject:** My mother / **Verb:** seems / **Complement:** satisfied 8. **Subject:** Cecilia / **Verb:** became / **Complement:** a high school teacher

Exercise 6.33

1. angry / adj 2. sad / adj 3. absent / adj 4. kind / adj 5. easy / adj 6. delicious / adj 7. satisfied / adj 8. high school teacher / n

Exercise 6.34

Answers will vary.

Quiz

1. might / may 2. has / has got / is supposed 3. can't / isn't able to 4. this 5. Those 6. yours 7. there 8. here 9. hair 10. A postponed event

Chapter 7   Health and Medicine

Exercise 7.1

1. have been taking   2. has been drinking   3. have been feeling   4. has been recovering
5. have been resting   6. has been eating   7. has been reading   8. has been feeling

Exercise 7.2

1. They've been feeling   2. He's been recovering / My father's been recovering   3. They've
been resting   4. She's been eating / His sister's been eating   5. He's been reading / Sam's been
reading   6. She's been feeling / Carolina's been feeling

Exercise 7.3

1. since yesterday   2. for a long time   3. all afternoon   4. the whole summer   5. since he got
the flu   6. lately

Exercise 7.4

1. Kristi has been studying all night for her exam tomorrow.   2. Cathy and Ned have been
meditating for 30 minutes.   3. Recently, we have/we've been waking up late.   4. Lately, you
have/you've been eating a lot of fast food.   5. I have/I've been exercising hard the whole
summer.   6. He has/He's been dieting since January.

Exercise 7.5

Answers will vary.

Exercise 7.6

1. has not been feeling   2. have not been singing   3. has not been shaving   4. have not been
having   5. has not been suffering   6. has not been going

Exercise 7.7

1. Solange hasn't been feeling very well all day. She's been sleeping.   2. The performers haven't
been singing traditional songs all semester. They've been singing new ones.   3. Mr. Foster hasn't
been shaving his face. He's been growing a beard and mustache.   4. Lately, we haven't been
having fun. We've been working too hard.   5. My daughter hasn't been suffering from allergies.
She's been breathing easily.   6. Henrietta hasn't been going to church this past month. She's
been recovering from a broken leg.

Exercise 7.8

1. They have not been coming to the sales meetings lately. / They haven't been coming to the
sales meetings lately.   2. They have not been checking e-mail for two weeks. / They haven't
been checking e-mail for two weeks.   3. I have not been going to the dog park since Monday.

/ I haven't been going to the dog park since Monday.   4. He has not been relaxing since he retired. / He hasn't been relaxing since he retired.   5. He has not been playing golf in Los Angeles for weeks. / He hasn't been playing golf in Los Angeles for weeks.   6. She has not been sleeping since she had the baby. / She hasn't been sleeping since she had the baby.

Exercise 7.9

1. QUESTION: Has he been recovering from his surgery?
   LONG ANSWER: Yes, he has been recovering from his surgery.
   SHORT ANSWER: Yes, he has. / Yes, he has been.   QUICK ANSWER: Yes.

2. QUESTION: Has Jigar been enjoying his vacation so far?
   LONG ANSWER: Yes, he has been enjoying his vacation so far.
   SHORT ANSWER: Yes, he has. / Yes, he has been.   QUICK ANSWER: Yes.

3. QUESTION: Have you been suffering from allergies in the past week?
   LONG ANSWER: No, I haven't been suffering from allergies in the past week.
   SHORT ANSWER: No, I have not. / No, I haven't. / No, I haven't been.   QUICK ANSWER: No.

4. QUESTION: Have Joey and Carlos/they been playing baseball all spring?
   LONG ANSWER: Yes, Joey and Carlos/they have been playing baseball all spring.
   SHORT ANSWER: Yes, they have. / Yes, they have been.   QUICK ANSWER: Yes.

5. QUESTION: Has Marion been taking her medicine since the doctor's visit?
   LONG ANSWER: No, she hasn't been taking her medicine since the doctor's visit.
   SHORT ANSWER: No, she has not. / No, she hasn't. / No, she hasn't been.   QUICK ANSWER: No.

6. QUESTION: Has she been preparing dinner for an hour?
   LONG ANSWER: Yes, she has been preparing dinner for an hour.
   SHORT ANSWER: Yes, she has. / Yes, she has been.   QUICK ANSWER: Yes.

Exercise 7.10

1. QUESTION: Where has Prisca been working with international professionals?
   LONG ANSWER: She's been working with international professionals in Switzerland.
   SHORT ANSWER: In Switzerland.

2. QUESTION: How long have Danielle and Mike been planning a round-the-world trip?
   LONG ANSWER: They've been planning a round-the-world trip for a month.
   SHORT ANSWER: For a month.

3. QUESTION: Why has Hailey been seeing her doctor every week?
   LONG ANSWER: She's been seeing her doctor every week for back pain.
   SHORT ANSWER: For back pain.

4. QUESTION: How much have Eveline and Paul been saving for a new house?
   LONG ANSWER: They've been saving half of their paychecks every month.
   SHORT ANSWER: Half of their paychecks every month.

5. QUESTION: How long has Michelle been teaching yoga in her new studio?
   LONG ANSWER: She's been teaching yoga in her new studio since January.
   SHORT ANSWER: Since January.

6. QUESTION: Where has Gerard been visiting his mother?
   LONG ANSWER: He's been visiting his mother in Florida.
   SHORT ANSWER: In Florida.

Exercise 7.11

1 / j	2 / g	3 / m	4 / k	5 / n
6 / b	7 / c	8 / a	9 / e	10 / d
11 / h	12 / o	13 / i	14 / l	15 / f

Exercise 7.12

1. Hair   2. Forehead   3. Sinus   4. Hand   5. Wrist   6. Elbow   7. Lungs   8. Eyes
9. Nose   10. Mouth   11. Throat   12. Heart   13. Thumb   14. Index finger   15. Middle
finger   16. Ring finger   17. Pinkie   18. Stomach   19. Intestines   20. Thigh   21. Knee
22. Ankle   23. Foot

Exercise 7.13

1. A little pain   2. Kind of hurts   3. Really hurts   4. Severe pain

Exercise 7.14

1. You should drink more water every day.
   You had better drink more water every day.
   You ought to drink more water every day.
   You might want to drink more water every day.

2. Melody should get eight hours of sleep every night.
   Melody had better get eight hours of sleep every night.
   Melody ought to get eight hours of sleep every night.
   Melody might want to get eight hours of sleep every night.

3. They should pay the rent on time.
   They had better pay the rent on time.
   They ought to pay the rent on time.
   They might want to pay the rent on time.

4. Fawn should do her homework every night.
   Fawn had better do her homework every night.
   Fawn ought to do her homework every night.
   Fawn might want to do her homework every night.

5. He should take his antibiotics every day until they're gone.
   He had better take his antibiotics every day until they're gone.
   He ought to take his antibiotics every day until they're gone.
   He might want to take his antibiotics every day until they're gone.

6. You should go to the dentist soon.
   You had better go to the dentist soon.
   You ought to go to the dentist soon.
   You might want to go to the dentist soon.

7. I should talk to my supervisor about the problem.
   I had better talk to my supervisor about the problem.
   I ought to talk to my supervisor about the problem.
   I might want to talk to my supervisor about the problem.

8. She should make an appointment with the doctor.
   She had better make an appointment with the doctor.
   She ought to make an appointment with the doctor.
   She might want to make an appointment with the doctor.

Exercise 7.15

1. had better / should / ought to   2. had better   3. should / ought to   4. might want to

Exercise 7.16

Answers will vary. Be sure to use *to* with *ought* and *might want*.

Exercise 7.17

1. QUESTION: Should she clean the house *today*?
   LONG ANSWER: Yes, she *should* clean the house today.
   SHORT ANSWER: Yes, she *should*.   QUICK ANSWER: Yes.

2. QUESTION: Should Trevor take this *job*?
   LONG ANSWER: Yes, he *should* take this job.
   SHORT ANSWER: Yes, he *should*.   QUICK ANSWER: Yes.

3. QUESTION: Should Marlene and Joyce *eat* at the new *restaurant*?
   LONG ANSWER: No, they *should*n't eat at the new restaurant.
   SHORT ANSWER: No, they *should*n't. / No, they should *not*.   QUICK ANSWER: No.

4. QUESTION: Should Cheryl join the *gym*?
   LONG ANSWER: Yes, she *should* join the gym.
   SHORT ANSWER: Yes, she *should*.   QUICK ANSWER: Yes.

5. QUESTION: Should Bobby fix his *car*?
   LONG ANSWER: No, he *should*n't fix his car.
   SHORT ANSWER: No, he *should*n't. / No, he should *not*.   QUICK ANSWER: No.

6. QUESTION: Should Jeanine color her *hair*?
   LONG ANSWER: Yes, she *should* color her hair.
   SHORT ANSWER: Yes, she *should*.   QUICK ANSWER: Yes.

Exercise 7.18
Answers will vary.

Exercise 7.19

1. QUESTION: When should Myron take his medication?
   LONG ANSWER: He should take his medication every morning.
   SHORT ANSWER: Every morning.

2. QUESTION: Where should Nick and Sara buy a house?
   LONG ANSWER: They should buy a house in Peabody.
   SHORT ANSWER: In Peabody.

3. QUESTION: Which car should Peter and Jeanine buy?
   LONG ANSWER: They should buy the red car.
   SHORT ANSWER: The red car.

4. QUESTION: When should David go to bed?
   LONG ANSWER: He should go to bed now.
   SHORT ANSWER: Now.

5. QUESTION: What should Jackson study?
   LONG ANSWER: He should study economics.
   SHORT ANSWER: Economics.

6. QUESTION: Where should Stacey move?
   LONG ANSWER: She should move to California.
   SHORT ANSWER: To California.

Exercise 7.20

Answers will vary.

Exercise 7.21

1. Can I watch TV now? / Can I please watch TV now? / Can I watch TV now, please?
   May I watch TV now? / May I please watch TV now? / May I watch TV now, please?

2. Can I wear your necklace to the party? / Can I please wear your necklace to the party? / Can I wear your necklace to the party, please?
   May I wear your necklace to the party? / May I please wear your necklace to the party? / May I wear your necklace to the party, please?

3. Can I get a new pair of shoes, Mom? / Can I please get a new pair of shoes, Mom? / Can I get a new pair of shoes, please, Mom?
   May I get a new pair of shoes, Mom? / May I please get a new pair of shoes, Mom? / May I get a new pair of shoes, please, Mom?

4. Can I take a vacation in July? / Can I please take a vacation in July? / Can I take a vacation in July, please?
   May I take a vacation in July? / May I please take a vacation in July? / May I take a vacation in July, please?

Exercise 7.22

Answers will vary.

Exercise 7.23

1. d 2. f 3. i 4. g 5. b 6. l 7. a 8. e 9. m 10. c 11. j 12. k 13. h

Exercise 7.24

1. came down with / getting over it 2. are looking over / are making sure 3. is taking care of 4. crossed / out 5. ran out of / called around 6. took care of

Exercise 7.25

Answers will vary.

Exercise 7.26

1. Rohit   2. He has the flu.

Exercise 7.27

Following is one example of active reading. There are many ways to mark up a passage.

Rohit's Illness

Rohit Malisetty was very sick. One Saturday, he woke up feeling awful. He had a sore throat, a headache, and a fever of 101°F. His body ached, and he couldn't stand up or walk around easily. He had to move very slowly because his body and head hurt so much. Sometimes, Rohit felt very hot. Other times, he got the COLD chills and shivered. He took some aspirin and stayed in bed all day. However, the next day he felt worse. To make sure he was all right, Rohit called his doctor. The doctor asked Rohit some questions, and Rohit described his symptoms. The doctor confirmed that Rohit had the flu. He had never had the flu before. The doctor prescribed bed rest, lots of liquids, and a fever-reducing painkiller? Rohit followed the doctor's orders. Seven days later, he got over the flu. He was very sick, but he finally recovered.

Exercise 7.28

1. Rohit got sick.   2. He had a sore throat, a headache, body aches, a fever, and chills.

Exercise 7.29

1. He called the doctor. The doctor confirmed flu. The doctor prescribed bed rest, lots of liquids, and fever-reducing painkillers.   2. His fever was 101°F.

Exercise 7.30

1. He had the flu.   2. No.   3. Sore throat, headache, fever, chills, and body aches
4. He rested and took fever-reducing painkillers.   5. Seven days.

Exercise 7.31

Rohit Malisetty was very sick.

Exercise 7.32

There are 15 supporting sentences.

Exercise 7.33

He was very sick, but he finally recovered.

Quiz

1. ought / might want   2. yesterday / Friday   3. one week / two days   4. Severe pain
5. True   6. Can I borrow your pen, Joan?   7. came down with   8. Dizziness   9 First
sentence   10. Middle of the paragraph

Chapter 8   Shopping and Clothing

Exercise 8.1

1. is going to do   2. will have   3. are going to hit   4. is seeing   5. will hold   6. is going to
be   7. will finish   8. will win   9. are going to clean   10. departs   11. is meeting   12. will
pick up

Exercise 8.2

1. He's going to do /Jack's going to do   2. You'll have   3. You're going to hit   4. He's seeing
/ Fred's seeing   5. I'll hold   6. It's going to be   7. I'll finish   8. You'll win   9. We're going to
clean   10. It departs / The 56 bus departs   11. He's/She's meeting   12. I'll pick up

Exercise 8.3

1. before class   2. None   3. None   4. this Tuesday morning   5. None   6. today   7. noon
tomorrow   8. this year   9. this weekend   10. in a few minutes   11. later   12 this afternoon

Exercise 8.4

1. I will/I'll complete the report by Monday night.   2. The train/It arrives in an hour.   3. I will/I'll
help you with homework after class.   4. Tomorrow night, we are/we're going to eat dinner at
the new restaurant.   5. You will/You'll be famous someday soon.   6. Ella is/She is/She's meeting
with her tutor tomorrow afternoon.

Exercise 8.5

Answers will vary.

Exercise 8.6

1. will not go   2. is not going to buy   3. will not write   4. is not going to work   5. will not
read   6. are not going to subscribe

Exercise 8.7

1. She won't go to the mall this afternoon.   2. She's not going to buy any more clothes online. / She isn't going to buy any more clothes online.   3. He won't write on a chalkboard.
4. She's not going to work next week. / She isn't going to work next week.   5. He won't read the newspaper on his tablet.   6. We're not going to subscribe to any more fashion magazines. / We aren't going to subscribe to any more fashion magazines.

Exercise 8.8

1. She's not going to come to my party today. / She isn't going to come to my party today.   2. They won't spend money on food tonight.   3. I'm not going to practice English every day here. (**Remember:** We cannot contract *am* and *not*.)   4. You won't attend the play at the theater tonight.

Exercise 8.9

1. QUESTION: Will they have a yard sale this Sunday?
   LONG ANSWER: No, they will not/won't have a yard sale this Sunday. It's on Saturday.
   SHORT ANSWER: No, they will not/won't. It's on Saturday,   QUICK ANSWER: No. It's on Saturday.

2. QUESTION: Is Lee going to lease a new car next year?
   LONG ANSWER: No, he's not/isn't going to lease a new car next year. He's going to buy a new car.
   SHORT ANSWER: No, he's not/isn't. He's going to buy a new car.   QUICK ANSWER: No. He's going to buy a new car.

3. QUESTION: Will you please show me some evening dresses?
   LONG ANSWER: Yes, I will show you some evening dresses.
   SHORT ANSWER: Yes, I will.   QUICK ANSWER: Yes.

4. QUESTION: Are Liam and Shelby going to rent a boat this summer?
   LONG ANSWER: Yes, they are/they're going to rent a boat this summer.
   SHORT ANSWER: Yes, they are.   QUICK ANSWER: Yes.

Exercise 8.10

1. QUESTION: Where will my brother fix her bicycle?
   LONG ANSWER: He'll fix her bicycle in the garage.
   SHORT ANSWER: In the garage.

2. QUESTION: When will she do her homework?
   LONG ANSWER: She'll do her homework after dinner.
   SHORT ANSWER: After dinner.

3. QUESTION: Which classes is Christian going to take this summer?
   LONG ANSWER: He's going to take art and history.
   SHORT ANSWER: Art and history.

4. QUESTION: Why are Evie and Lorraine going to buy a new stove?
   LONG ANSWER: They're going to buy a new stove because their stove is broken.
   SHORT ANSWER: Because their stove is broken.

Exercise 8.11

1. Can I help you look for something?   2. Can I help you with that luggage?   3. How may I help you, ma'am/sir?   4. Can I help you find something?

Exercise 8.12

Answers will vary. Here are some possible answers:
1. How may I help you this afternoon?   2. Can I help you find something? / Can I help you look for something?   3. Can I help you find a train? / Can I help you with the schedule?

Exercise 8.13

Answers will vary. Here are some suggestions:
1. Excuse me. Can you help me, please? I can't find the restrooms.   2. Pardon me. Could you help me, please? I can't find my room key.   3. Excuse me. Can you help me, please? I can't decide what to order.   4. Pardon me. Could you help me, please? I can't make a copy.

Exercise 8.14

Answers will vary. Here are some possible answers:
1. Excuse me. Can you help me, please? I can't find the price of this shirt. / Excuse me. Can you help me find the price of this shirt, please?   2. Pardon me. Could you help me, please? I can't read the train schedule. / Pardon me. Could you help me read the train schedule, please?
3. Excuse me. Can you help me, please? I can't find the library. / Excuse me. Can you help me find the library, please?

Exercise 8.15

1. a. Baseball cap   b. T-shirt   c. Shorts   d. Socks   e. Sneakers / Tennis shoes / Athletic shoes   f. Sweatshirt / Hoodie   g. Jeans / Pants / Trousers

2. a. Tank top   b. Skirt   c. Flip-flops   d. Dress   e. Belt   f. Boots   g. Shirt / Blouse / Top h. Sweater / Jumper   i. High-heeled sandals   j. High-heeled shoes

3. a. Coat / Raincoat / Trench coat   b. Umbrella   c. Rain boots / Galoshes / Wellies   d. Gloves

4. a. Hood   b. Winter jacket   c. Hat   d. Scarf   e. Mittens

Exercise 8.16

1. c   2. i   3. e   4. g   5. a   6. h   7. d   8. f   9. b   10. j

Exercise 8.17

1. is going to send / back   2. is coming apart   3. will grow into   4. is trying / on   5. put on   6. pick out

Exercise 8.18

1. in / in   2. at   3. in   4. in   5. on / on   6. for / on   7. in   8. in

Exercise 8.19

1. it   2. him   3. her   4. them   5. you   6. it   7. me   8. us

Exercise 8.20

1. Jenny and Lori shopped for them.   2. She likes them.   3. My aunt got a good deal on it.   4. I like shopping with her.   5. I found a T-shirt for him.   6. How much money does it cost?

Exercise 8.21

Answers will vary.

Exercise 8.22

Possible answers.
1. I think that dress is very pretty on you.   2. I think that outfit is too casual for the party.
3. I think your shoes are so lovely today!   4. I think that coat is quite trendy.

Exercise 8.23

1. trendier than   2. more/less casual than   3. wider than   4. more/less professional than
5. more/less beautiful than   6. more/less expensive than

Exercise 8.24

1. the trendiest   2. the most casual   3. the widest   4. the least professional   5. the most beautiful   6. the least expensive

Exercise 8.25

1. I think it's perfect.   2. It's too small. Maybe you could try a bigger size.   3. I think it's professional.   4. It's too loose. Maybe you could try a smaller size.

Exercise 8.26

Answers will vary.

Exercise 8.27

1. Julia   2. She bought a new pantsuit/outfit/suit.

Exercise 8.28

Julia's New Outfit

Reason

Julia went shopping and bought a new outfit. She just got a job as a secretary, so she needs new clothes. She's very excited about this outfit. It is her first pantsuit. She shopped around for a week. Finally, she found a store that carried pantsuits and was not expensive. Julia tried on many pantsuits. She picked out a navy blue one. It is the most professional-looking and the most comfortable. She bought a few blouses to wear with the suit—a white one, a tan one, and a green one. Julia also got a new pair of black shoes with flat heels. They were the most comfortable shoes she tried on. Julia is very happy with her purchase. She looks really good in her new pantsuit. She's glad she bought a new outfit.

Exercise 8.29

1. Julia bought a pantsuit, blouses, and shoes.   2. She is excited.   3. She got a new job as a secretary.   4. No, it wasn't expensive.   5. She shopped around for one week.

Exercise 8.30

Julia bought a new outfit.

Exercise 8.31

1. Yes   2. 13

Exercise 8.32

1. Julie went shopping and bought a new outfit.   2. She's glad she bought a new outfit.

Exercise 8.33

This paragraph will vary. Be sure to follow the instructions carefully and use the paragraph about Julia to guide you.

Quiz

1. are going to go   2. will help   3. am not going to fail / will not fail   4. leaves   5. are getting married / are going to get married   6. the fluffiest   7. the most talented   8. smarter than 9. 3   10. What do you think? / What do you think of . . . ?

Index

393